IMAGES
of America

NIPPENOSE VALLEY

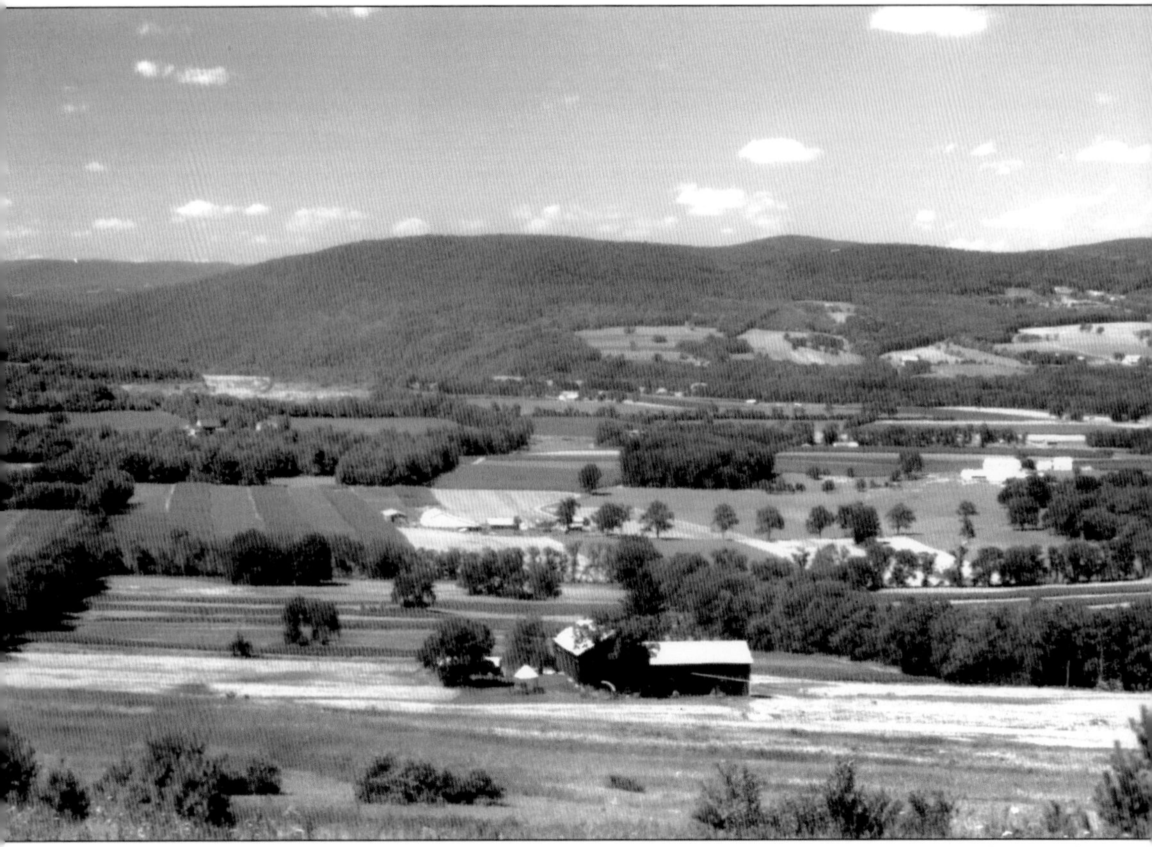

Many who live in Nippenose Valley consider it to be a beautiful little piece of Mother Earth. Tom Yorks said it like this: "I really believe God made the earth in six days, and did not get around to making the valley until near the end of the last day—after He had everything just right." This view is from Paul Reading's farm.

On the cover: Please see page 121. (Author's collection.)

IMAGES
of America

NIPPENOSE VALLEY

Wayne O. Welshans

ARCADIA
PUBLISHING

ISBN 978-0-7385-5782-3

Published by Arcadia Publishing
Charleston, South Carolina

Printed in the United States of America

Library of Congress Catalog Card Number: 2008922535

For all general information contact Arcadia Publishing at:
Telephone 843-853-2070
Fax 843-853-0044
E-mail sales@arcadiapublishing.com
For customer service and orders:
Toll-Free 1-888-313-2665

Visit us on the Internet at www.arcadiapublishing.com

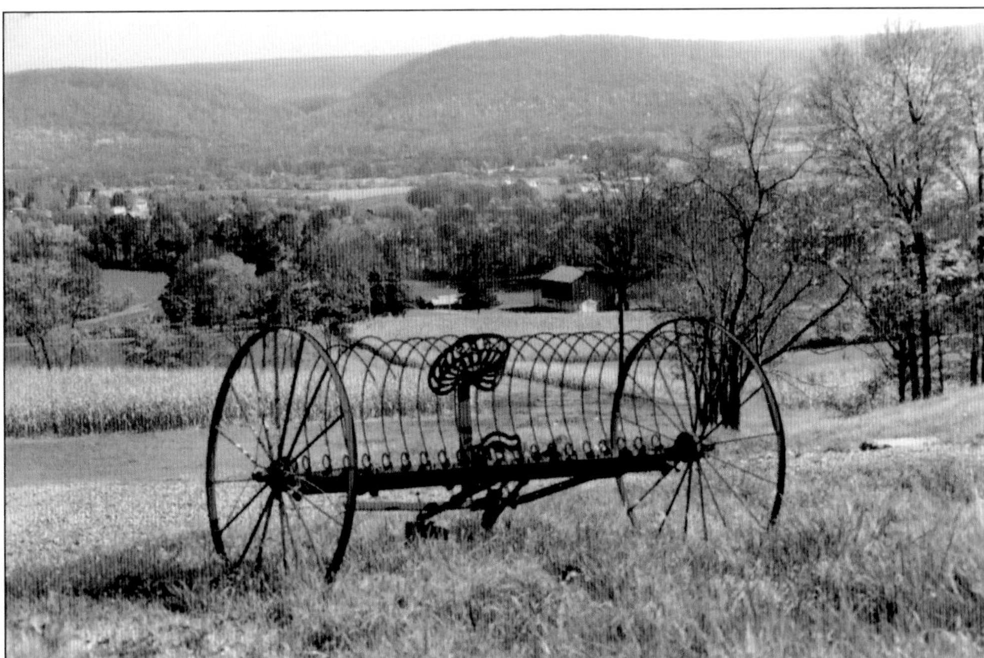

This is a southerly view of the valley from High Meadows Farm. The 300-acre land warrant, No. 561, was surveyed by John Lukens and entered to Mary Field on April 3, 1769. In 1787, the land deed was registered to Joseph Yates of Lancaster County. The 306-acre parcel was called Piedmont Situate and remained in this family for 62 years. The warrant was split in 1850 when purchased by Abraham Conrad Welshans and has been in the family since. The Jones dump rake, made by the Plano Manufacturing Company of Illinois, was last made in 1902, and this company was absorbed by International Harvester.

Contents

ACKNOWLEDGMENTS

The historic photographs and information accompanying them have come from ancestors of the original core families that settled and lived in this valley since the Civil War. This book contains a small sample of what has been gathered over the last 40 years. My visits with these older people were incredibly pleasant and successful, as they told their stories and gathered their photographs and memorabilia that allow us to better understand early times in Nippenose Valley.

Those who contributed include Byron and Evelyn Welshans, Abram and Mary Welshans, Joseph and Evelyn Welshans, John and Evelyn Jenkins, Myron and Jane Sweitzer, Harold and Florence Welshans, Frank Meixel, Tom and Isabel Yorks, Cliff Meixel, William Meixel, Mary "Dolly" Eck, David and Ruth Ann Hallow, Dean and Virginia Lehman, Gene Lehman, Harry Lehman, Marvin Bixel, Gerald Moore, Fred Hampe, Raymond Eck, Alfred and Esther Stopper, John Haas Jr., Howard and Dorothy Knarr, Charles Dorwart, Henry and Madeline Dorwart, Odessa Schlotman, Robert and Ann Barrett, Doris Schramm, Ruth Philabaum, Robert and Doris Thompson, Betty Snyder, William and Martha Thompson, Louis and Olive Kaufman, Harriet Ruch, John and Evelyn Buttorff, Frank and Pauline Schuler, Louie and Harriet Williams, Pastor John Dean, Charles and Susan Stopper, Raymond and Olive Gilhart, Paul and Margaret Reading, Grace Callahan, Robert and Josephine Clark, Gerald and Phyllis Fleisher, Donald Keeler, John Bixel, Lorraine and Fanny Davidson, Dale and Edna Kemmerer, Ray and Lydia Wynn, George Overdorf, Martha Vairo, Richard Welshans, Charles N. Welshans, Bruce and Ellie Welshans, Philip Winter, Robert Winter, Joseph Seewald, Orrin Engler, Benjamin Croyle, Clarence and Ruth Danneker Jr., Steve Danneker, Jeff Wenner, William and Margaret Garrett, Joseph Waldman, Tim and Julie Dapp, Gene and Betty Nau, John Youngman Sr. and John Youngman Jr., Ned and Harriett Sweitzer, Merrill Sweitzer, Nathan Welshans, Ron Phleger, Robert and Joan Harer, Jack Harbach, and Peggy Brewster. A special thanks to my wife, Janice, for her support in this endeavor.

Written sources include church histories; two valley newspapers, the *Oval Ledger* by H. J. Moore and the *Nippenose News* by Leonard Wright; D. J. Stewart's *History of Lycoming County*; John F. Meginness's *History of Lycoming County*; D. S. Maynard's *Historical View of Clinton County*; census records; James and Vincent Smith photographs; Cleo Barclay's historical notebook; school records; and Stevenson W. Fletcher's *Pennsylvania Agriculture and Country Life, 1840–1940*. Local research facilities include the Jersey Shore Historical Society, the Jersey Shore Library, the Taber Museum, the James V. Brown Library, and the Ross Library in Lock Haven.

The symbol x is used to indicate marriage.

INTRODUCTION

Nippenose Valley, Mosquito Valley, and Cades Cove in Tennessee are unusual geological features in that they are enclosed by mountains as opposed to being open ended like most in the Appalachian Mountain range. This oval-shaped valley is about seven miles long and three miles wide and trends in a southwest to northeast direction. The bottom of the valley is made of karst (soluble) limestone characterized by sinkholes, disappearing streams, and an underground labyrinth of passageways. No streams flow over the valley floor but tend to "sink" at about 870 feet of elevation where surface limestone first appears. Most of the valley floor is comprised of good farmland soils, but above this lays a narrow band of shale followed by the durable sandstone mountains. The valley floor is about 800 feet in elevation, and the mountains rise as high as 1,900 feet.

According to stories collected by John F. Meginness, the first white men to enter the valley assumed that the land was barren, as the valley floor did not support a lush forest like neighboring Sugar Valley. Instead they found a burned over area of downed yellow pine with a dense thicket of white thorn growing from apparently inhospitable land. Since reliable sources of water were not to be found on the valley floor, the first settlers lived near the foot of the mountains where natural springs were found. There were no roads but only paths made by Native Americans leading in and out of the valley. Travel was difficult, and it was a long time before wagon roads were made by widening the paths. The first products coming from the valley were pine knots salvaged from the burn area that were transported to Jersey Shore to be used for night fishing on the river, street lighting, and fireplaces. Some of the pine was burned in kilns to produce tar and lampblack. These marketable products were transported Native American style by horse and on the heads of women. Names of the earliest settlers were not recorded, but the names John and William Winland, and John, Francis, and Thomas Clark are considered first. William Winland's son, Joshua, born in 1791, was the first recorded birth in the valley. The Clarks were at first living in fair play territory on the north side of the river in disputed Native American land outside the jurisdiction of Great Britain and the Penns. Francis was accused of stealing a Native American's dog and found guilty of the offense. His sentence was either a lashing with a whip or banishment from the territory. The Clarks left and headed into Nippenose Valley. John developed the first improved land in what became the Upper End of the valley in 1776. He left the valley during the Big Runaway but returned in 1784. The mystery of underground caverns was experienced early on by the Winlands when, upon digging a well, they punched through a large flat rock with nothing but space below. Upon testing to 30 feet and finding nothing but space and darkness, they became afraid and covered the hole.

The 1700s began with William Penn's ownership of a vast wilderness. The first map of the state, the Thornton map of 1681, only showed the beginnings of white settlement around Philadelphia. The "Sasquahana" River was shown flowing north into a vast wilderness, and the southern boundary of the state was placed 40 miles too far south. That got Penn in trouble with the Calverts of Maryland, and the boundary was not settled until the Mason-Dixon survey was completed 100 years later.

The Nicholas Scull map of 1759 began to sketch in the mountains and showed that there was both a North Branch and a West Branch to the river. William Scull produced a better map in 1770 and presented it to Thomas and Richard Penn. The map still did not show the valley but did register "Nippenuce" Creek flowing north out of the mountains. He named the island at Jersey Shore Cowichanwane and identified Pine Creek (not Tiadaghton) and Larty's Creek to the east.

The first map to show Nippenose Valley was produced in 1792 and is known as the Reading Howell map. The valley was labeled "Nepanose," and the map clearly shows it as an enclosed place rather than open-ended like the other valleys. Thirteen streams were identified as flowing from the mountains and disappearing through the valley floor. His updated map of 1811 shows each little stream ending in a circle, the symbol used to indicate sinking streams. The map also showed the Great Island Path running the length of the valley. It extended from Sunbury to Great Island where Lock Haven later developed. It came over the White Deer Mountain and along Rattling Camp Stream, likely following the pathway of Middle Road today. The 1811 edition of the map showed the settlements of Jersey Shore (not Waynesburg), Newberry, and Williamsport. The name Larty's Creek was still in use.

This section of the country was part of Berks County from 1752 to 1772, at which time the valley became part of Northumberland County. Things were getting better because land and other legal transactions could be completed at Sunbury rather than Reading. Lycoming County was created in 1795, and the first county map places the valley in Nippenose Township, one of the original seven established in the county. Antes land was noted on all these early maps.

Twenty-six years after this land was legally acquired from the Native Americans and land sales opened up, a warrantee map was produced for the county showing who owned these large pieces of land at that time. The Treaty of Fort Stanwix went into effect on November 5, 1768, and the land office opened on April 3, 1769. On that day, the first white man, Ralph Forster, applied for the first warrant in Nepanose Valley. A warrant was an application for a survey, and at the time, John Lukens was surveyor general, and the deputy surveyor for land on the south side of the river was Charles Lukens. William Scull processed the warrants on the north side of the river beginning after the second treaty of Fort Stanwix, which legally opened fair play land north of the river in 1784. The names of these men are found on many legal land documents of the time. Such an application cost $1 plus a small fee for hiring a scout to find the desired land. In this area, Hawkins Boone was the main guide. If the warrant and survey were approved, the applicant received a deed to the land.

Nippenose Valley became part of Adams Township in 1824 and thus separated from Nippenose Township. What is called the Upper End of the valley was taken from Lycoming County in 1839 with the formation of Clinton County. It then became part of Wayne Township until 1841 and then became part of Crawford Township. In 1835, the name of Adams Township changed to Limestone.

The following photographs are a small sample of what has been collected; nevertheless, they provide insight into the valley's people and their accomplishments between 1880 and 1935.

One

In the Beginning

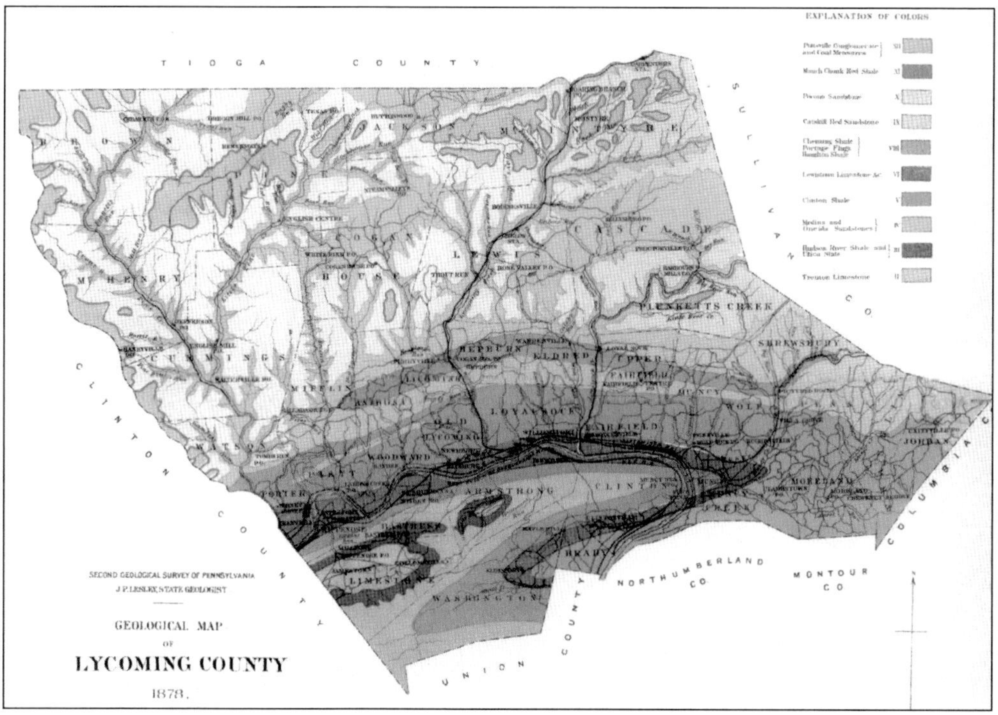

The oval shape of Nippenose Valley is nearly unique in the Appalachian Mountain range except for neighboring Mosquito Valley and Cades Cove, Tennessee. The valley is surrounded by a double row of sandstone mountains and has a floor of karst limestone. The drainage system of the valley runs underground through limestone conduits, and surface features include springs, sinkholes, and a karst fenster. Antes Creek carries the water to the Susquehanna River three miles away.

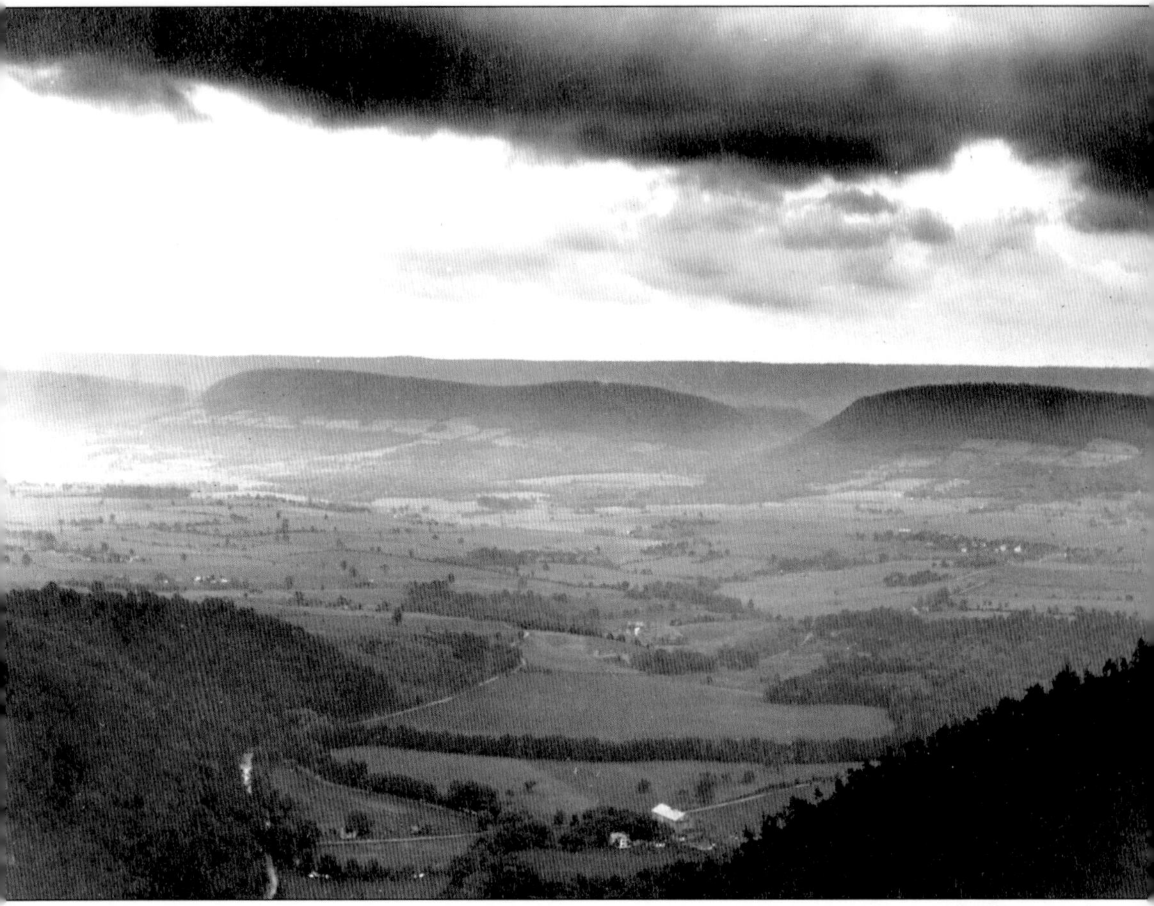

This is a view of the valley as seen from the north about 1908. The village of Millport and the oldest surveyed property in the valley, Lochabar, are directly below. On the other side of the valley runs North White Deer Ridge, which is fronted by small mountains called the Seven Sisters. The bottom is all farmland lightly scattered with houses and barns. The village of Jamestown and the Nygart and Sweitzer Gaps are seen in the distance.

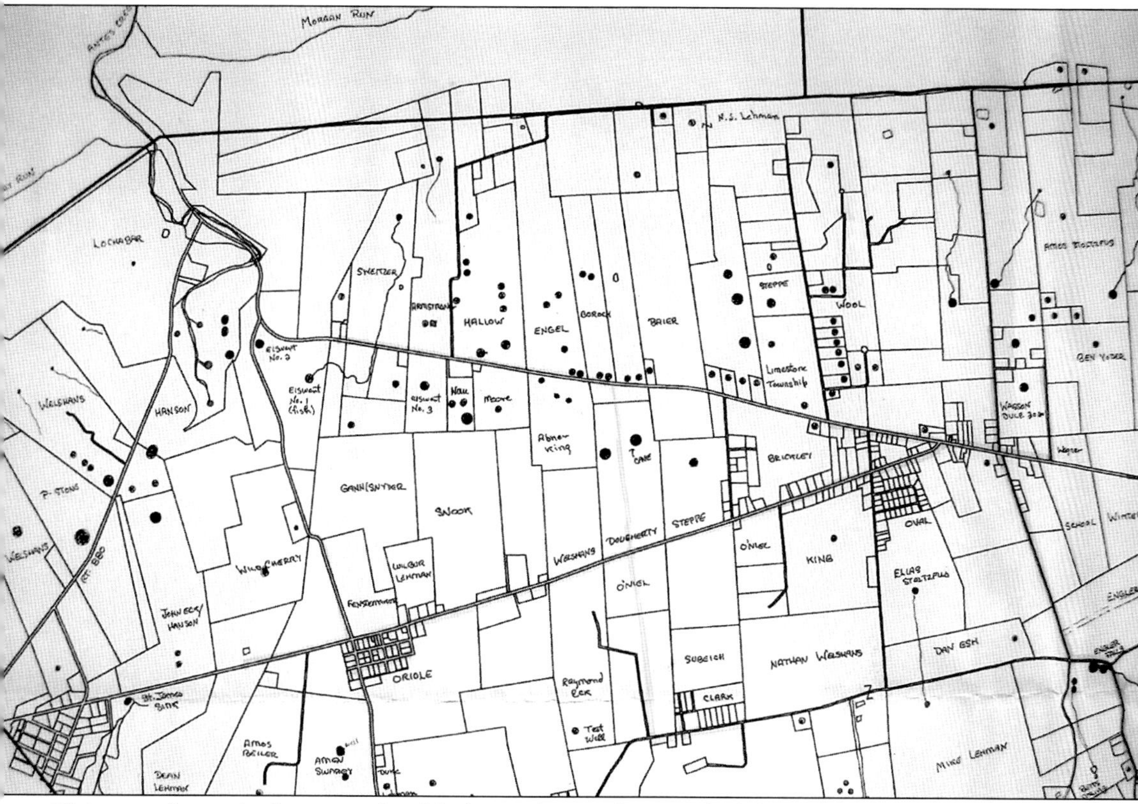

This map shows the location of sinkholes at the northern end of the valley. Thirteen streams enter from the mountains and begin sinking underground at about 870 feet of elevation. Being quite soluble, the karst limestone erodes away, leaving ever-larger caverns. Eventually the "ceilings" fall, leaving surface depressions that lead into the underground water supply. Three community water systems deliver potable water to the villages and some farms.

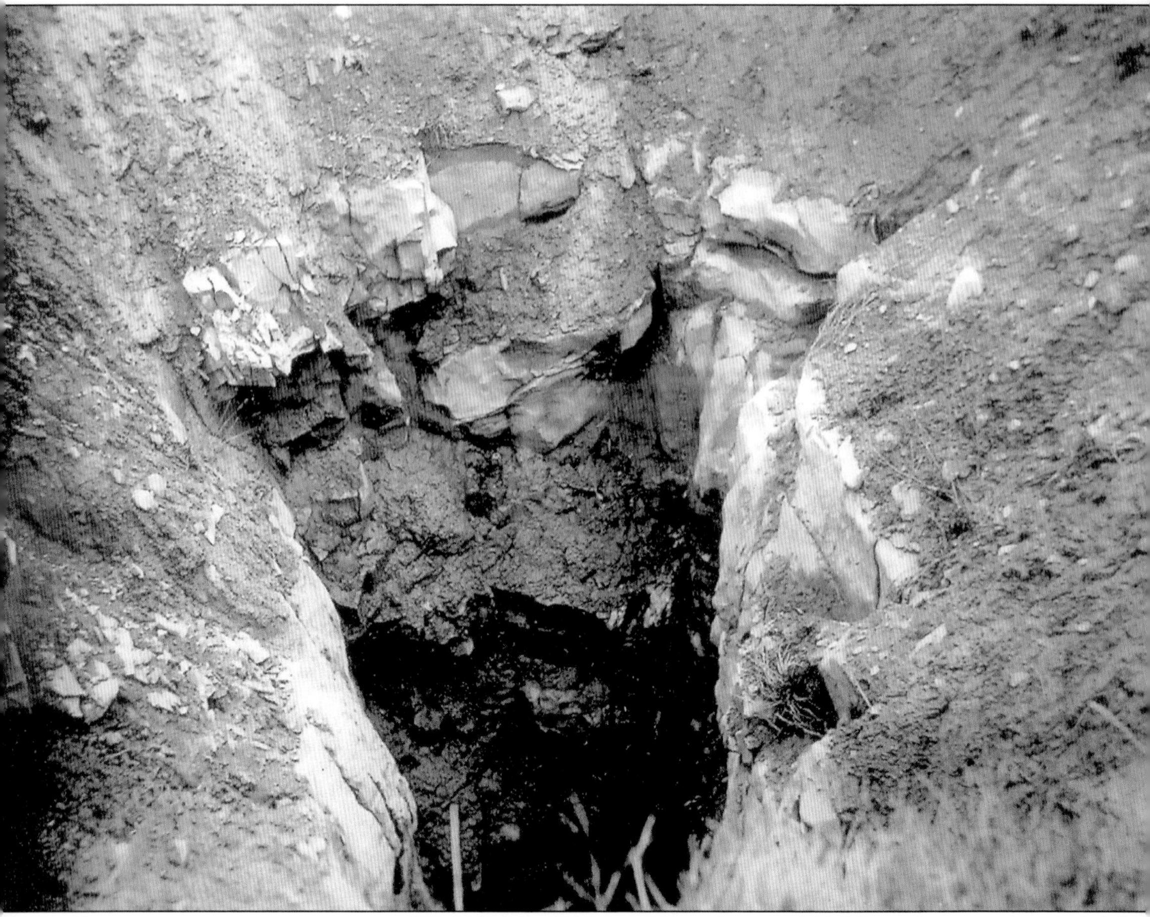

This large sinkhole formed on the Ira Dougherty farm in May 1928. It was known locally as "Doc's Hole" and brought thousands of curiosity seekers. At peak interest, a band played, hot dogs were sold, lights were strung, newsreels rolled, and the two caves at the bottom were explored. This sink, known as a cenote, opened at the highest point on the valley floor, providing a window into the underground flow of water toward the big spring.

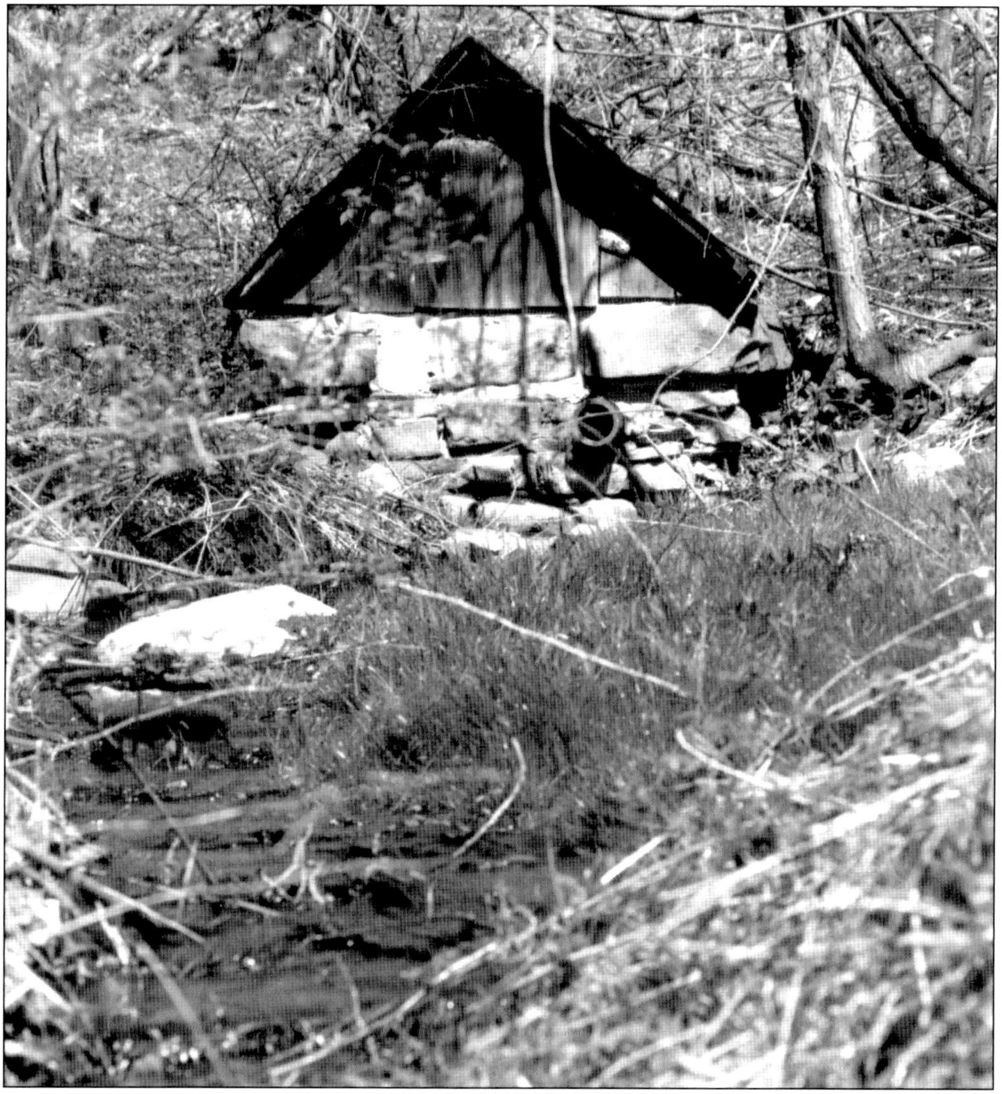

Springs and springhouses encircle the valley at the base of the mountains. Early settlers built their log cabins and barns beside them. There was no readily accessible water down in the valley. To live below, stone cisterns were built to hold rainwater from the house roofs, and shallow wells were dug. Some water was carried a distance from the spring through wooden or lead pipes. Such systems may be a mile long.

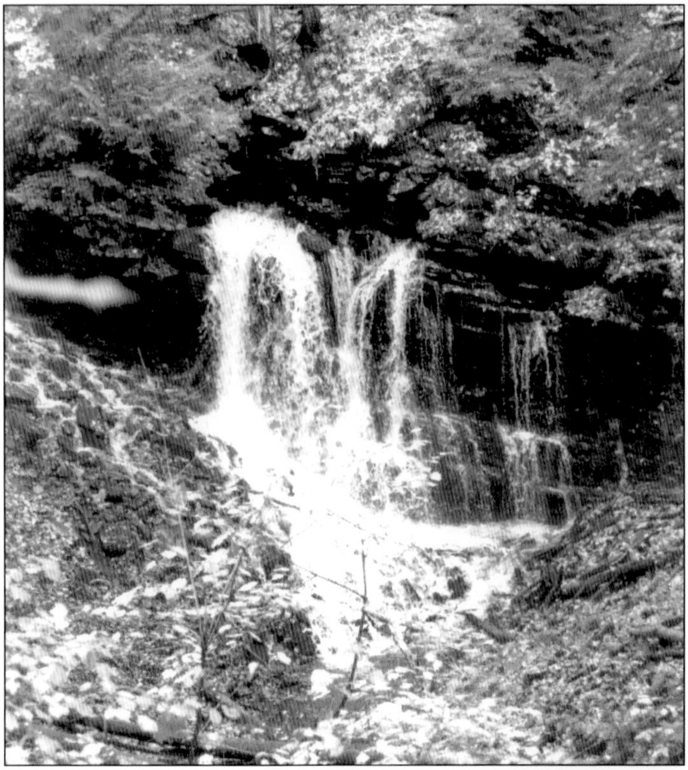

Engler Falls is located at the bottom of Nygart Gap just south of Collomsville. It is the only such waterfall in the valley with water dropping 20 feet or so into a sink and disappearing underground again. The Nippenose Valley watershed drains some 56 square miles of land, and the runoff is carried by 13 streams that feed the underground system. The larger streams are named Rauch's, McMurren's, Nygart's, Sweitzer's, and Rattling Camp.

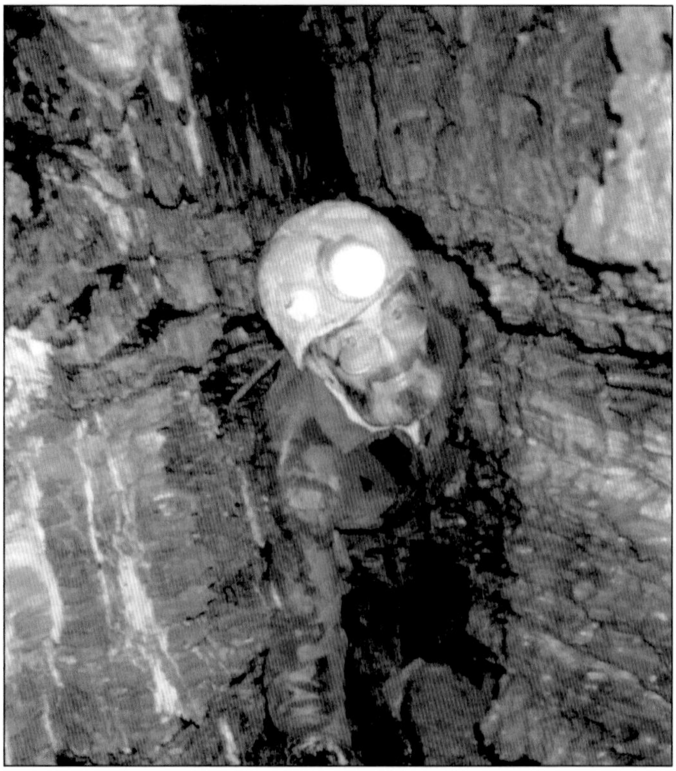

The larger, more accessible valley caves have been explored since the first settlers entered this place in the early 19th century. Caves generally lead into water channels that trend east to west, and the water level at any given time is often the limiting factor determining how far back in one can go. David Hollick is seen here in such a passageway. During heavy rain events, these channels fill up, forcing additional water to flow over the surface of the land.

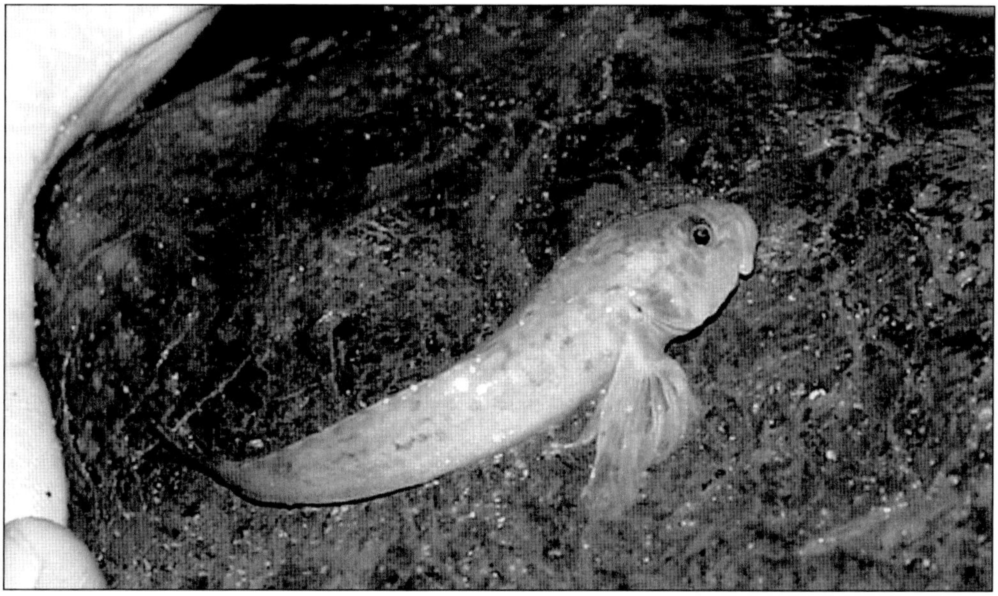

In 2003, the discovery and confirmation of a troglomorphic (cave adapted) fish, a species of sculpin, was announced. These valley sculpins represent the northernmost population of cave-adapted vertebrates in the world. By 2007, eight more invertebrate trogolomorphs were discovered, confirming the existence of a unique ecosystem under the valley floor. Dr. Luis Espinasa announced this discovery at a Nippenose Valley Watershed program presented to valley residents on January 15, 2008.

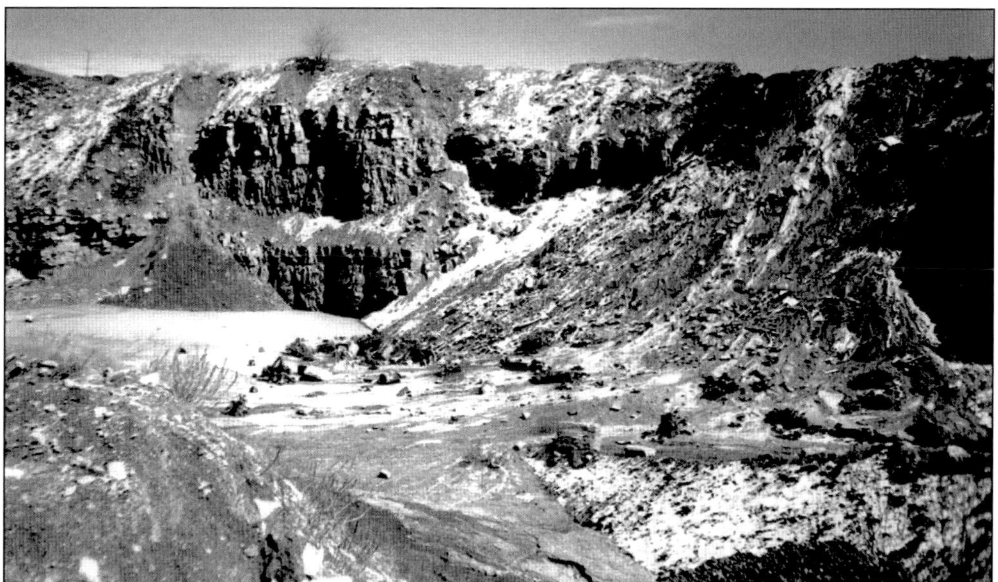

It was the limestone soils that attracted German farmers to the valley in the first place, and its primary use was that of fertilizer. Limekilns were built for this purpose, and many remain on the farms today. As time went on, the mined stone was crushed and used to pike mud roads. Since 1956, two large-scale surface mining companies have been at work, and nine farms have been (or will be) eliminated by these operations.

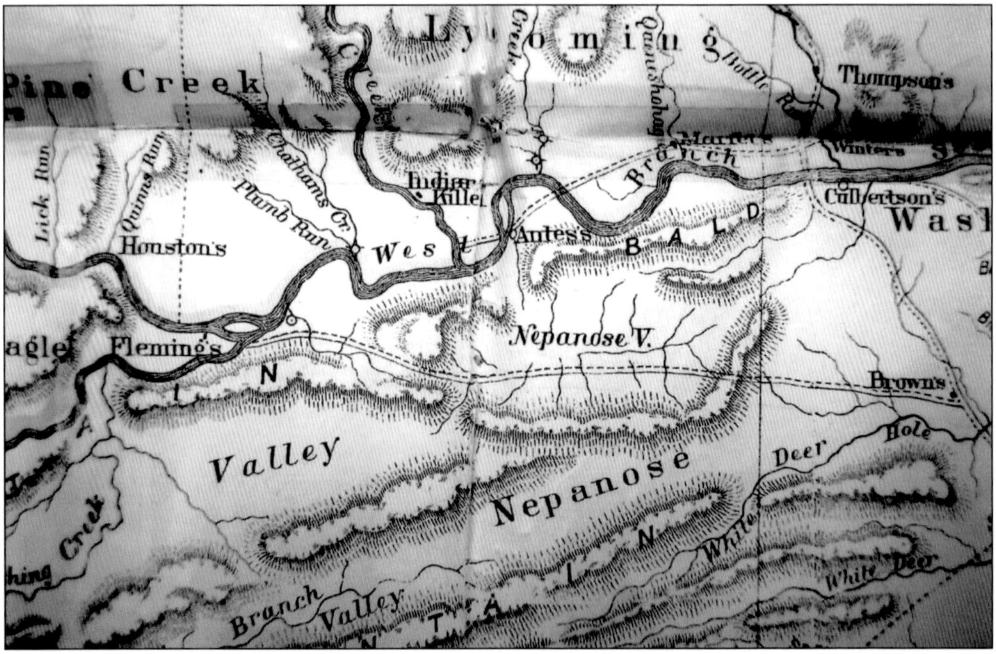

The first map of Pennsylvania was called the Thornton map, and it was made for William Penn in 1681. The 1770 William Scull map named the valley's outlet stream Nepanosis, and the Reading Howell map of 1792 was the first to show this oval-shaped valley and give it the name Nepanose. All 13 streams were plotted, and all ended with a circle that designates sinking streams.

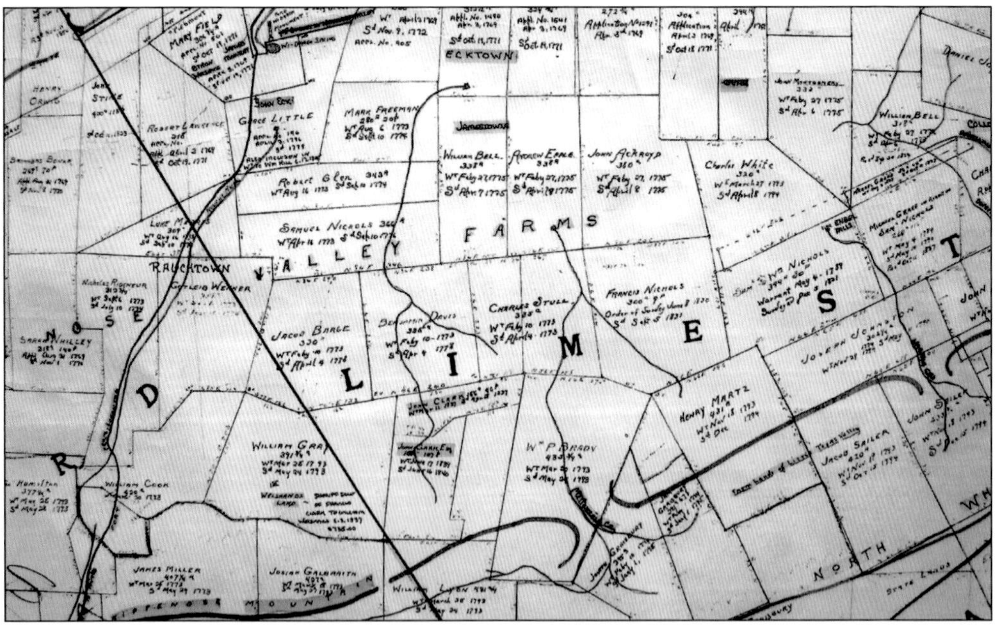

The first Treaty of Fort Stanwix opened the land for settlement here on November 5, 1768, and this warrantee map for Lycoming County was produced in 1795. The first survey in the valley was the Forster tract that was established on April 3, 1769. Charles Lukens was the surveyor, and Hawkins Boone was the guide. This map shows a total of 84 warrants for Nippenose Valley, with 52 for Limestone Township, 18 for Crawford Township, and 14 for Bastress.

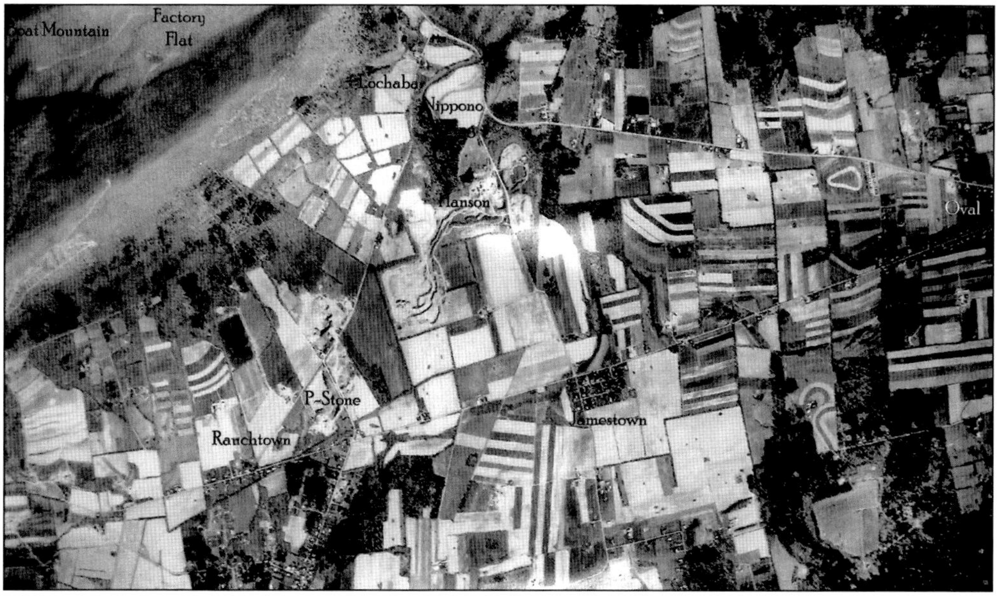

This aerial view shows the patchwork of fields that results from contour farming techniques. Many of the original warrants were split in half, resulting in about 130 farms here today. The limestone soils of the valley floor will support highly productive farms. The average size of these farms today is 134 acres with 42 percent of the land being harvested. The average age of a farmer is 54 years old, and 94 percent of the farms are family owned. (Photograph by Modern Explorer Products.)

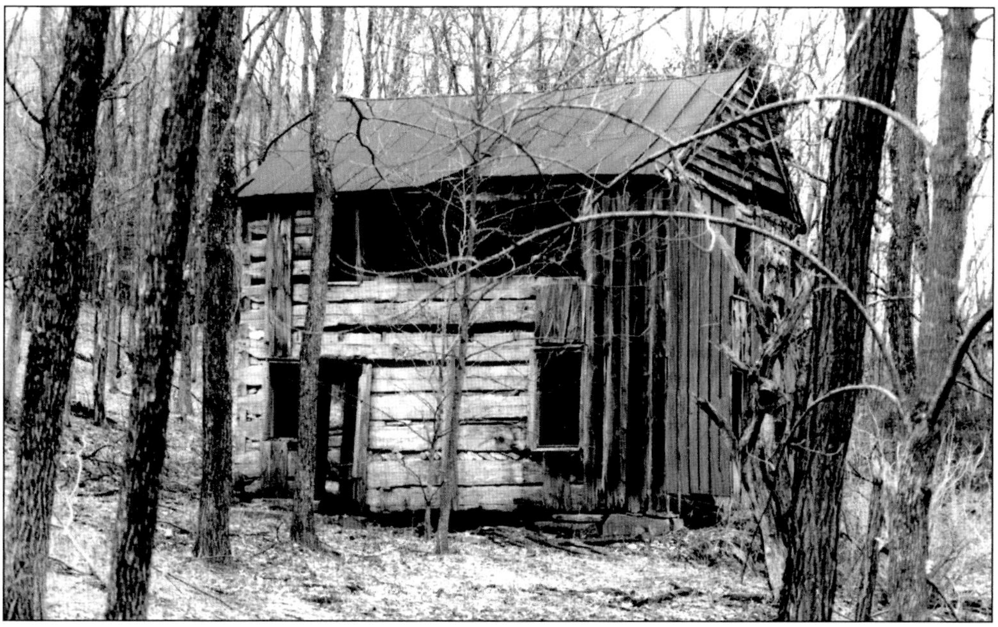

In the beginning, log houses and log pen barns were built from virgin timber growing on the sides of the mountains. This home was built by the Busler family. John Busler (1779–1844) and Margaret Busler (1790–1879) were listed as communicants of St. Peter Lutheran Church in 1842. Life was hard. The better land was bought up early, and such land as this was relatively cheap. Joseph and David Busler were the last to live here.

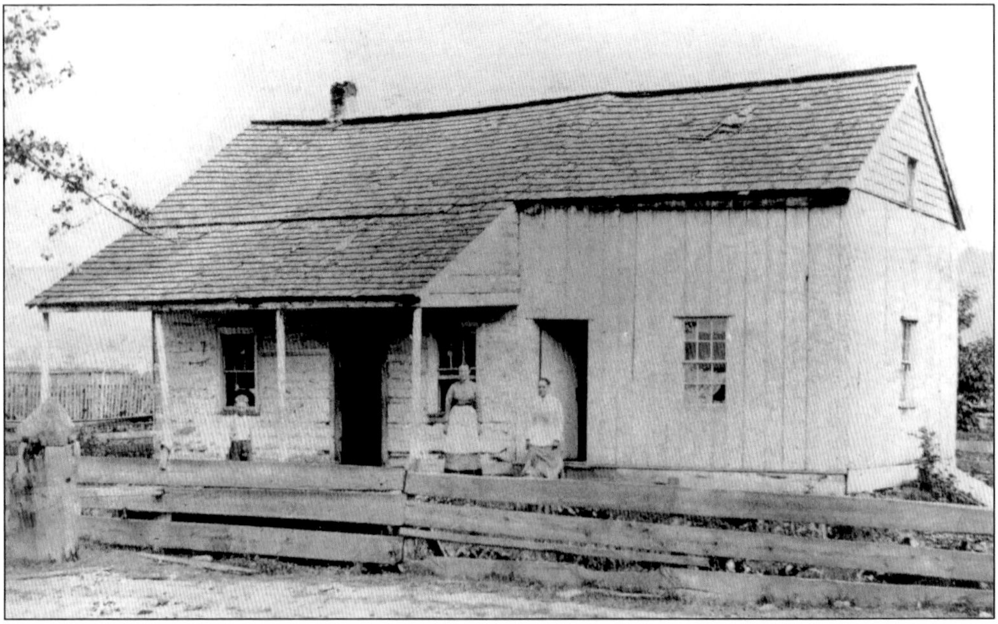

The John Gann family moved to the valley in 1808 and settled where Oval is today and built this log house. Gann bought 300 acres of land at $1.25 per acre, and he and his wife, Catherine, raised eight children here. The water supply for this place flowed through wooden water pipes from a spring. The water diverter, visible at left, directed the flow on to other places. This log house was dismantled in 1975 and reassembled at Coatesville, Pennsylvania.

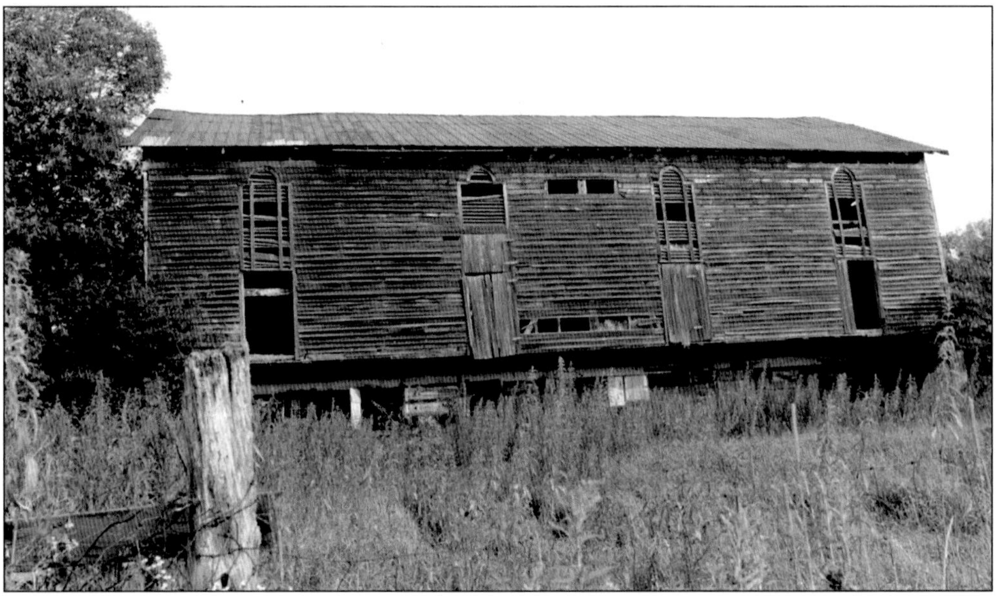

German ancestors built Pennsylvania bank barns, the design of which they brought from the old country. These very large and overbuilt barns were generally constructed before the house and were always the heart of the farm. This 40-by-80-foot barn was built in 1850 by Abraham Welshans. The barn was banked into the land, making for easy access to the threshing floors and hay mows. The older barns were sided with chestnut clapboards rather than vertical boards and battens.

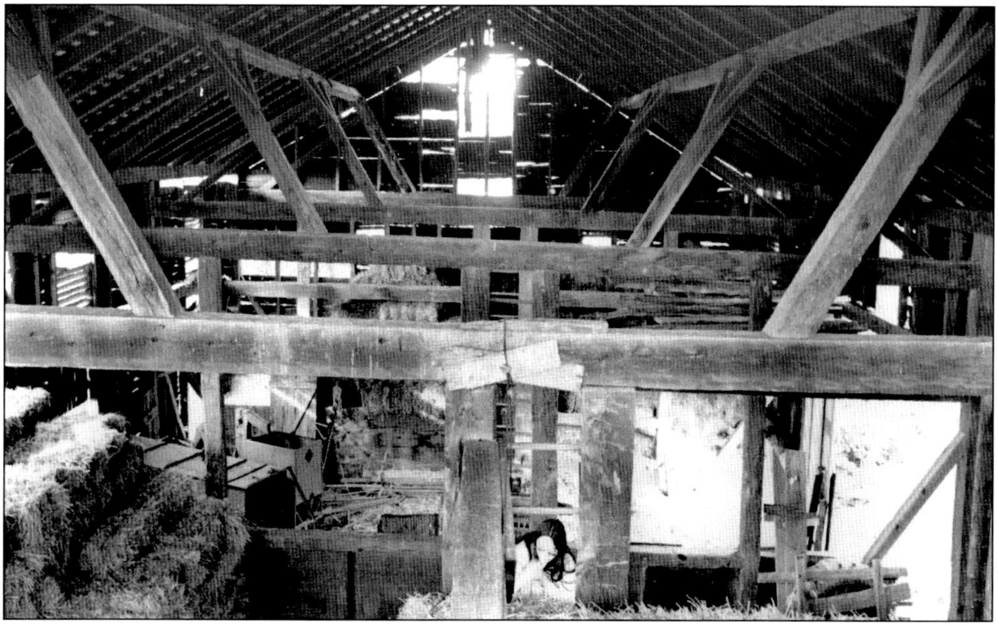

The skeletons of these barns were made of large timbers that were hewed and adzed to dimension. They were fitted together with mortise and tenon joinery and held into place with hardwood treenails, fitting square pegs into round holes. The rafters seen here were 25 feet long, cut to a four-by-six dimension, and supported midway with purlines. This barn survived for three generations before falling in March 1999.

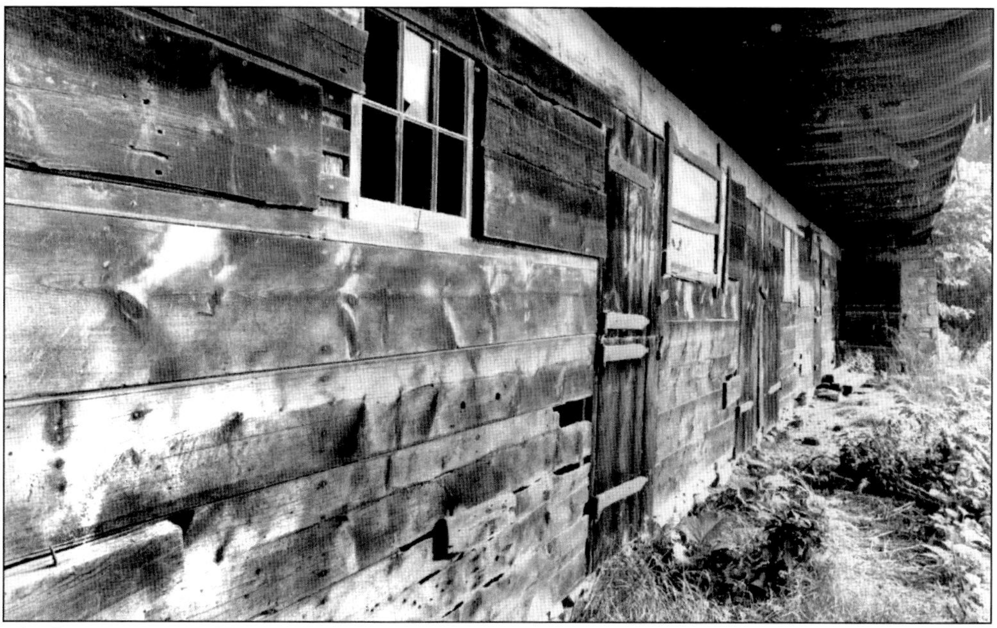

The basement or stable area of the bank barn was surrounded by thick stone foundation walls that supported the massive structure above. This barn was 18 feet high to the square. The barn faced south, and the overhang gave some shade in the summer and kept snow away from the stable doors in winter. The doors swing on massive steel hinges that were forged by a valley blacksmith. As with the Amish today, barn raisings were accomplished by family and neighbors.

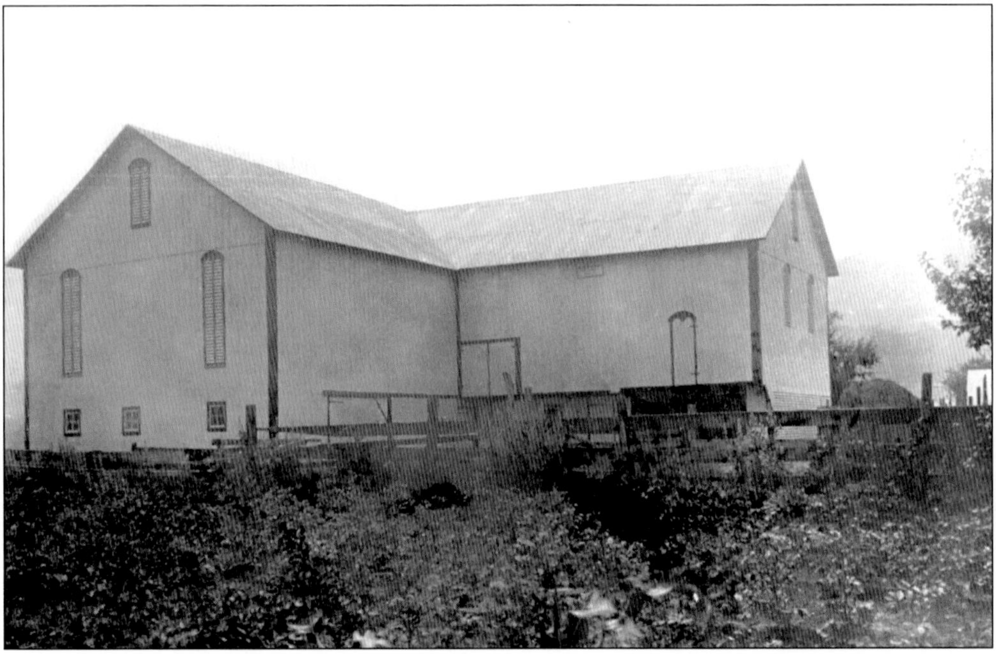

This was a new barn built on the Henry Laubach farm in 1913 after the 1889 barn burned. The timbers for the main barn came from an old barn standing at the upper crossroads in Rauchtown. A sizable straw shed was attached to the front, and both sections were sided with vertical boards and battens. Prior to 1889, the original log house and log pen barn stood on this farm.

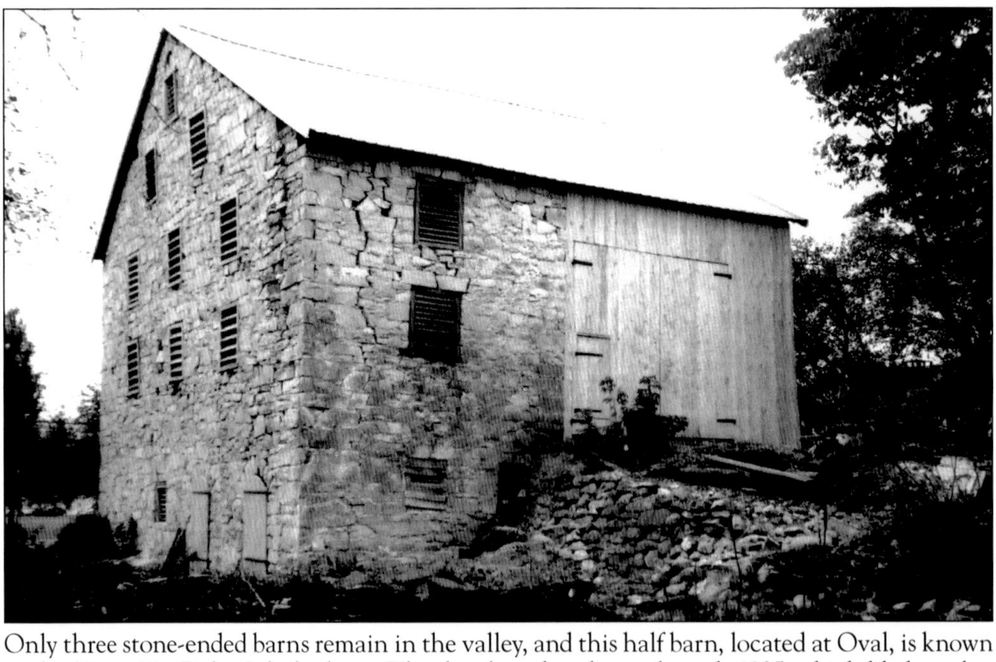

Only three stone-ended barns remain in the valley, and this half barn, located at Oval, is known as the Gann-VanDyke-Schuler barn. The date board at the peak reads 1835, which likely makes it the oldest standing barn in the valley. The 1861 Walling landowner map shows it belonging to John Gann, but the Beach-Nichols map of 1873 shows it belonging to his son Israel. The crack in the wall was due to a lightning strike. Note the owl hole at the peak.

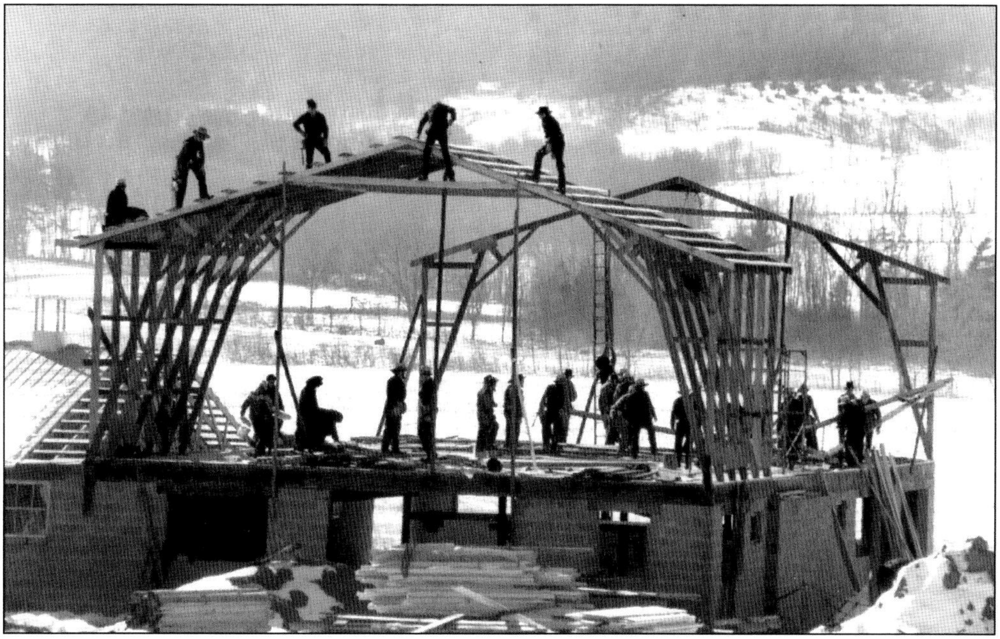

Amish families began moving into Nippenose Valley in 1985 and are shown here in March 1996 building a new barn on the Levi Stoltzfus farm at Oval. This farm belonged first to John Gann then George Clark, George Hampe, and Fred Hampe. Although not of bank barn design, new barns are built with a design better suited for today's farming practices. The yellow brick house on this farm was built around 1865.

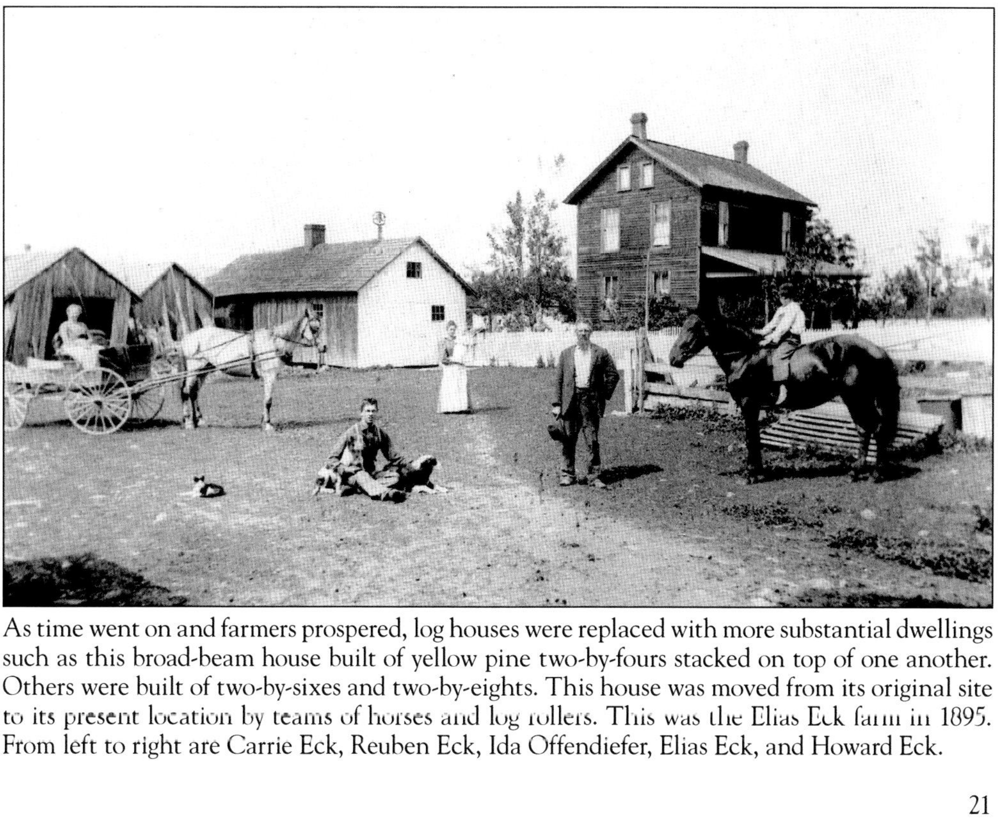

As time went on and farmers prospered, log houses were replaced with more substantial dwellings such as this broad-beam house built of yellow pine two-by-fours stacked on top of one another. Others were built of two-by-sixes and two-by-eights. This house was moved from its original site to its present location by teams of horses and log rollers. This was the Elias Eck farm in 1895. From left to right are Carrie Eck, Reuben Eck, Ida Offendiefer, Elias Eck, and Howard Eck.

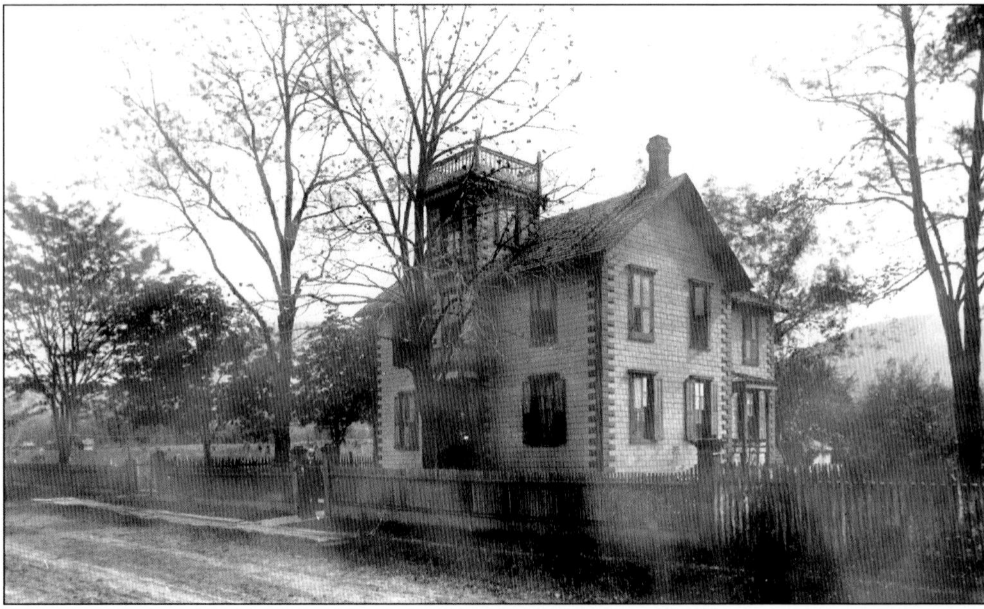

This was the Jacob and Elizabeth Zerbe Homan place in Collomsville, built around 1870. It was a plank house built around a beam skeleton. The main two-inch-thick vertical planks ran from bottom to top, and the outside was covered with horizontally running scored planking. Facing in were one-inch-wide boards to which lath was nailed and covered over with horsehair plaster, rough coat, and smooth. This is where Steinbacher Demolition is located today. The house burned when Emanuel Laubach lived here.

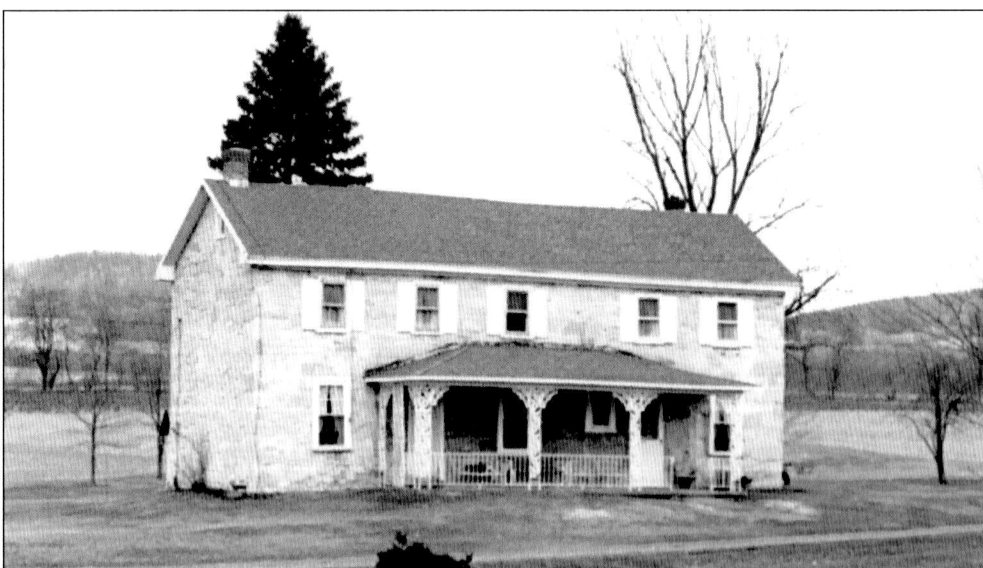

This stone house at Collomsville is one of the oldest in the valley. The original patent was to William and Margaret Bell, dated December 5, 1776. In the 1830s, it was owned by John Bixler and was known as the Bixler Hotel. In 1844, it belonged to John Kaufman; in 1864, it belonged to John A. Gamble; in 1885, it belonged to Robert Homler; in 1913, it belonged to David and Magdalena Eck; in 1945, it belonged to Charles and Winnifred Hallow; and in 1955, Benjamin and Mary Jane Croyle bought the place. It is still called the Dave Eck place by many.

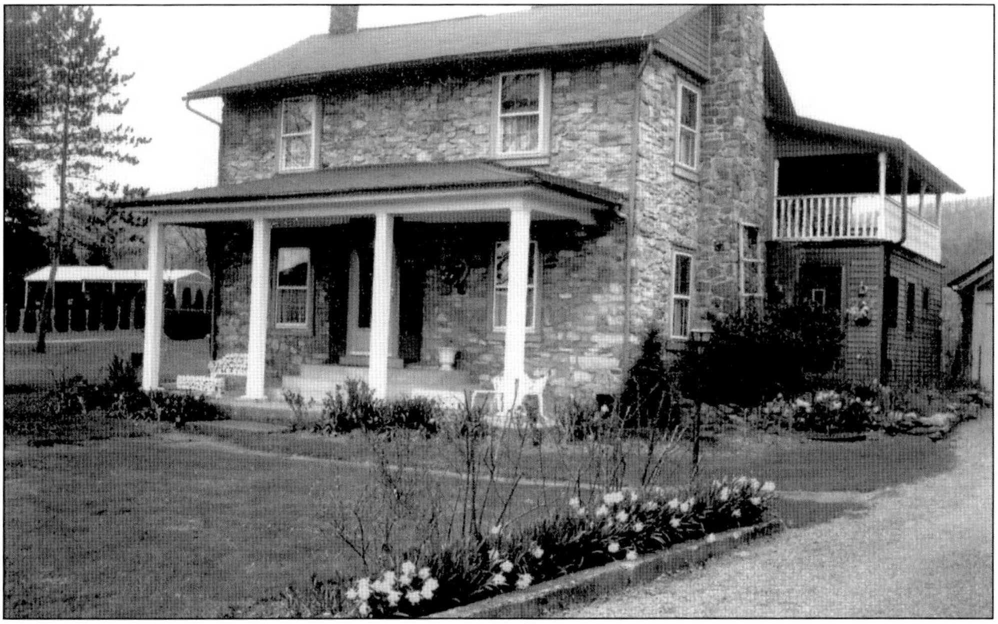

There are not many stone houses remaining in the valley, but this was the farmhouse of Augustus Eck that was built around time of the Civil War. The 1873 map shows Joel, William, Augustus, and Nathan Eck living close by, and for over 100 years, this stretch of road leading from Millport Hill to Oval was called Ecktown. Augustus married Frances Dougherty in 1856, and together they raised 12 children here.

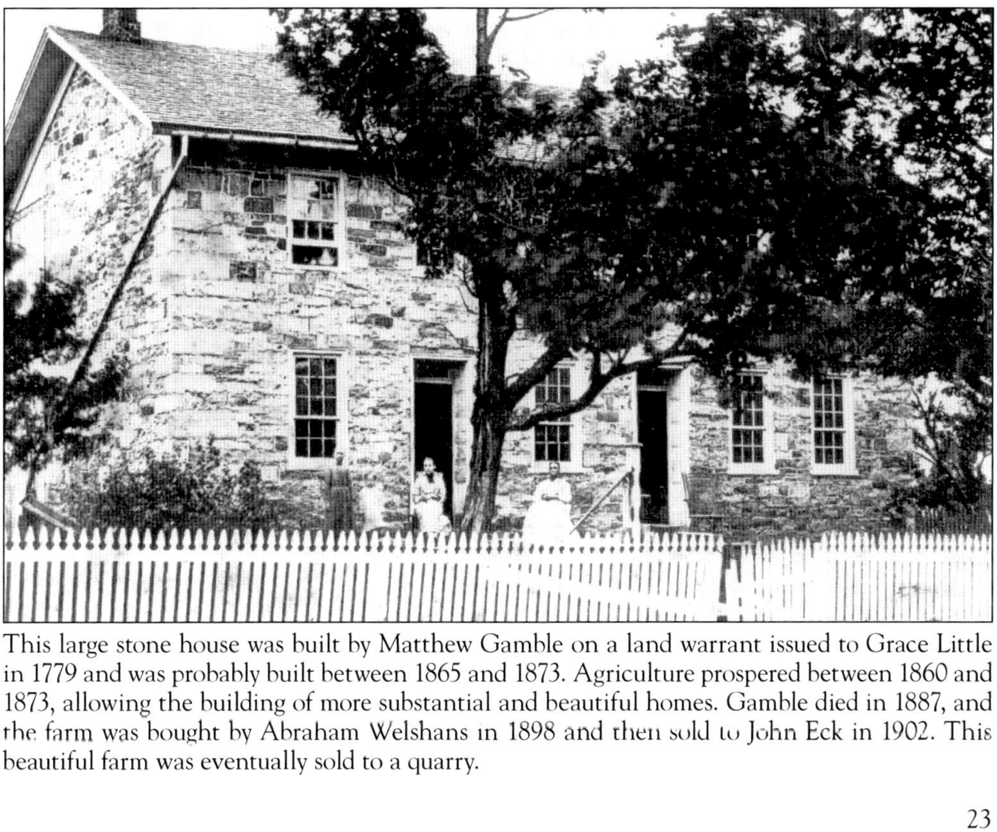

This large stone house was built by Matthew Gamble on a land warrant issued to Grace Little in 1779 and was probably built between 1865 and 1873. Agriculture prospered between 1860 and 1873, allowing the building of more substantial and beautiful homes. Gamble died in 1887, and the farm was bought by Abraham Welshans in 1898 and then sold to John Eck in 1902. This beautiful farm was eventually sold to a quarry.

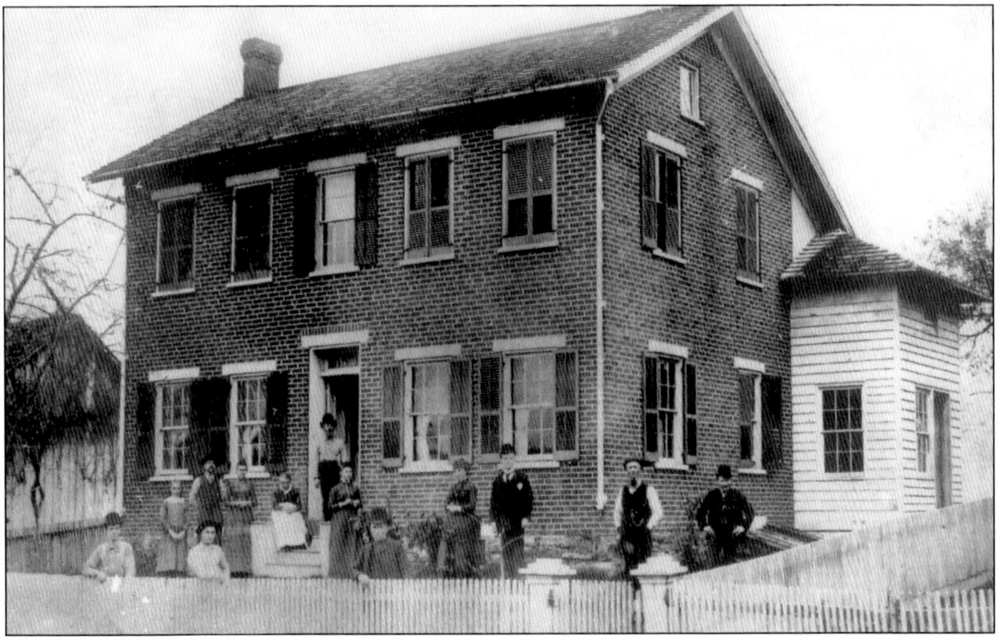

Few brick houses were built in the valley, but for those that were, the bricks were often made on site. This photograph shows the Hullar home in Collomsville. The family came from Germany and arrived here in 1852. This place sat between William Clark's/ DeFrain's General Store and the Collomsville Hotel. Others that lived here include Augustus Lehman, Fred Miller, and the Stiffler, Engel, and Waldman families.

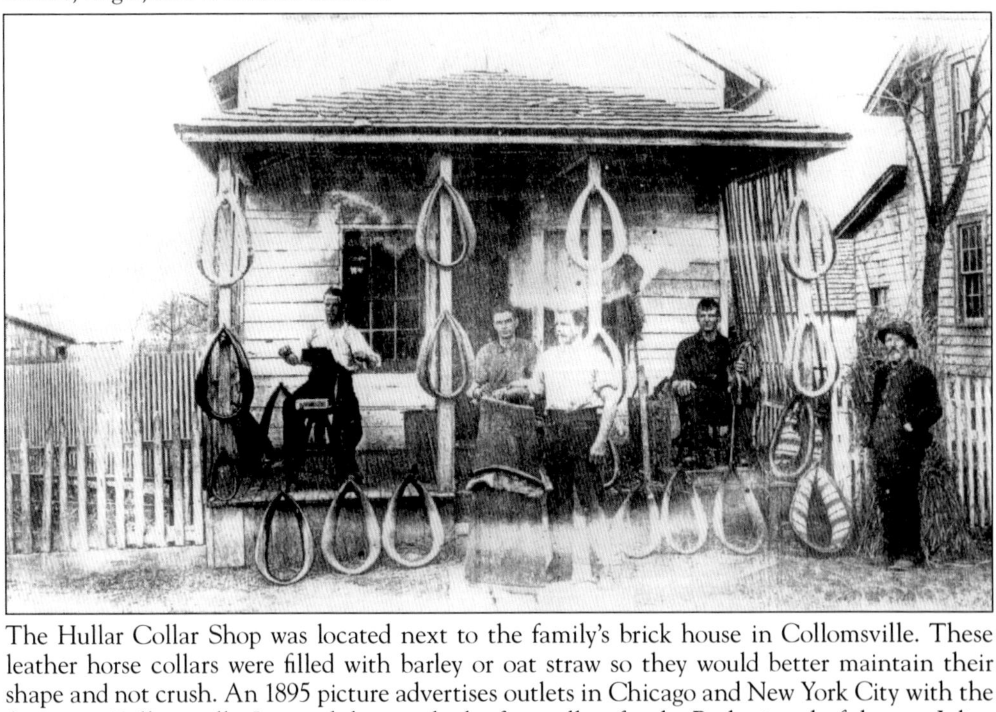

The Hullar Collar Shop was located next to the family's brick house in Collomsville. These leather horse collars were filled with barley or oat straw so they would better maintain their shape and not crush. An 1895 picture advertises outlets in Chicago and New York City with the factory at Collomsville. It is said they made the first collars for the Budweiser draft horses. Julius Hullar later built a larger shop that sat further back on the property.

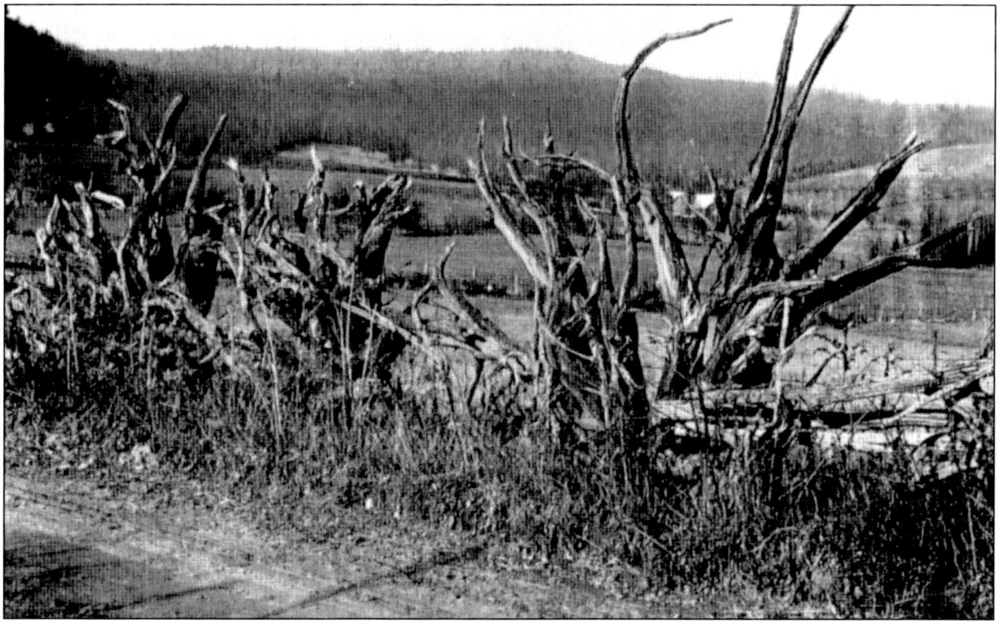

Homesteading a piece of land involved clearing the ground and building the barn, a house, a springhouse, a wood shed, a smokehouse, implement sheds, and so on. As the farmland was cleared, fences were built to keep neighboring free-ranging livestock out of the fields and to divide the farm into roughly 10-acre sections. Until 1889, Pennsylvania operated under the fence law of 1700, which was based on the idea that fences were made to keep livestock out, not in.

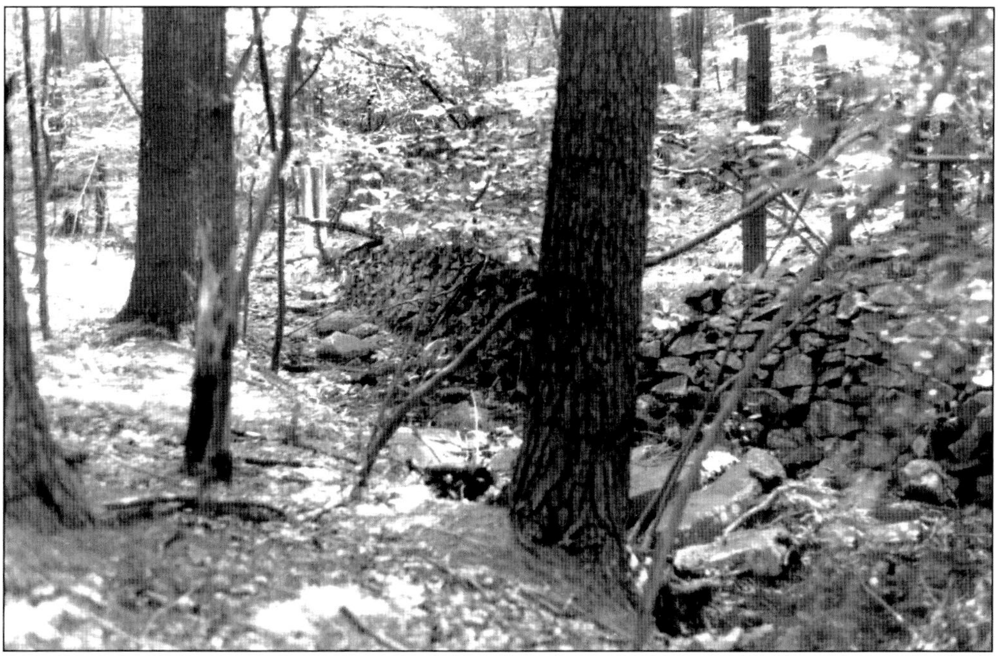

Clearing the fields also involved moving big stones, using a stone boat or wagon. Stone piles were often formed in the center of a field or were used to build stone fences like this one. Some were thrown, others were laid. Henry Miller said to the fellows picking stone for him, "Clap them rocks good boys, there ain't any too much dirt here now."

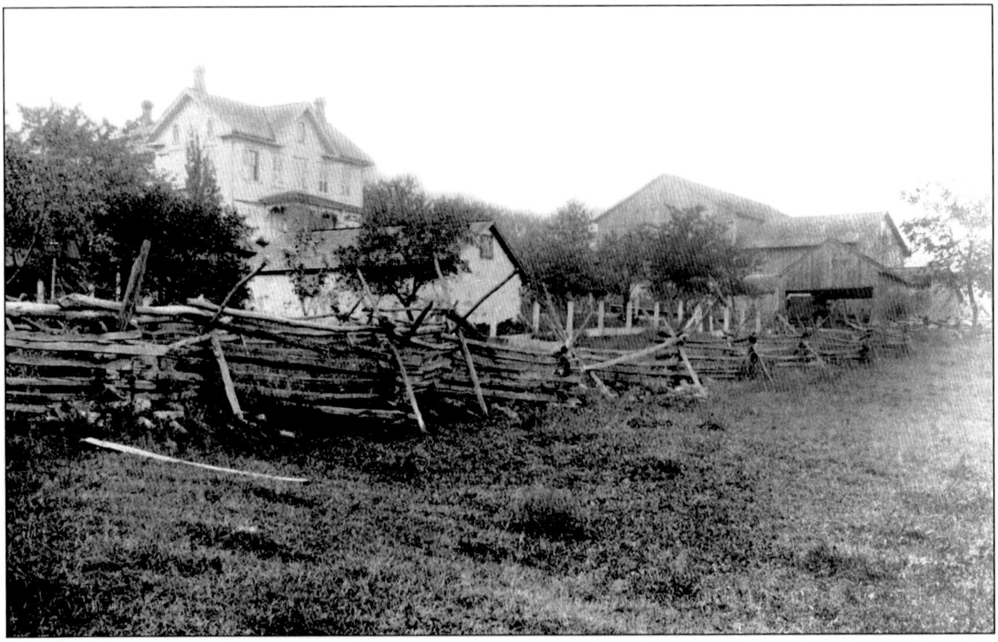

This was the Nicholas Schular farm along Stopper Road in Bastress. The place burned in the 1920s. Wood was plentiful at the time and was the universal building material. Stake and rider, or worm fencing, is shown here. It was easy to erect and repair but took up a lot of space and sheltered many weeds and rodents. Chestnut was the wood of choice, but the blight of 1908 killed them all. A chestnut post lasted 40 years or more if sunk into a stone row.

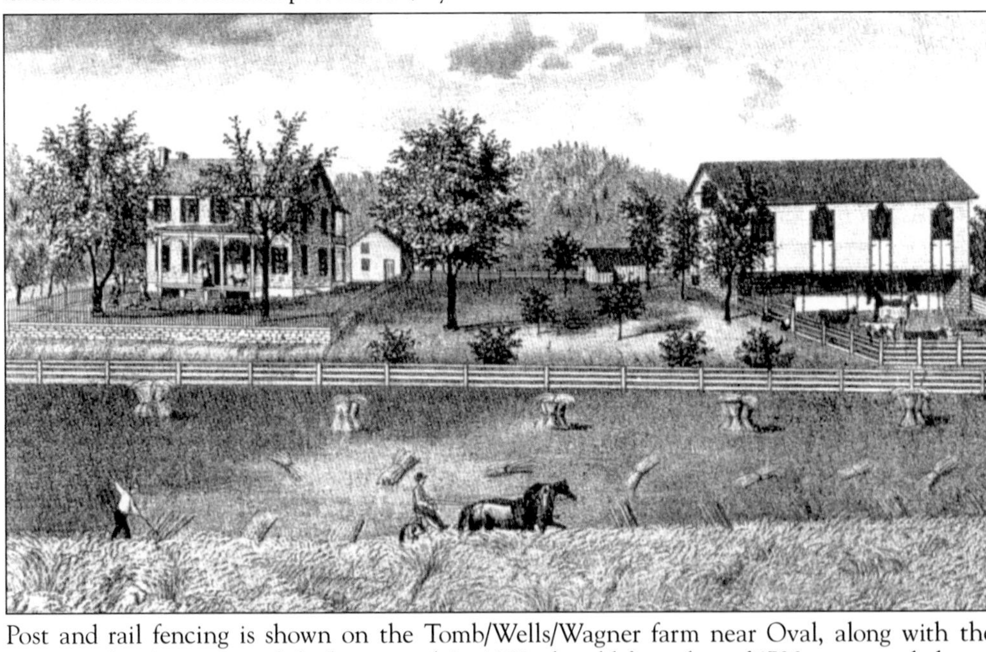

Post and rail fencing is shown on the Tomb/Wells/Wagner farm near Oval, along with the square picket fence around the home yard. In 1889, the old fence law of 1700 was repealed, and common law, which predated it, took effect. After this, fences were constructed to keep livestock penned in, and they were no longer allowed to range freely. In 1874, barbed wire was patented and gradually replaced wooden fences, many of which were used as fuel during butcherings.

Two

Antes Gap to Millport

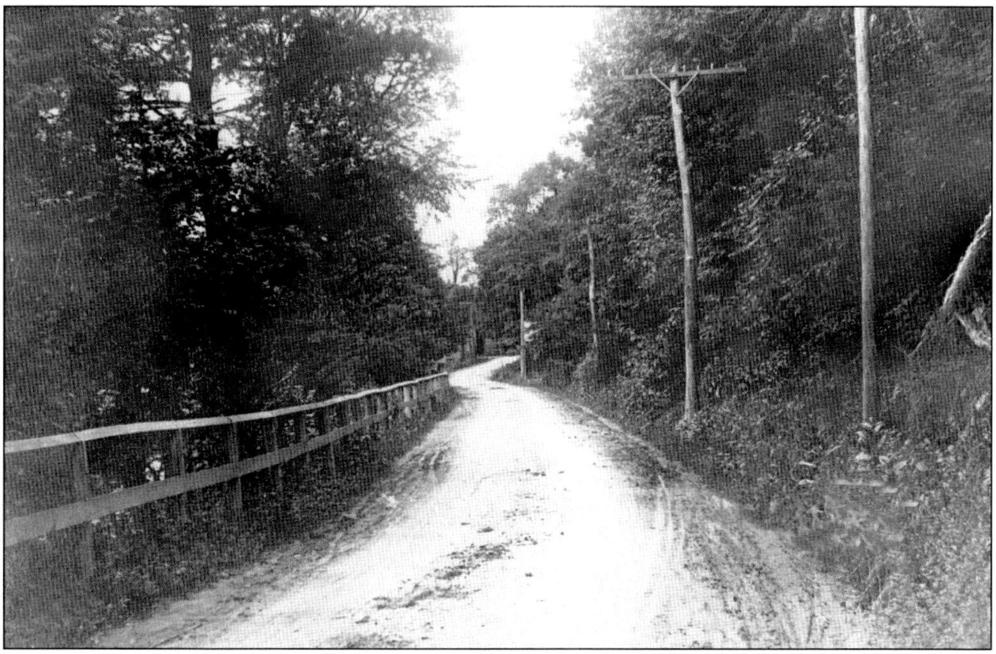

In the early 20th century, the road between Jersey Shore and the valley looked like this. It was called the Youngman Road, named for the family that owned most of what was originally called Nepanose Creek. In 1816, Amelia Antes, daughter of John Henry Jr., was married to Elias P. Youngman by Rev. John Hays Grier. It was their son George Washington Youngman who built the woolen mill halfway through the gap in 1865.

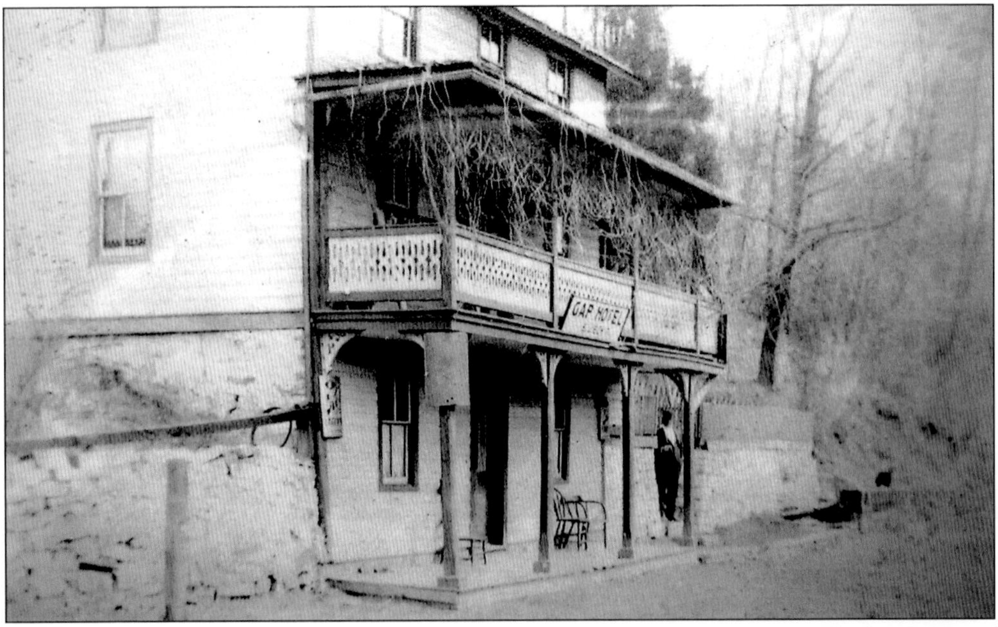

Seen here as it looked in 1904, the Gap Hotel stood along the Youngman Road. The first owner of record was Joseph Ferrar, who ran this establishment from 1885 to 1902. Then came Edward Eck from 1902 to 1906, Joseph Frederick from 1907 to 1913, and Albert Lorsong from 1913 to 1934, followed by Lewis Bardo and Joel Hennigan. A watering trough for horses was located here, and valley dairy farmers delivered their milk here to be picked up by the Jersey Shore Creamery.

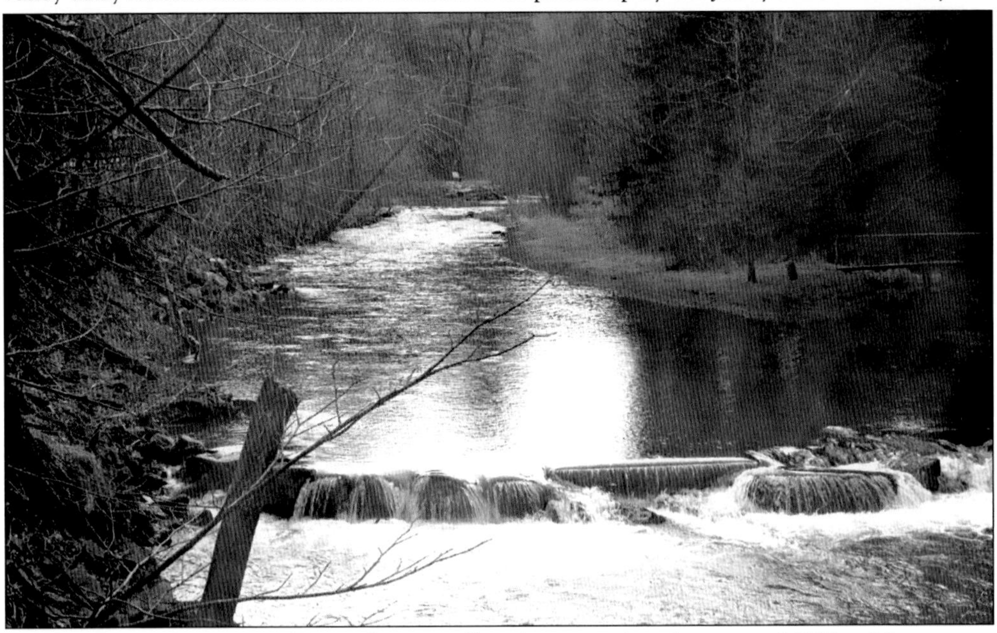

This creek was first mapped by William Scull and appeared on his map of 1770 as Nipennoses Creek. The Reading Howell map of 1792 named it Nepanose Creek, and it was still called Nippenose Creek on the Beach-Nichol's map of 1773. Sometime after this, the name was changed to Antes Creek. By 1865, there were three dams along this creek that powered two gristmills and one woolen mill.

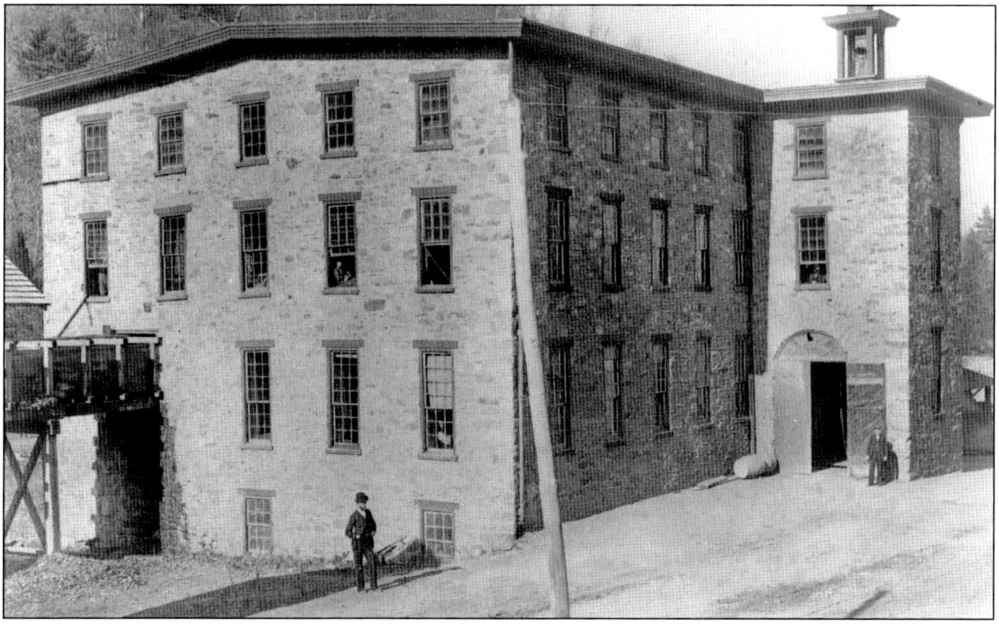

This stone building, measuring 105 feet by 51 feet, was built by George Washington Youngman in 1865 as the Nippenose Woolen Mill. It was four stories high and lit by 100 windows. It took two years to build the mill that went into operation on January 1, 1868. In 1873, it was producing 1,500 yards of material per week, using 20,000 pounds of wool. Philadelphia and New York City were major outlets for their goods.

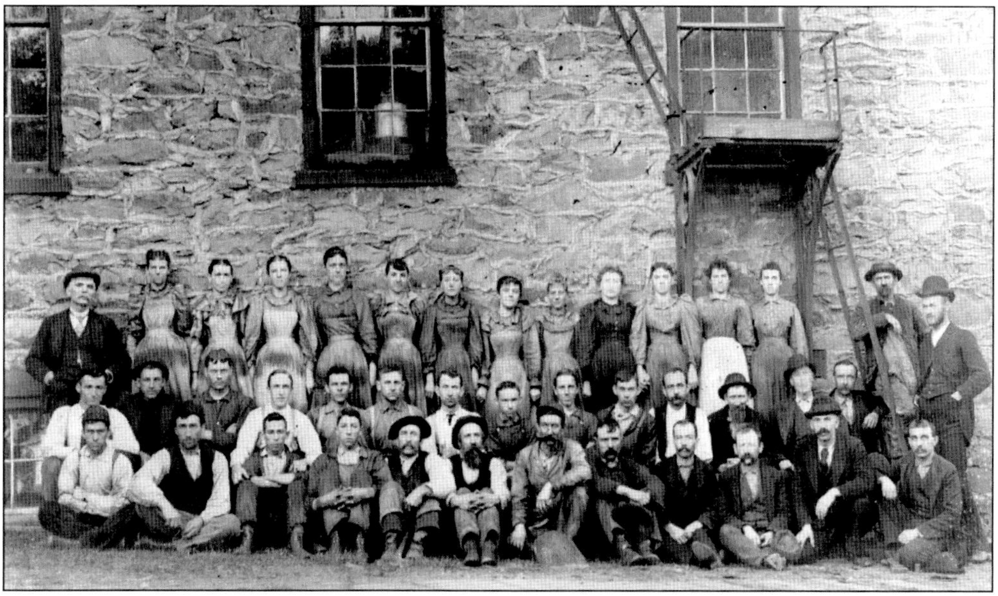

These were mill workers around 1891. Brothers William and George Washington Youngman went out of business after the disastrous June 1, 1889, flood. They lost their homes, which were located across the creek from the mill, and nine family members. From 1890 to 1902, the mill was run as the Leinbach Woolen Mill. It was this family disaster that prompted John Youngman Sr. to lead the fight for Williamsport's flood protection plan, which was completed in 1955, some 50 years later.

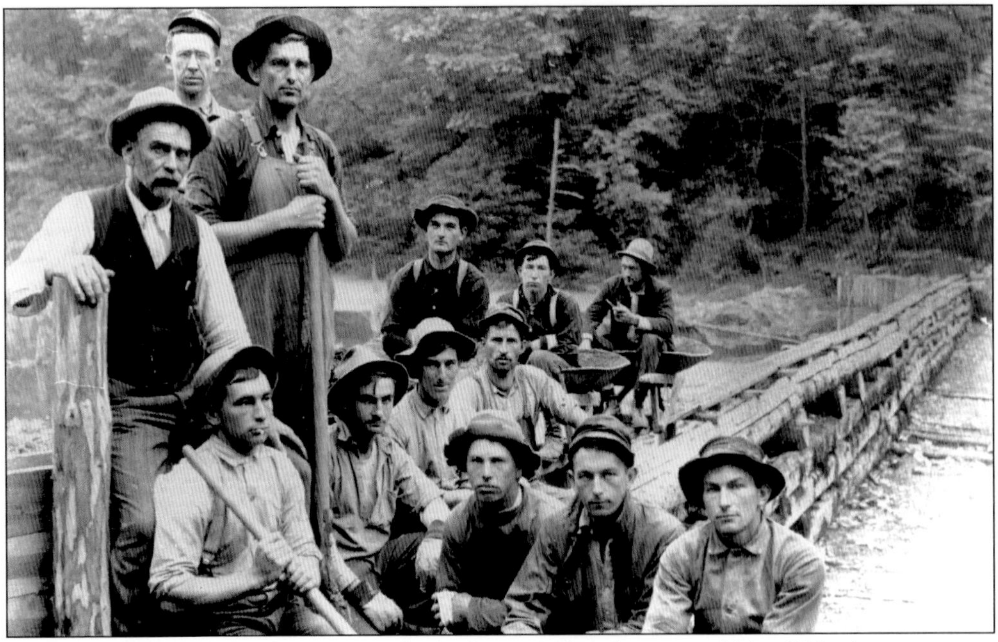

The original milldam and flume were built about 1866 and getting old by 1911 when someone, fishing with dynamite, blew up the dam. It is shown being rebuilt. From left to right are (first row) Ed Hanner, Charles Pearson, Floyd Blair, and Jake Hanner; (second row) unidentified, Clyde Laubach, and Marion Tomb; (standing) Christian Hess (builder), Harry C. Williams, and Harry Yarrison; (third row) Ercel Ramsey, John Hanner, and Charlie Weikert.

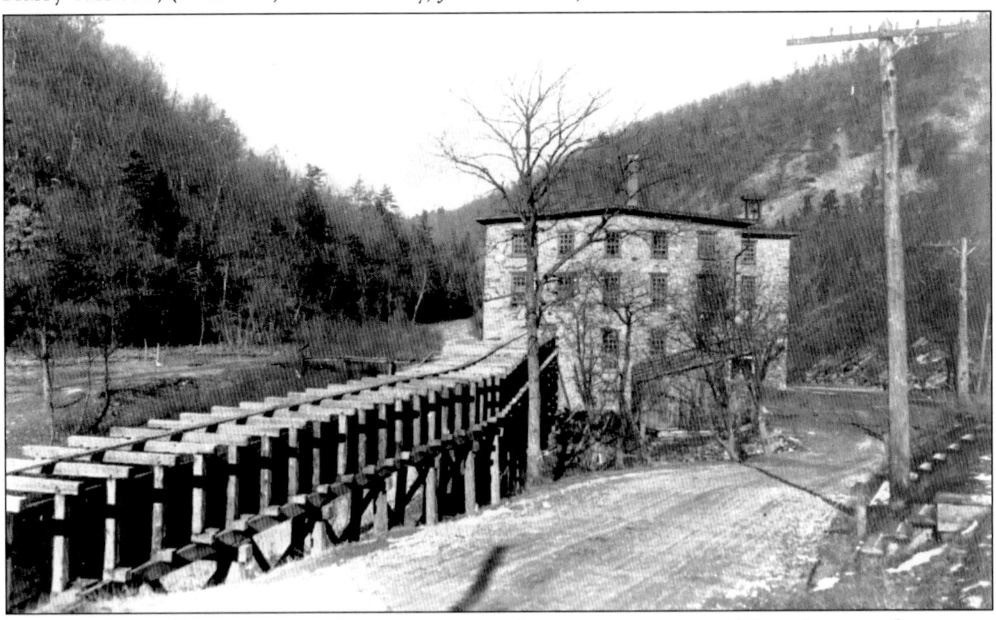

This woolen mill was converted to a stone-grinding operation in 1907, and a new flume was constructed to carry water to the overshot waterwheel. The new (1916) Fitz waterwheel could deliver up to 200 horsepower to the line shaft. One of the products produced by the crushers, grinders, and pulverizers was used as a base for gray paint, which was used to paint American battleships during World War I, hence the name paint mill.

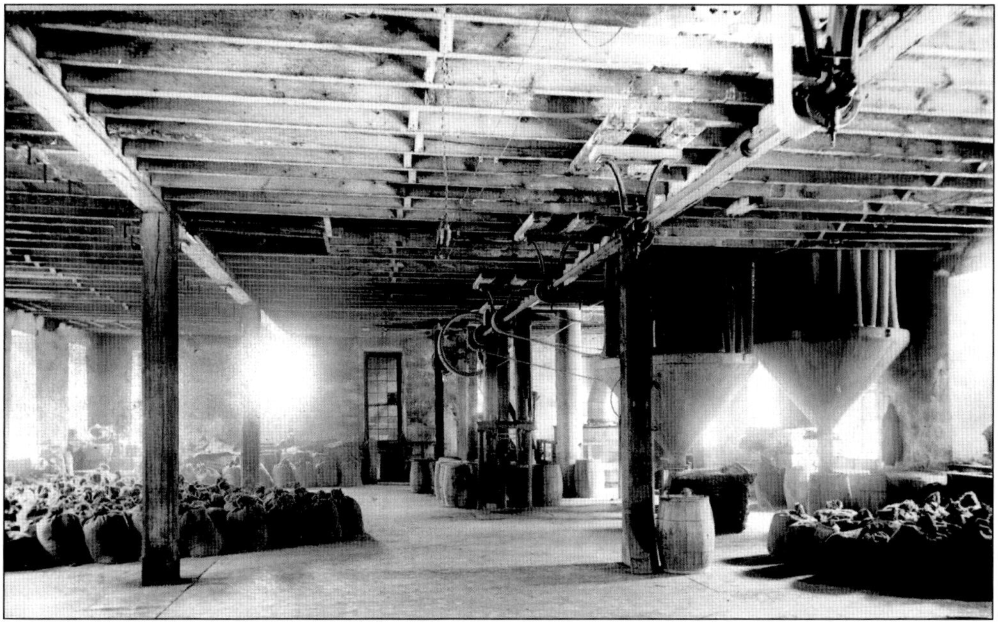

This is a view of the north end of the basement floor in the paint mill. Each 10-hour day produced 20 tons of finished product. The ground rock material was packaged in 400-pound barrels, 200-pound burlap sacks, and 75-pound paper sacks. John Garrett hauled stone to the mill from a quarry by horse and wagon and delivered five barrels of product per load to the railroad station in Antes Fort. Ercel Ramsey fed stone to the grinders.

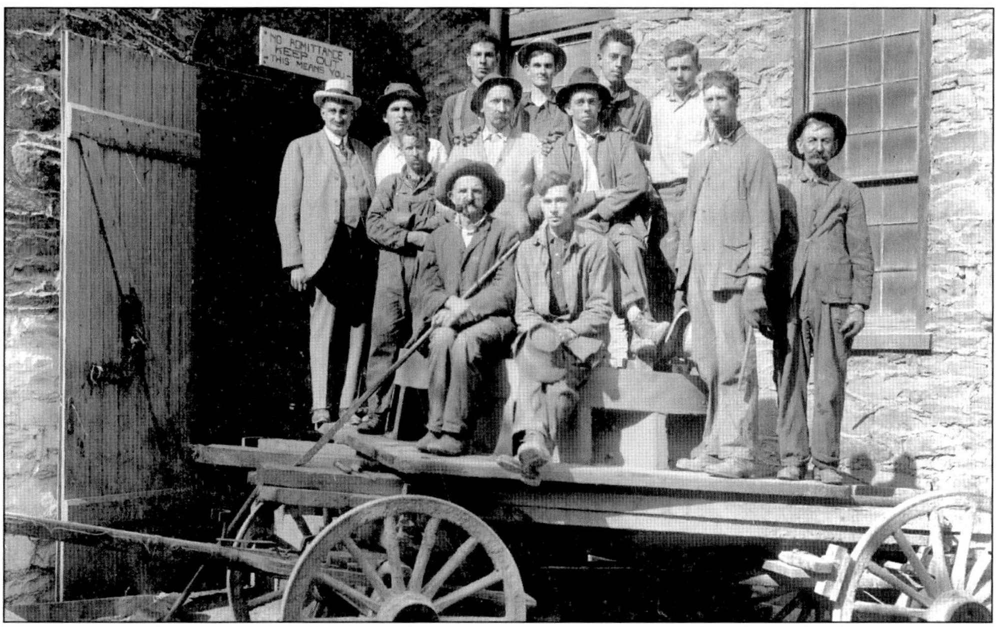

These men were about to install a new pulverizer in the mill in 1916. Pictured from left to right are (first row) Chris Miller and Verus Fenstemaker; (second row) Mike Tomb, Bill Brownlee, Fred Eoute, Asher Tomb, and Mike Barner; (third row) Mr. Cook, Harry C. Williams, Charles Fenstemaker, Ercel Ramsey, Walter Keeler, and Stuart Welshans. Welshans's team and wagon brought the machinery from the train station.

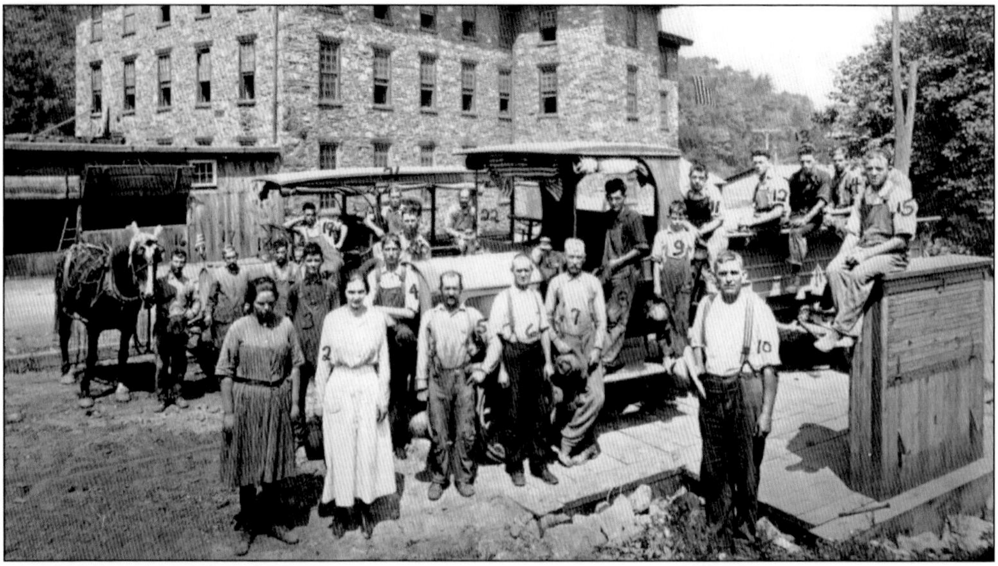

This is a picture of the paint mill crew taken during World War I. From left to right are (first row) Harriet Williams, Florence Williams, Ambrose Grambly, Jesse Gheen, Bill Garrett, Harry C. Williams, and Lute Smith (sitting on scales); (second row, from the horse) Bill Bennett, Mike Barner, James Showers, Ercel Ramsey, Guy Barner, Walter Keeler, Charles Pearson, Ellery Fenstemaker, and Henry Ludwig; (third row, from the truck cab) Walter Overdorf, Harry L. Williams, Dick Koons, Dayton Kaufman, Ollie Steinbacher, and Ambrose Eiswert. The truck in front is a Mack, and the one behind is a Selden.

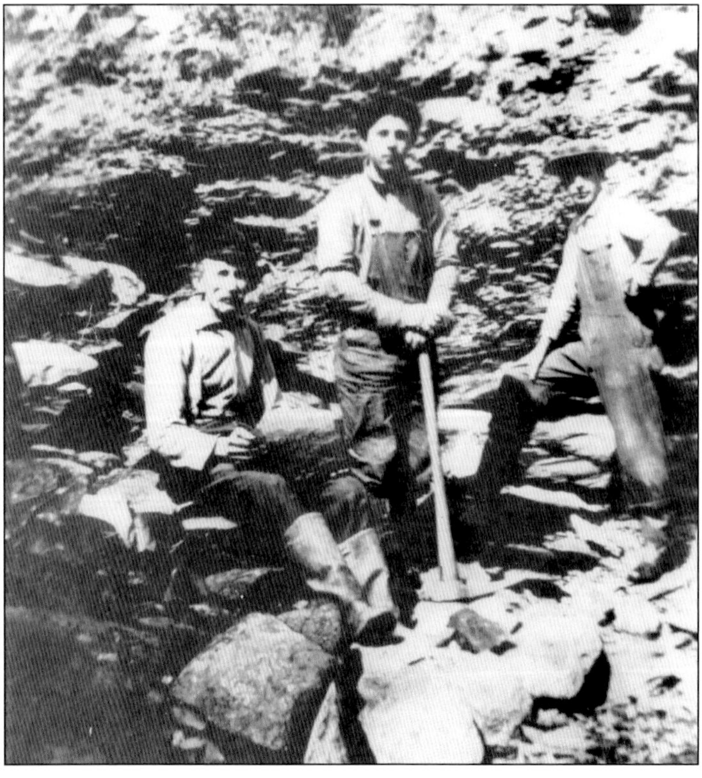

These three men were mining rock for the paint mill when such work was done by hand. This was known as the Black Hole Mine, which was located at the Overdorf farm in the Upper End. The shale rock is soft enough to be crushed by hand and is full of plant fossils. From left to right are Daniel Showers, John Smith, and Frank Kirby. Kirby was also a valley barber and on Saturday walked to Antes Fort and cut hair in the bottom of the Antes Fort Hotel.

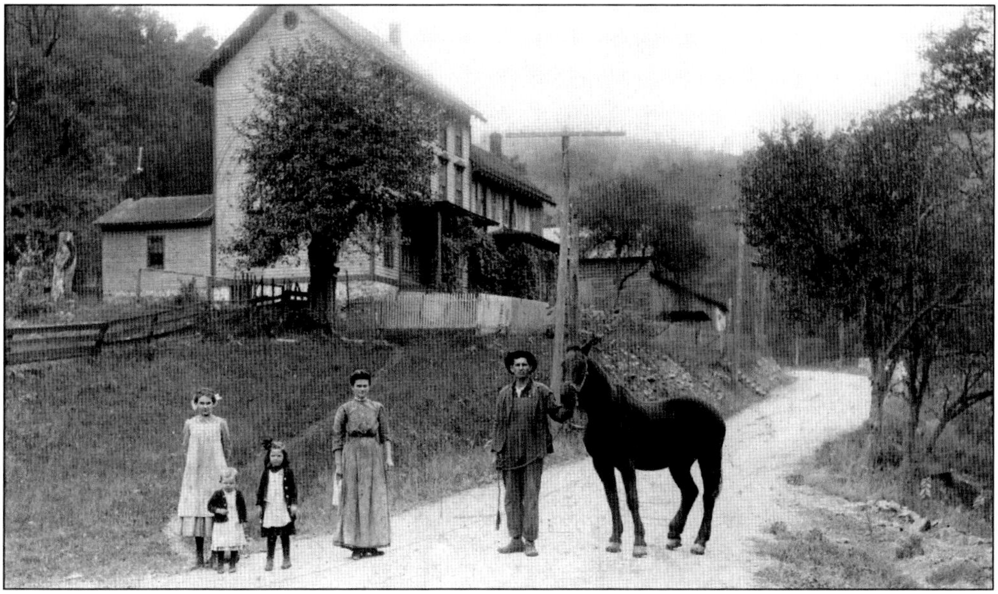

Harry C. Williams was associated with the stone business since 1907 and bought the business in 1932. The family lived in the superintendent's house, which was built in 1872, and in this picture, the old three-story boardinghouse was still attached. He married Clara Siegel of Larryville on December 22, 1896. The Williams family is seen here in 1910. From left to right are Florence, Harry L., Harriette, Clara, Harry C., and Maud the horse. The family continued the operation until the Agnes flood of 1972.

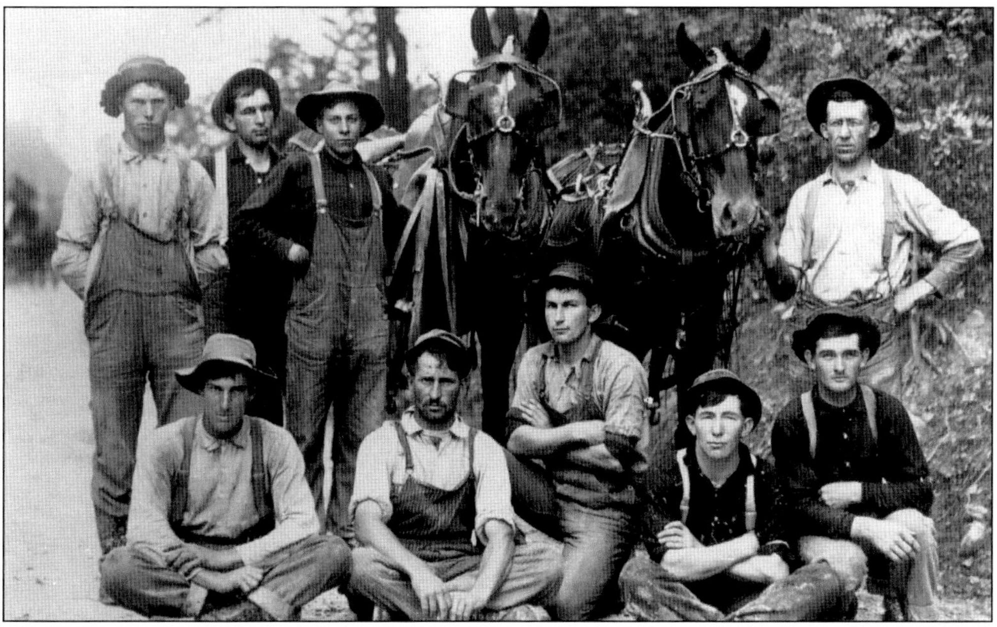

These men posed for a picture near the mill in 1911. From left to right are (first row) Clyde Laubach, Marion Tomb, Jake Hanner, John Hanner, and Ercel Ramsey; (second row) Charles Pearson, Ed Hanner, Sees Welshans (with team), and Harry Yarrison. Byron Welshans worked here in 1922 when the pay was $3.50 per 10-hour day, six days a week. When the woolen mill workers were here, they were paid in gold coin.

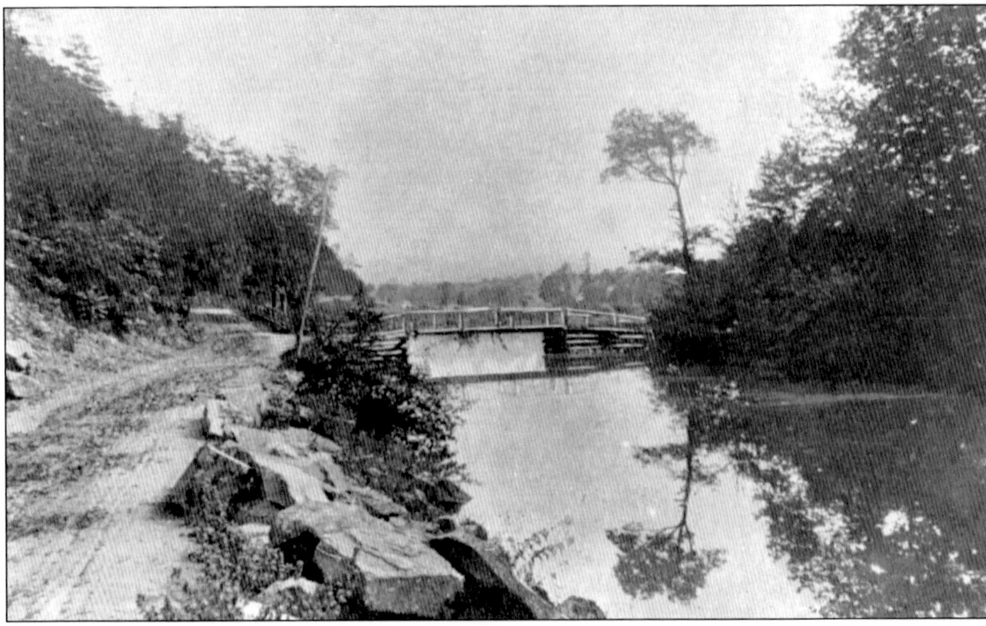

The southern end of Antes Gap opens into the northern end of Nippenose Valley at a village called Millport. The first bridge encountered was the Merriman bridge, which connected to an old road that snaked westward along the foot of the mountain, meeting up with what is the Thompson Road today. Six or so springs are located along this old road, where early settlers such as John Tomb, John Yates, Henry Wensel, and Jacob Smith built their log homes.

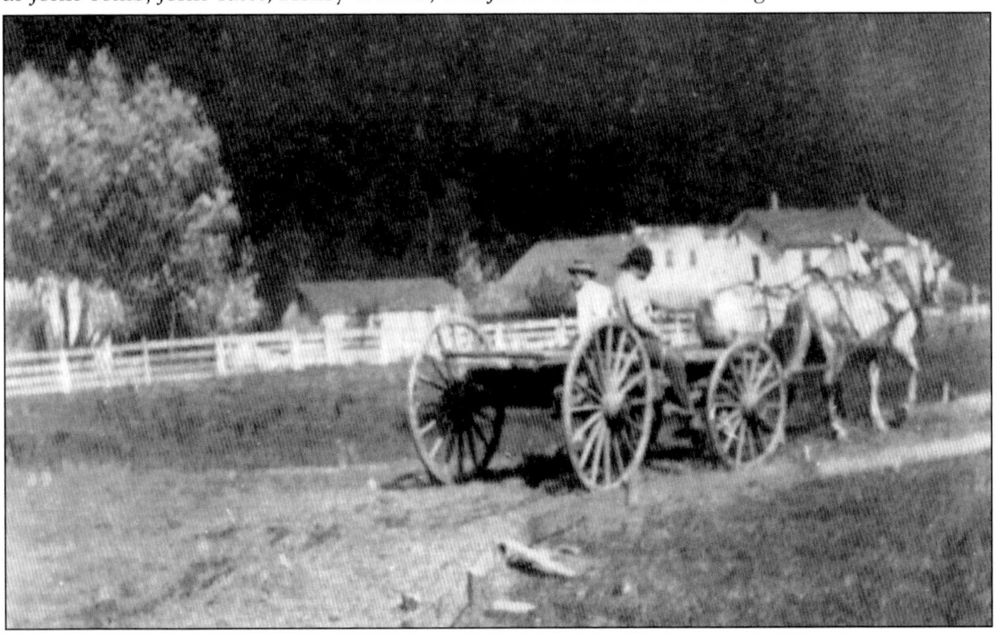

Millport was laid out as a town in 1837, and about a dozen homes were built. Around 1820, a gristmill was build by Jacob Sallada for John Henry Antes Jr., and Antes built a covered bridge over the creek in 1823. Here the Sanderson family built a large general store in which the first post office in the valley opened in 1828. It was named Nippenose, and the postmaster was Daniel Antes. The village was destroyed by the 1889 flood.

This is the only known picture of the Millport gristmill that may have been built as early as 1817 by Jacob Sallada. In 1847, John J. Sanderson advertised in the *Jersey Shore Republican* newspaper, "The mill is now prepared to grind corn on the cob." An 1880 advertisement stated that Reuben Bower had leased the Sanderson flour mill and added new machinery. Jacob Sees was the last miller.

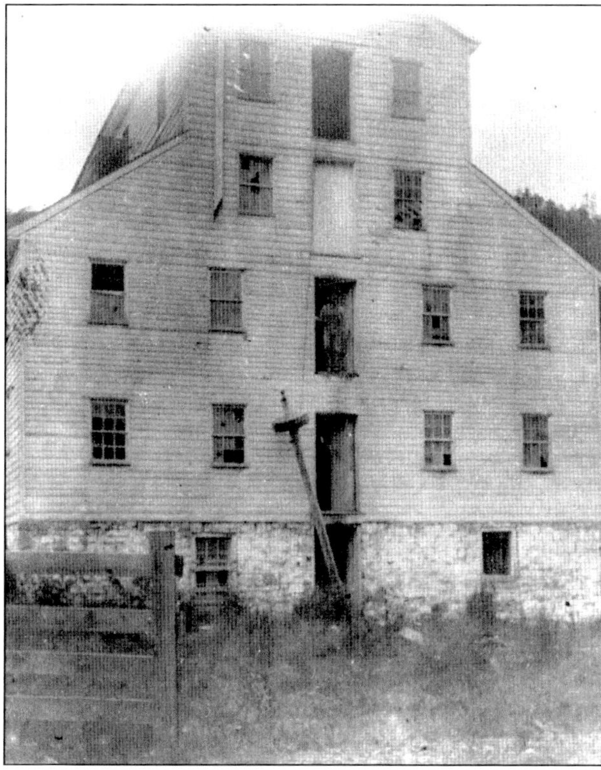

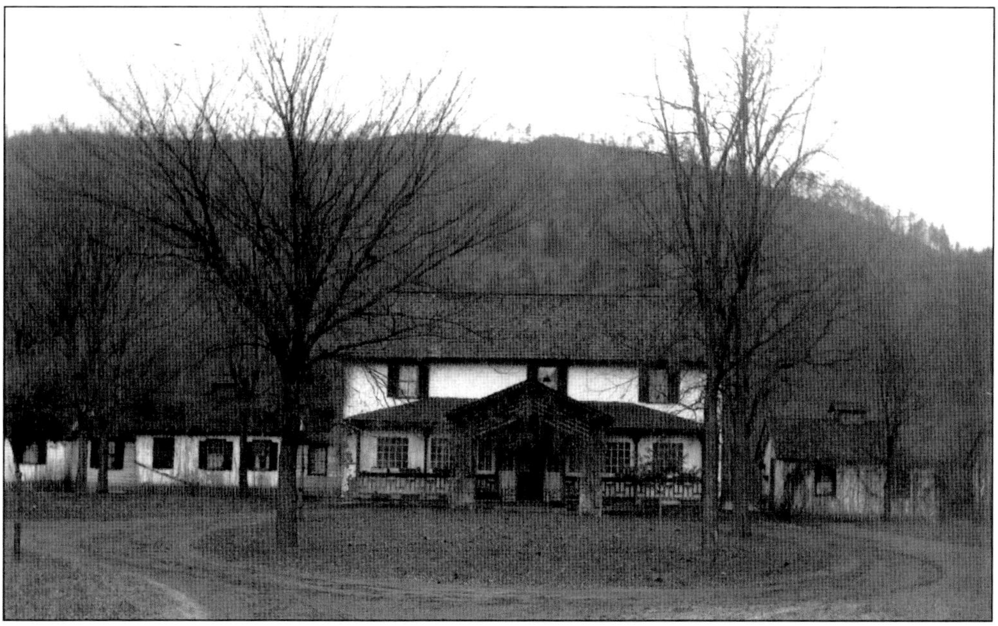

This is the oldest house in Nippenose Valley and may be one of the oldest in Lycoming County. The cornerstone of the stone house is said to have been laid in 1769, the year William Penn's sawmill tract No. 1724 was deeded to Robert Forster. It belonged to the Antes family from 1798 to 1848, the Sanderson family from 1848 to 1921, and then the Barclay/Sweitzer families to the present.

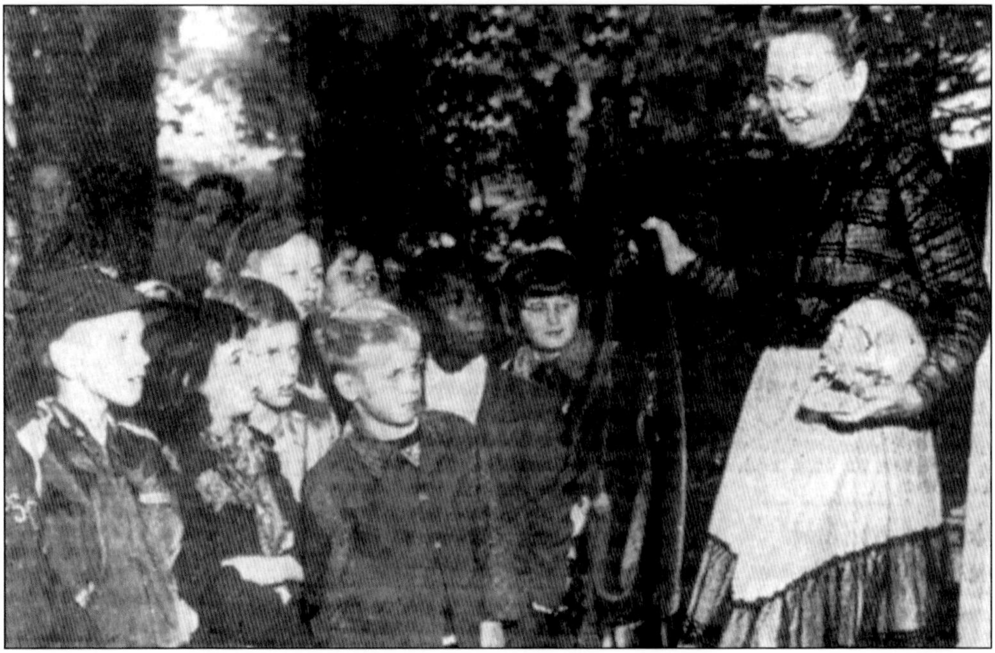

This photograph appeared in the *Williamsport Sun-Gazette* on October 14, 1952. Schoolchildren were bused to local areas of historic interest, and a most memorable experience was had by all when Cleo Barclay showed the skull and sword of a Hessian soldier George Sanderson had found in a walled-up section of the basement in 1876. During the Revolution, the place was called Fort Forster and was considered a protective haven from marauding Native Americans.

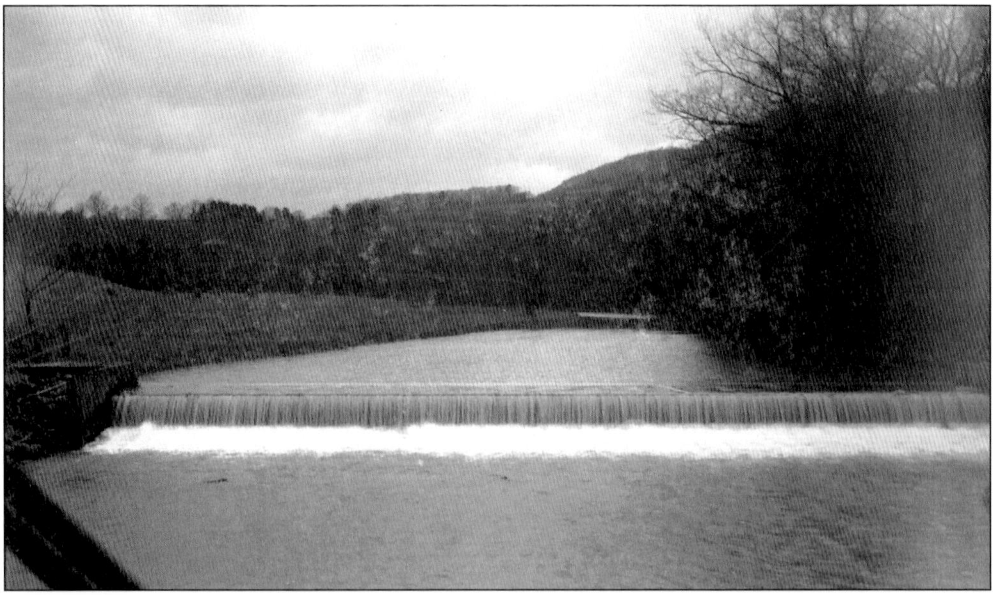

This was the Sanderson dam that was built at the foot of Millport hill. Nepanose, or Antes Creek, flows out of the ground a short distance above and, at the time, coursed a mile and a half through Lochabar property—some 1,500 acres. Near the cabin were fish boxes capable of handling 15,000 small trout. This limestone stream was always noted for its trout and in 2007 was given the highest stream rating in Pennsylvania, exceptional value (EV).

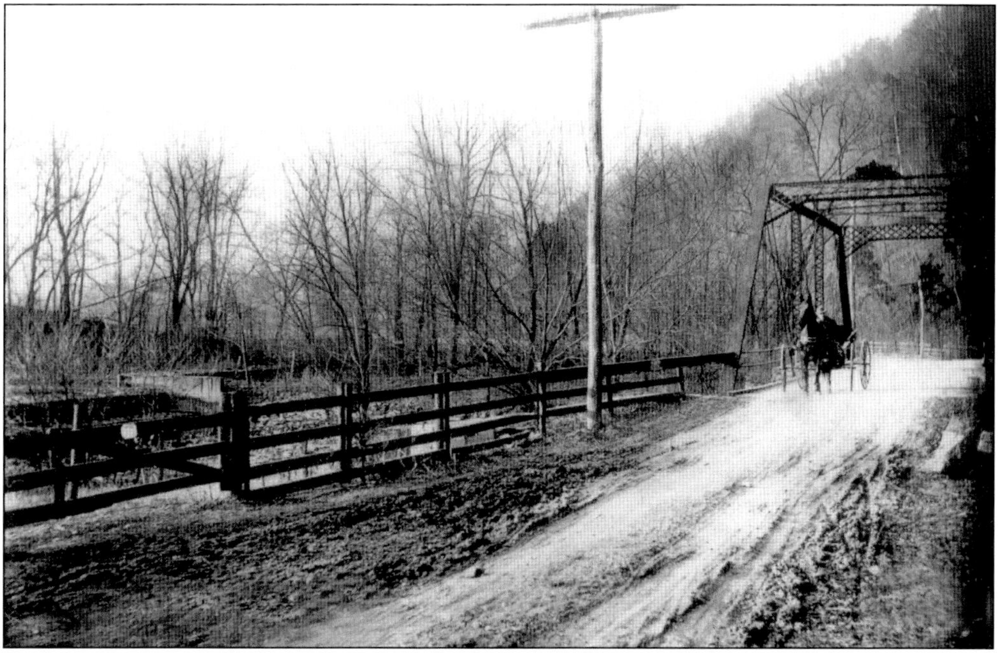

This steel bridge crossed Antes Creek just below Sanderson dam on the Lochabar property. The year was 1908, and the man in the buggy was William Camerer. His father, Robert, moved to the United States from Germany in 1867 and owned and operated the planing mill in Jersey Shore where many doors, windows, and shutters were made for local housing.

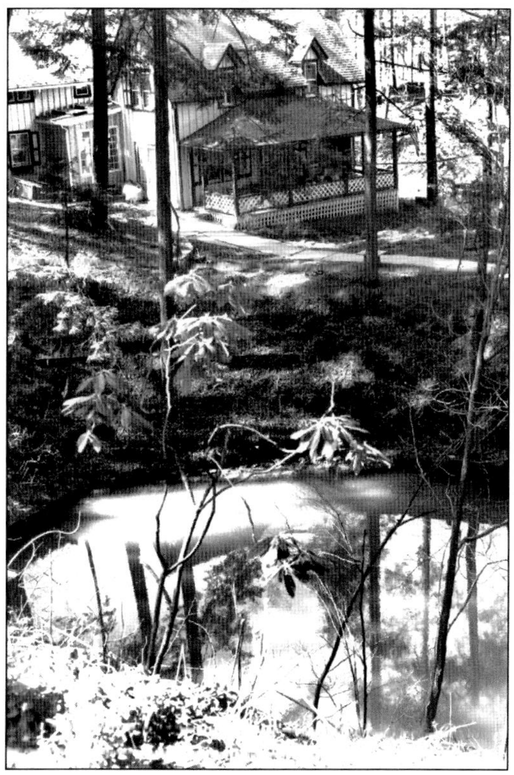

Lochabar spring, the headwater of Antes Creek, is the largest spring in the state. It produces an average of 18,000 gallons of water per minute or 25 million gallons per day. Robert Covenhoven, a Revolutionary War soldier, called it "Widow's Spring," because the two land warrants surrounding it were owned by women whose husbands had been killed during the war. Their names were Mary Field (Welshans farm) and Grace Little (John Eck farm).

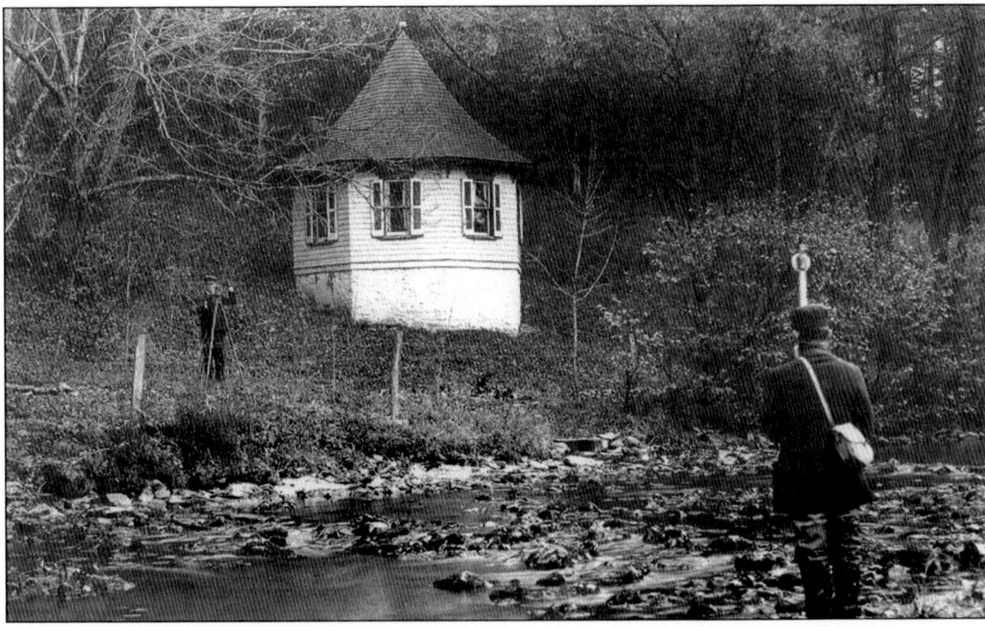

Antes Creek has always been a private fishing stream. George Sanderson's private fish preserve was guarded against fishing by a watchman who made use of two such watchtowers—one at the Millport bridge, the foundation of which is still there, and the other at the big bend in the creek near the Merriman bridge, which was washed away during the 1889 flood. Abe Welshans, a neighbor, was fined $100 for fishing the stream in 1895.

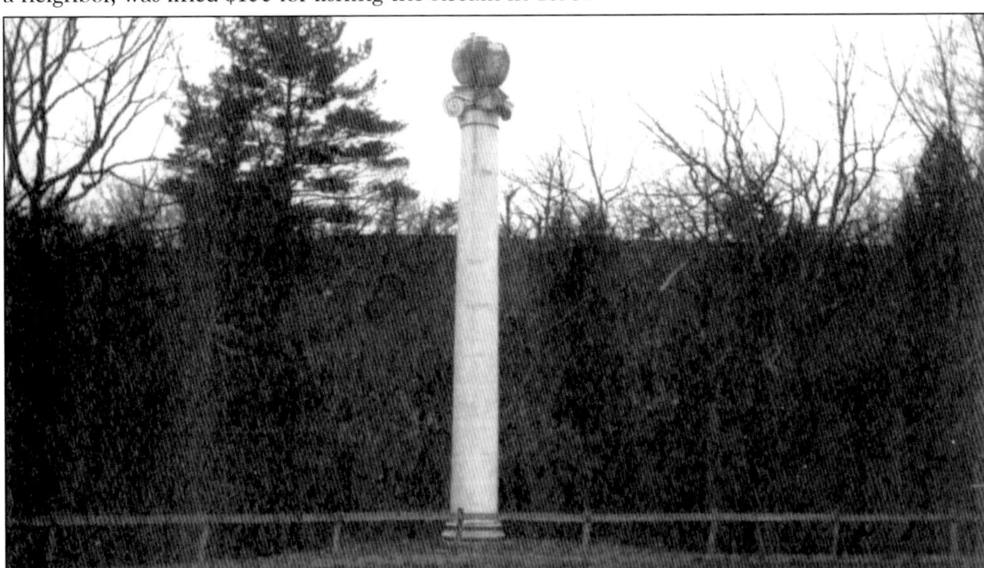

This pillar serves as a monument to Chief Wi-daagh who lived at the big spring prior to the Revolutionary War and sold Native American land in this area to the white man. His grave is marked by a pile of stones along the creek not far from this column. This was one of six pillars from the Pennsylvania Capitol Building, which burned in 1897. There is another in the Jersey Shore Cemetery and one at Linnwood Cemetery in McElhattan. Sanderson had this placed here in 1900.

This 45-foot-high column, weighing 41 tons, was placed as a memorial to Chief Wi-daagh and the Native Americans who once lived here. Uriah Cummings wrote a book for Sanderson named *The Song of U-ri-on-tah* in 1900. It seems it was written in riddles, making use of Native American names and places, and contains numerous drawings of Native Americans and their activities. His daughter Emily wrote in the front of her book, "My daddy and friends playing Indian. Some of this is true, which?"

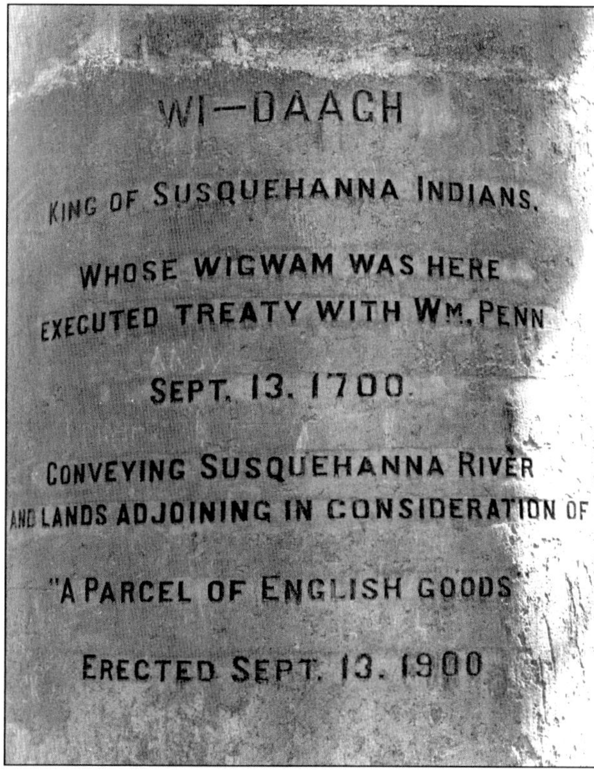

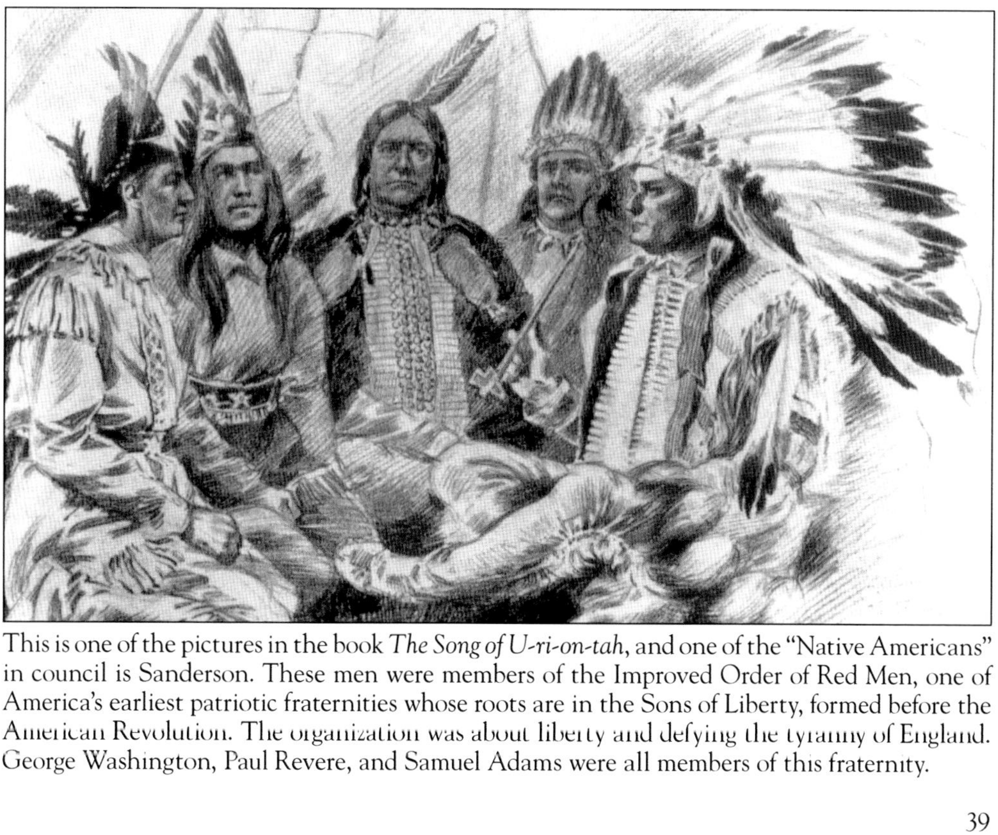

This is one of the pictures in the book *The Song of U-ri-on-tah*, and one of the "Native Americans" in council is Sanderson. These men were members of the Improved Order of Red Men, one of America's earliest patriotic fraternities whose roots are in the Sons of Liberty, formed before the American Revolution. The organization was about liberty and defying the tyranny of England. George Washington, Paul Revere, and Samuel Adams were all members of this fraternity.

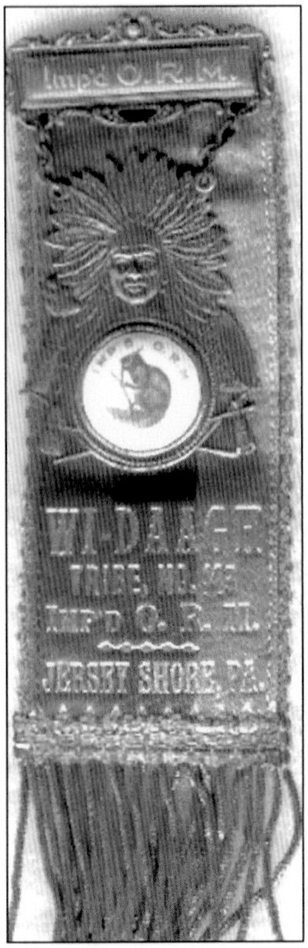

Benjamin Franklin studied the laws of the Iroquois Confederacy in 1744 and wrote his findings in the Albany Plan of Union as a guide to uniting the colonies. No one was interested until the Constitution was being written, at which time they discovered Iroquois law reflected such things as a system of checks and balances among chiefs and for allowing individual liberty. It promoted a strong central government but allowed for states' rights. The symbol of the eagle came from the Iroquois as well, but the American eagle is clutching 13 arrows instead of six.

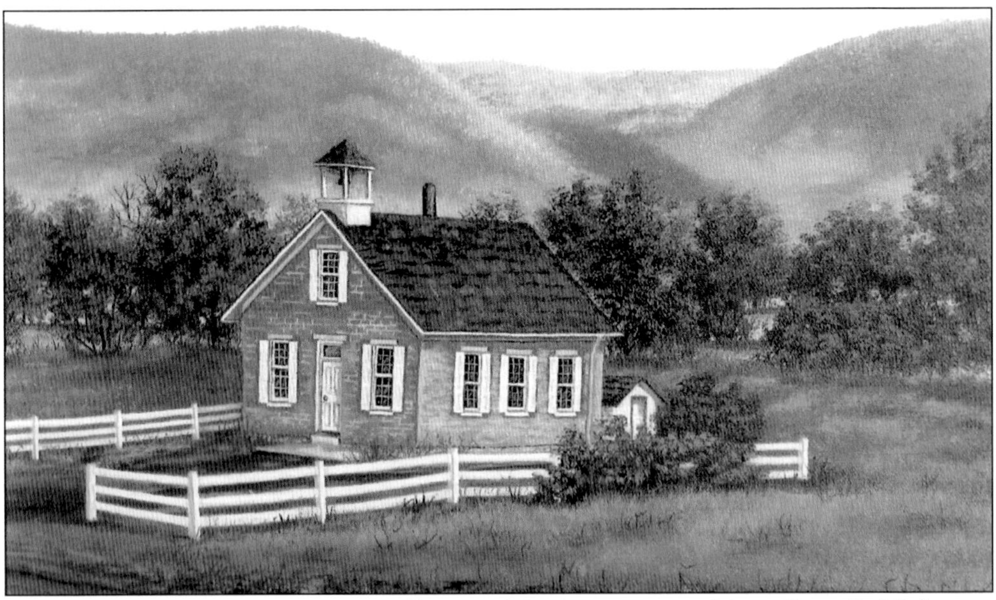

At the top of Millport Hill between Millport and Oval is a section of the valley called Ecktown. A school was established here before 1861, and this one replaced it around 1898 on a piece of ground sold to the Limestone Township School Board by Augustus Eck. It closed in 1921, and John Welshans got the contract to transport students from Ecktown to Oval the next year. At one time, there were 212 one-room schools in Lycoming County, and 9 of these were in the valley.

Three

OLD-TIME FARM LIFE

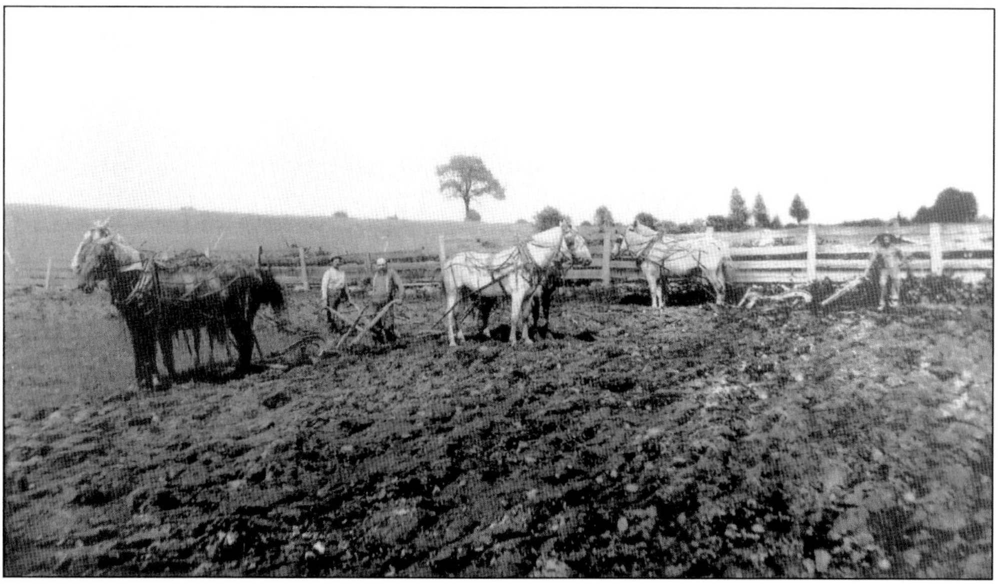

From left to right are Lawrence Wolfe, Newton Phleger, and John Phleger on one of three Phleger farms along the Voneida or Middle Road just east of Jamestown. Both Syracuse and Oliver plows were used in the valley. In 1840, plows were made by local blacksmiths, and by 1860, cast-iron plows were being replaced with steel plows. The manufacture of Syracuse plows began in New York in 1876, and the business was later bought out by Deere. Two horses pulled 10-inch plows, three horses pulled 12-inch plows.

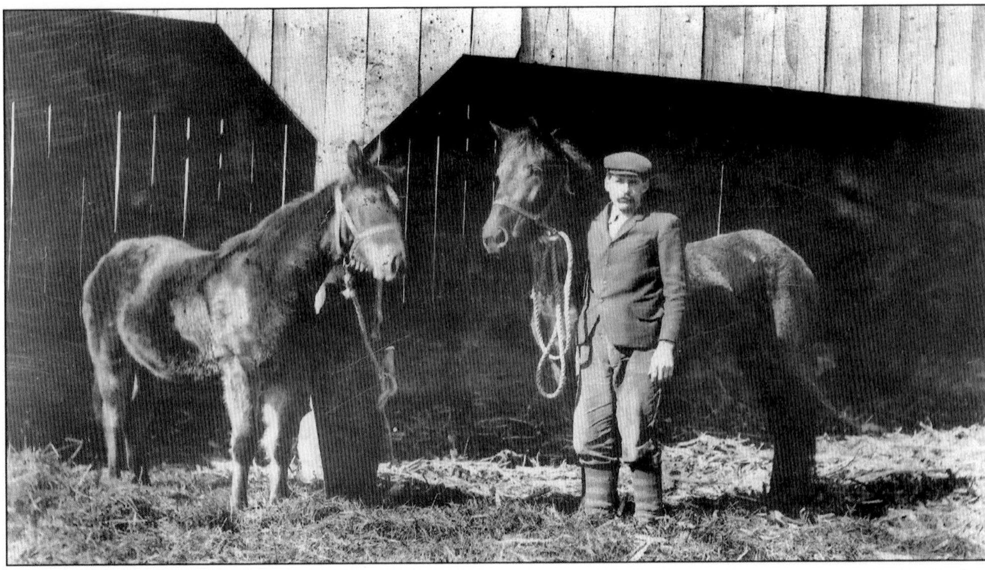

This picture shows Wilbert Lehman at his farm along Middle Road. It was not until 1865 that Pennsylvania farmers eliminated their oxen in favor of the horse. Between 1850 and 1890, the Pennsylvania horse population rose from 350,000 to 618,000, and there were never enough horses raised within the state. Valley farmers sometimes bought green broke horses from out west that came off the train at Antes Fort.

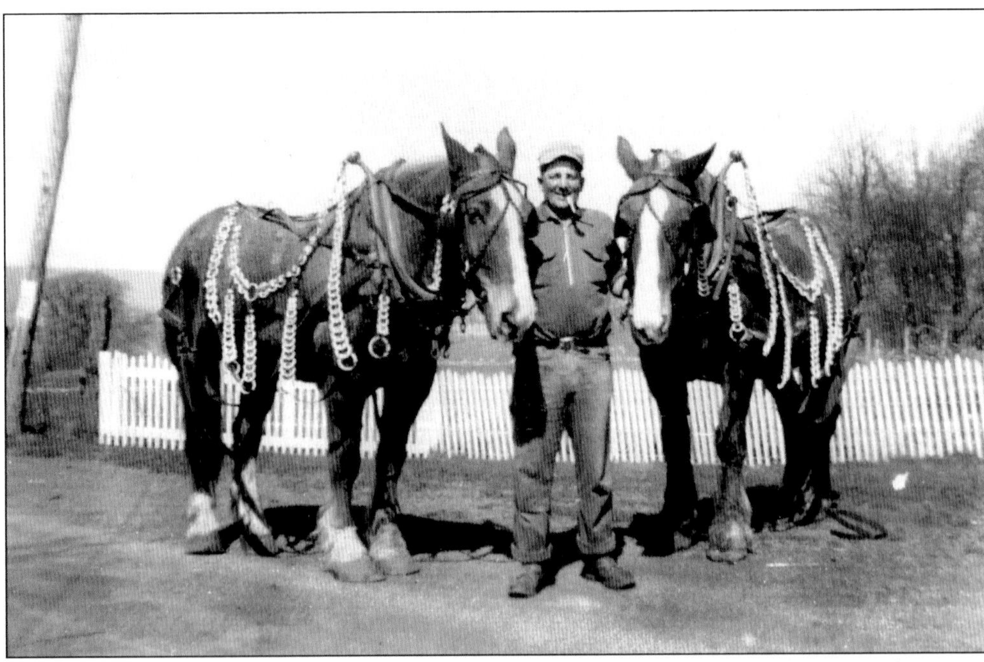

There were a number of farmers in the valley that were slow to give up their horses, and Leonard "Punk" Welshans was one of them. He is shown here with a fine set of workhorses at his farm south of Jamestown. Their names were Tom and Jack. Horse jewelry was common throughout the ages and made mostly of metal until the development and practical use of celluloid by 1870.

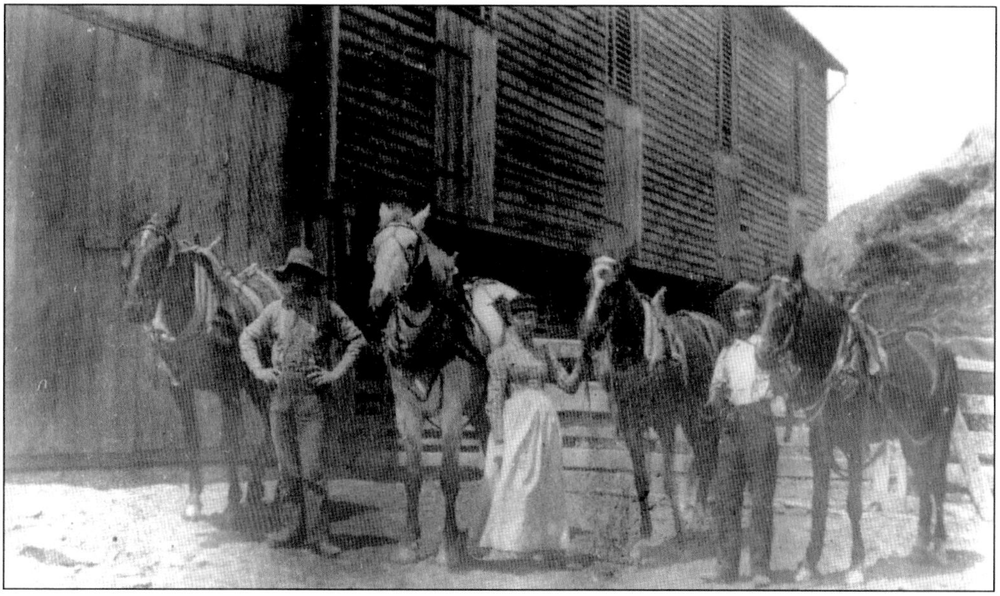

This picture was taken in front of the Hampe barn in Oval. From left to right are George Hampe, Elsie Sweitzer Hampe, and Merrill Koons. The horses at left were named Jim and Dandy, and those to the right were Ned and Rock. Horses were not taxed until they were four years old, at which time they could be profitably worked. In 1910, horses were the most valuable farm animals, quite a bit ahead of cows. Before tractors, yearly replacement of horses was about 50,000 animals. In 1940, two-thirds of all farms still had horses.

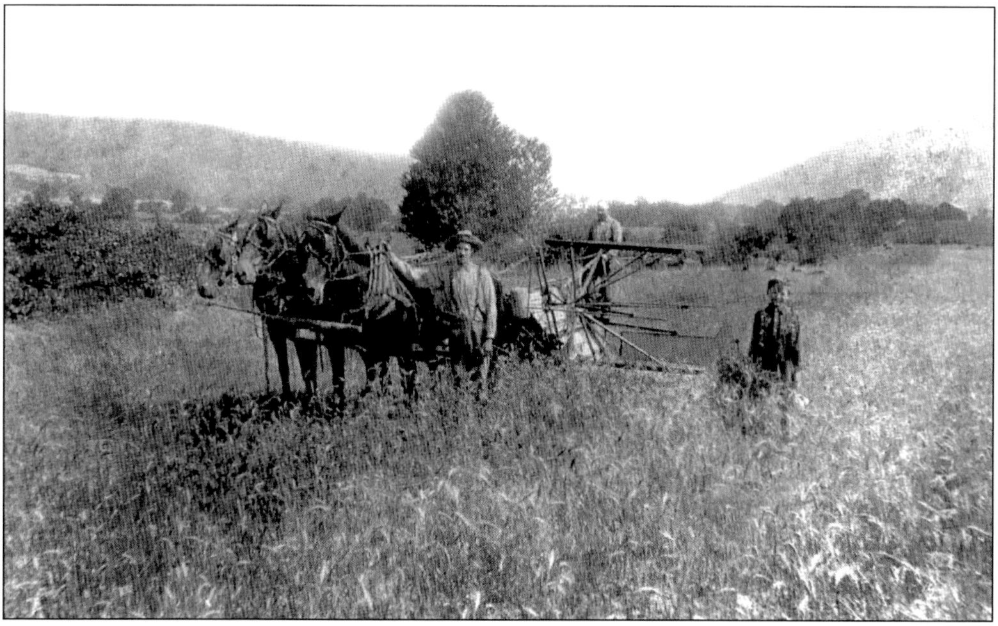

Here is Ulysses Grant Welshans on a McCormick grain binder in front of the family farm in 1900. His oldest son, Abram, stands at right, and Harvey Lehman of Fourth Gap is by the horses. Three horses harnessed together were known as a spike team. Hussey and McCormick reapers were developed in 1833 and 1834 but did not become popular until 1860. Up to that time, grain was harvested with a sickle or cradle and later threshed with a wooden flail on the barn floor.

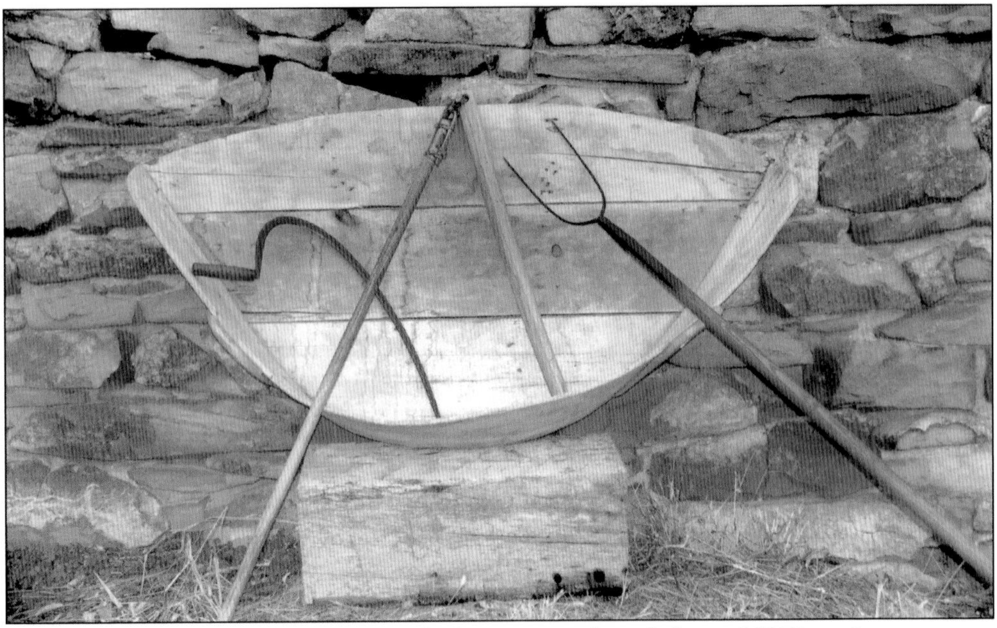

These are old-time grain harvesting tools that were used until the mid-1800s, or later on some valley farms. Such equipment was used for 1,000 years. Grain was cut with a reaping sickle, tied into sheaves, and stacked into shocks. The sheave fork loaded the sheaves onto a wagon, the sheaves were taken to the barn and flailed, and then they were scooped up with the winnowing tray and thrown into the air. A good breeze through the barn doors separated the grain from the chaff.

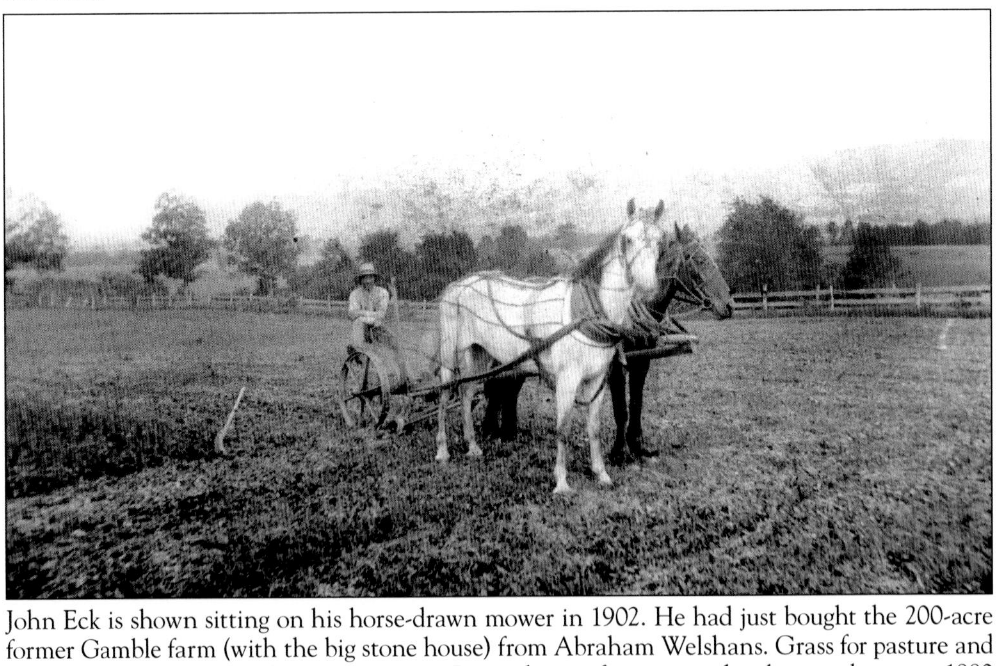

John Eck is shown sitting on his horse-drawn mower in 1902. He had just bought the 200-acre former Gamble farm (with the big stone house) from Abraham Welshans. Grass for pasture and hay had long been of high importance to Pennsylvania farmers, and only once between 1880 and 1930 was its value beaten by another crop. Timothy was the most valuable hay, as it was used to fuel the horses.

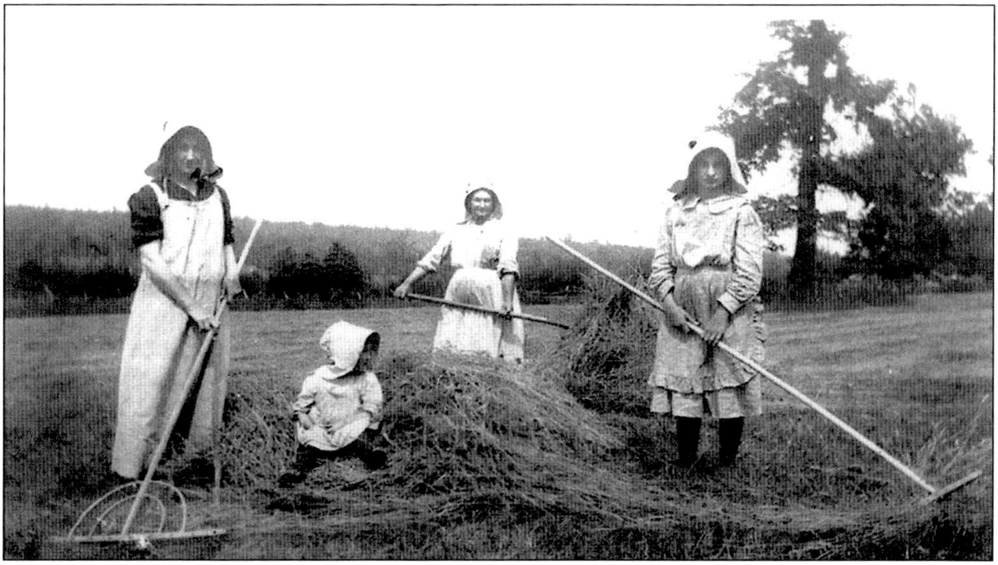

At one time, hay fields were raked by hand. With mechanization came the dump rake and side-delivery rake, and like the Amish today, the old German farmers wasted nothing. Here is a piece of field the rake did not catch. It is being hand raked by, from left to right, Mary Ulsamer, Barbara Dincher, and Margaret Ulsamer, with the child, Dorothea Bower, sitting on the pile.

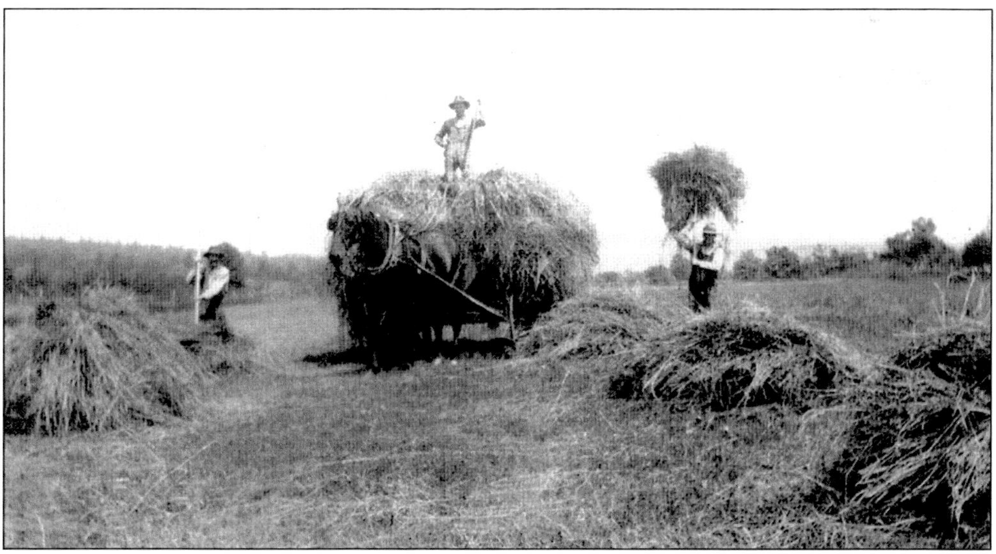

Low-slung hay wagons were piled high with hay, and the driver is also high up astraddle an upright. He drove the wagon to the barn hill where the horses were unhitched and the wagon hooked up to a pulley system that enabled the horses to pull it onto the barn floor. A large hay fork was dropped into the loose hay, pulled up, swung into the mow, and released at just the right moment.

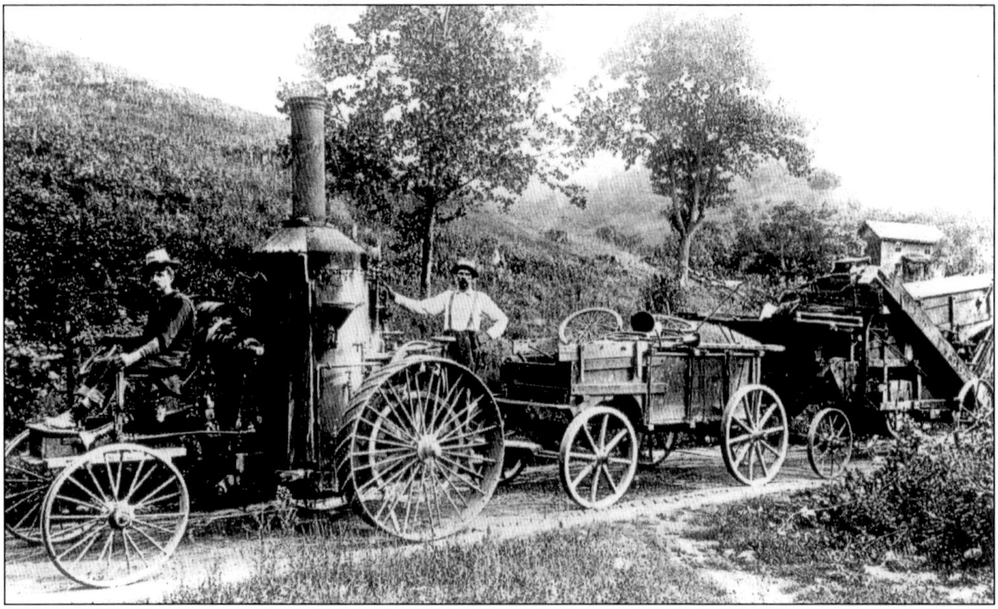

In 1853, Joseph Fawkes of Lancaster invented the first practical steam tractor. This one is likely a Westinghouse vertical boiler steam tractor that was first built by George Westinghouse, father of George Westinghouse Jr., the founder of the Westinghouse Company. The place is near Collomsville, and the photographer, D. Vincent Smith, and his bicycle are behind the boiler. The threshing machine follows, and the water wagon should be at the end of the train.

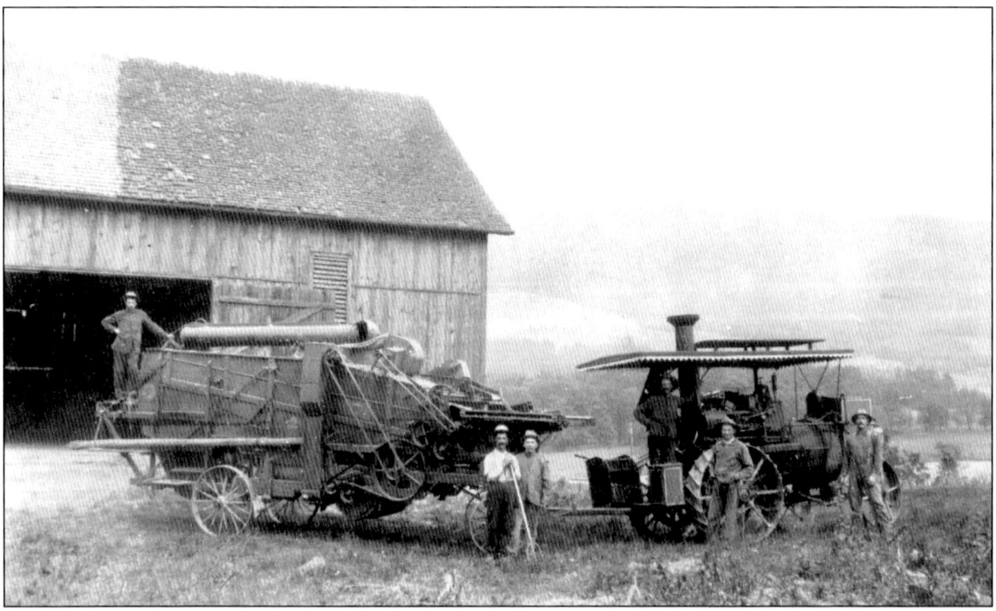

This picture shows John Bixel with his Huber steam tractor and threshing machine at the Oakland Welshans farm in 1912. The most successful years for these tractors were between 1880 and 1920, and 5,000 such tractors were built in 1900. Huber began building steam tractors in the 1890s, and its production line was second only to McCormick's. Huber built its last steam tractor in 1927, about the same time light gasoline-powered tractors were coming into common use.

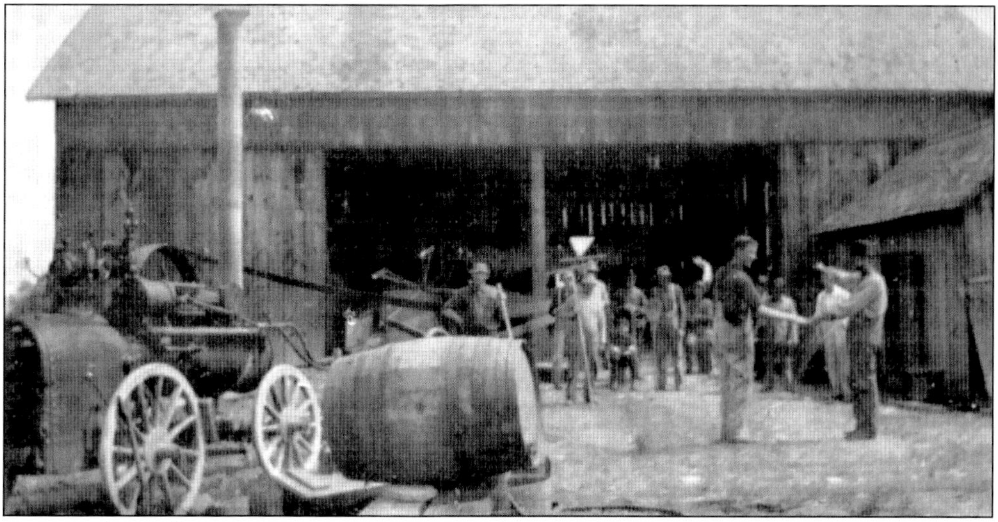

Here is a horse-drawn steam engine at the Frank Bower farm on Bastress Mountain. Rob Baier and Frank Bower Jr. are at front right. Between 1860 and 1883, steam farm tractors went from portable skid-mounted engines to horse-drawn engines with wagon wheels to self-propelled horse-guided engines to self-propelled and self-steering designs. The job of threshing was usually hot, humid, and dirty and required a lot of people, each with a specific job.

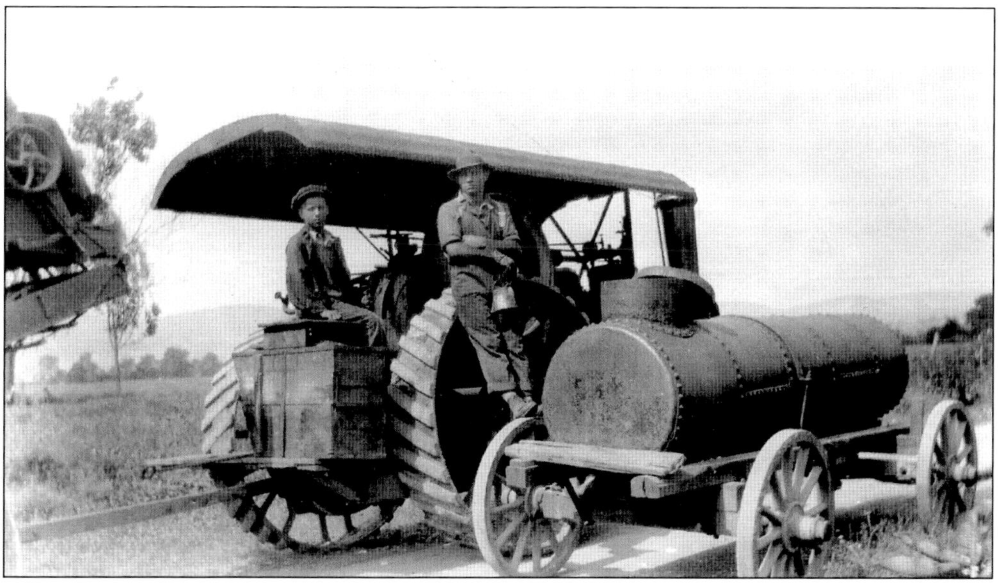

Stewart Eck (left) and Howard Eck are shown with their father's Frick steam engine, threshing machine, and water tank. George Frick began manufacturing such steam tractors in 1853 at Waynesboro, and the Frick Implement Company was formed in 1873 and became incorporated in 1885. Frick sold about 1,800 tractors a year. In 1885, Pennsylvania law required that all drivers of these machines must stop 300 feet from horse-drawn vehicles. John Eck traded this tractor on a Huber gasoline tractor in 1914.

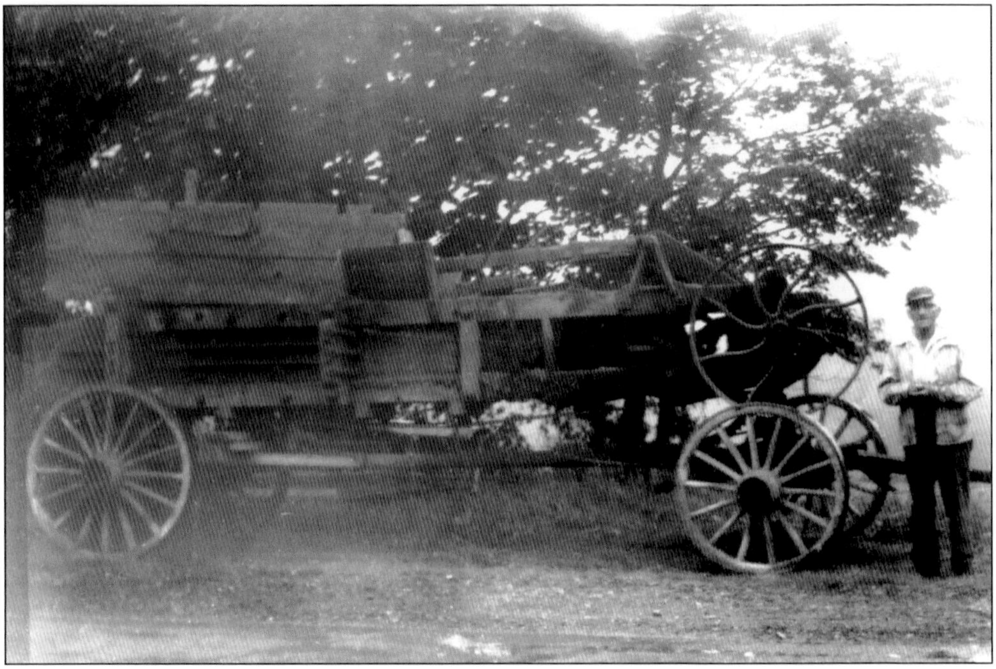

This picture shows Howard Eck standing beside a stationary baler on the John Eck farm. It is said to be the first baler in the valley. It was belt driven off the flywheel of John's Frick steam tractor. Hay was gathered from the field and brought to the baler where it was compressed by the plunger into 80- to 100-pound bales. Hand-threaded and looped baling wires held the bales together.

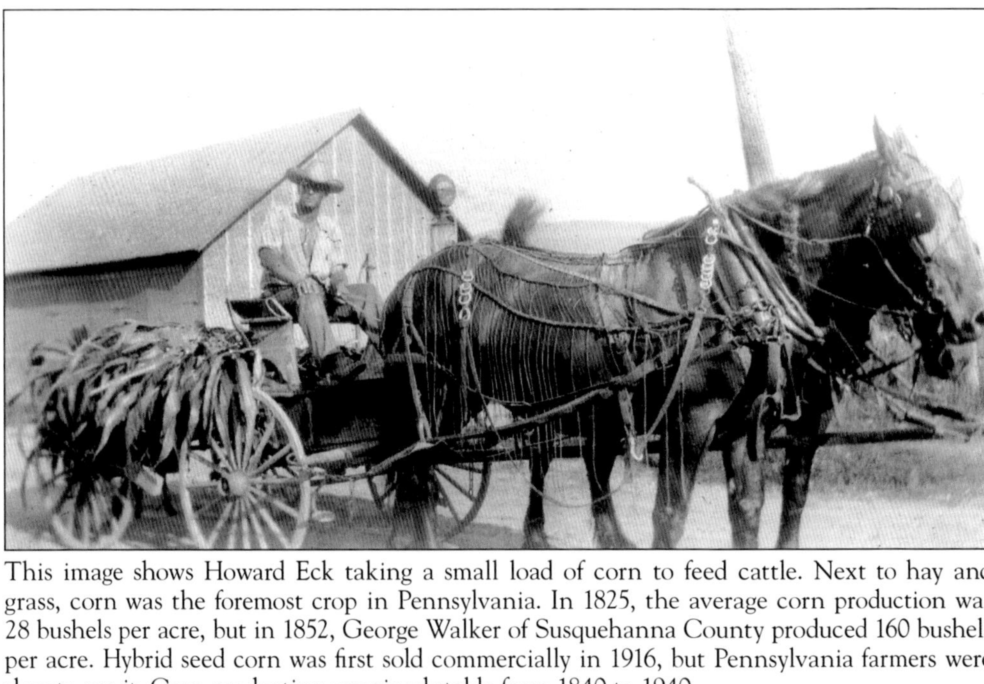

This image shows Howard Eck taking a small load of corn to feed cattle. Next to hay and grass, corn was the foremost crop in Pennsylvania. In 1825, the average corn production was 28 bushels per acre, but in 1852, George Walker of Susquehanna County produced 160 bushels per acre. Hybrid seed corn was first sold commercially in 1916, but Pennsylvania farmers were slow to use it. Corn production remained stable from 1840 to 1940.

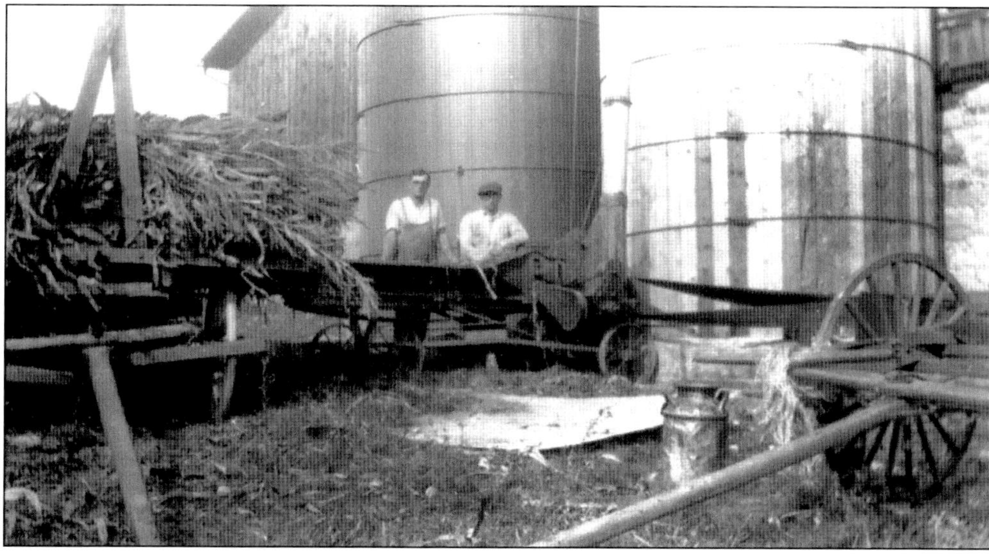

Here Howard and Stewart Eck are blowing ground corn plants into wooden silos to be used later as ensilage. Before 1880, most farmers milked their cows only during the pasture season. The silo changed the dairy industry by providing good food during the winter and allowed it to operate all year long. The first silo in Pennsylvania was built in Berks County in 1880, and by 1917, some 17,000 had been built in the state. Corn ensilage produces more energy per acre than any other crop.

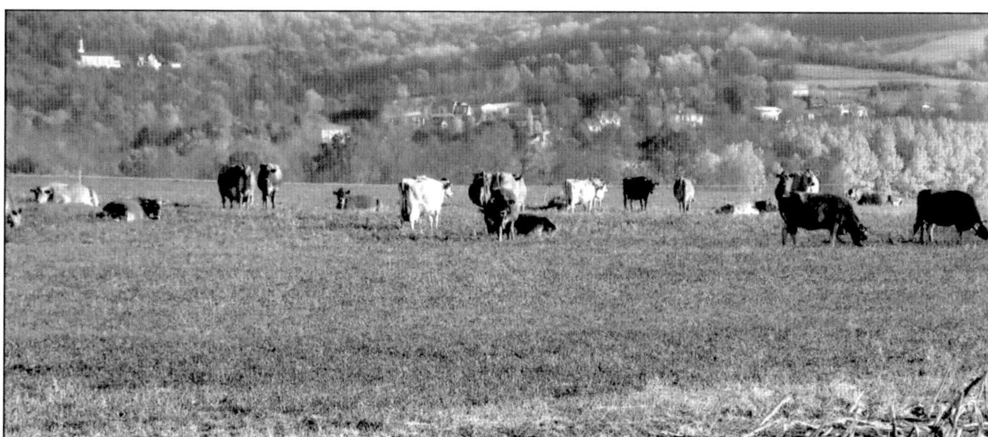

Before the Civil War, farming was more a way of life than it was a business. Farmers strived for self-sufficiency. By 1900, a growing demand for dairy products in Williamsport saw a rise in the number of milk cows in the valley. A 1913 census indicated 296 cows in the valley over four years old. By 1900, improved dairy herds consisted of Jersey, Guernsey, Holstein, and Brown Swiss. Newt Phleger had the first registered Holstein herd in Lycoming County.

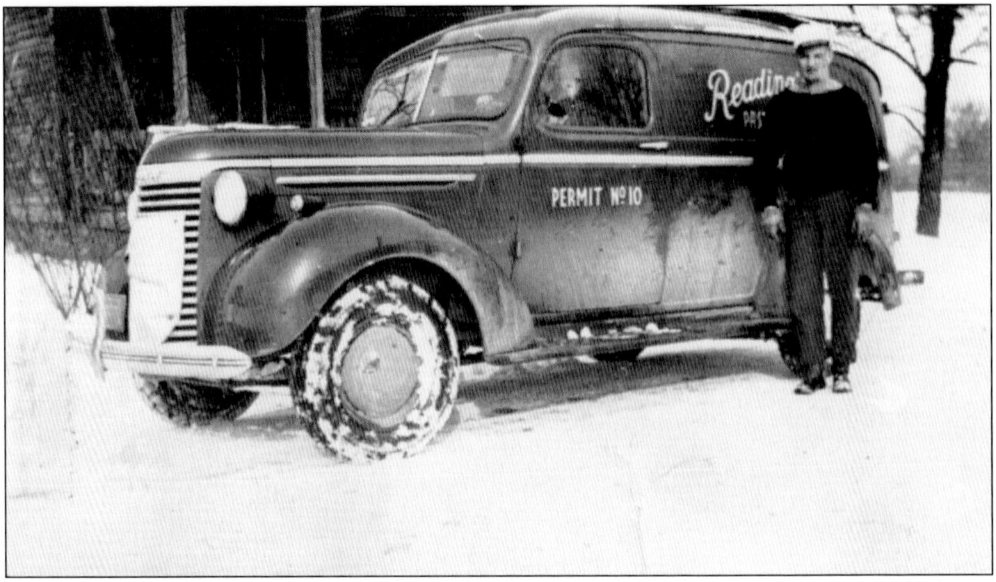

Reading's milk was peddled in the valley from 1920 to 1942. Milk was first delivered by horse and a milk wagon purchased from Bill Wagner of Jersey Shore. The picture shows Paul Reading standing beside his milk truck around 1940. About 500 quarts a day were sold, with 100 quarts going to the Civilian Conservation Corps (CCC) camp above Rauchtown. Pasteurization was required at this time. In 1920, milk sold for 7¢ a quart and increased to 16¢ by 1942.

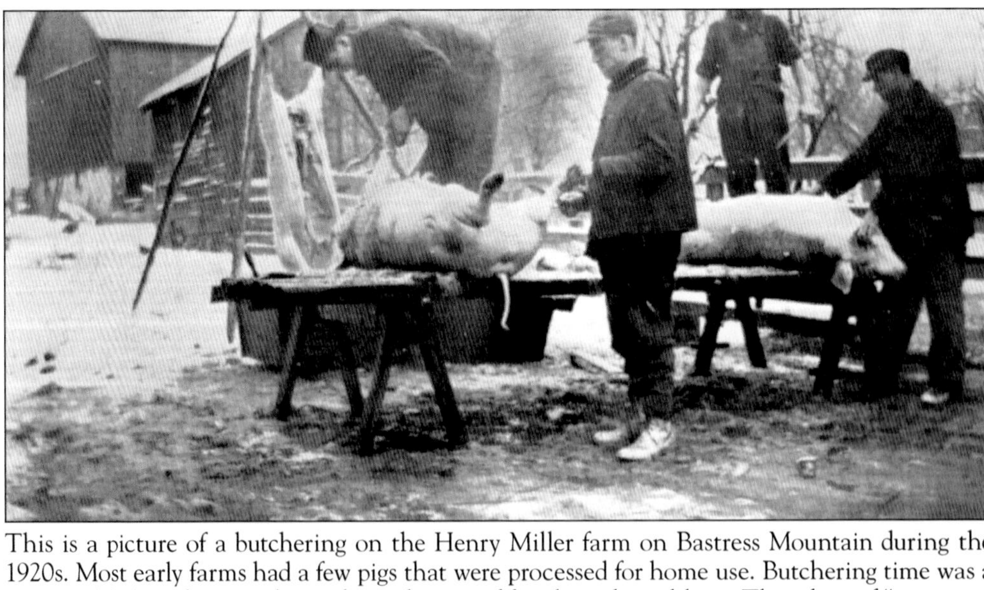

This is a picture of a butchering on the Henry Miller farm on Bastress Mountain during the 1920s. Most early farms had a few pigs that were processed for home use. Butchering time was a farm highlight, often involving the gathering of family and neighbors. The adage of "waste not want not" resulted in such products as souse, blutwurst, panhaus, pudding, lard, and cracklins. Hogs were big in those days, often reaching 700 pounds.

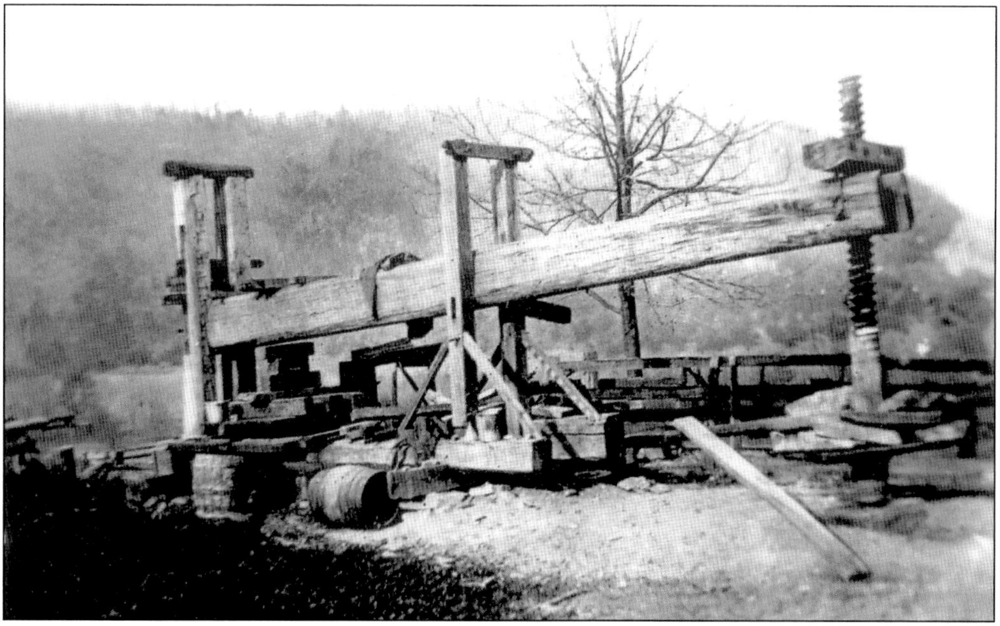

Oval had one of the largest cider and vinegar operations in Lycoming County, with one storage tank holding 30,000 gallons. It was started by Warren Clark and continued by George Hampe and his son Fred Hampe. This is a picture of the press used. Such farm production was essentially over by 1910, as the Pennsylvania Assembly enacted a law in 1897 stating that vinegar offered for sale must contain four percent acetic acid, a number farm-produced vinegar seldom reached.

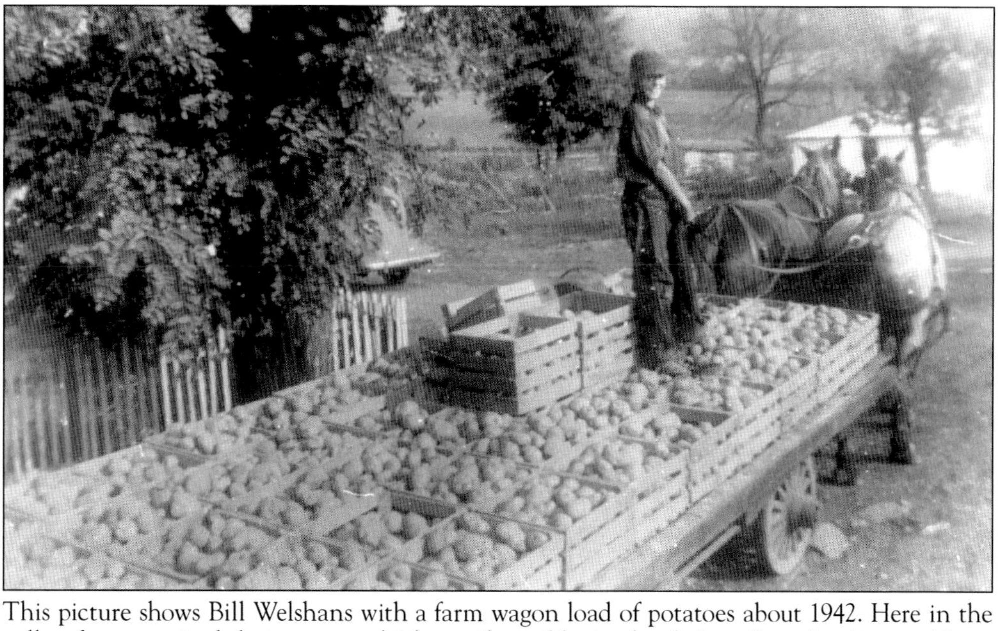

This picture shows Bill Welshans with a farm wagon load of potatoes about 1942. Here in the valley, farmers raised their potatoes high up, if possible, in the shale soil, as the dirt would not stick to them as much. In 1840, potatoes were mostly fed to livestock, but by 1940, they were the leading cash crop of the state. The potato blight, or rot, reached Pennsylvania in 1843 from Ireland, and the Colorado potato beetle arrived in 1872. Spraying with Bordeaux (copper sulfate) and dusting with Paris Green (arsenic) helped.

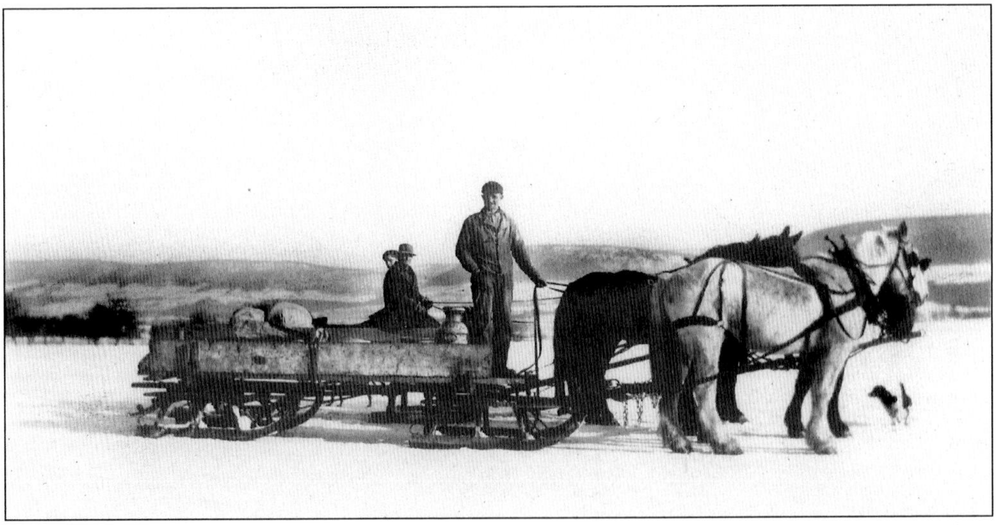

Another chore met by farmers involved cutting firewood for their room stoves and kitchen ranges from which they got their hot water. Every farm had a woodlot for that purpose, and here are Wilson, Merrill, and Nathan Sweitzer in a pair of pin bobsleds headed off to Sweitzer Gap. The work was all done by hand, including the felling of trees, bucking to length, and splitting to size.

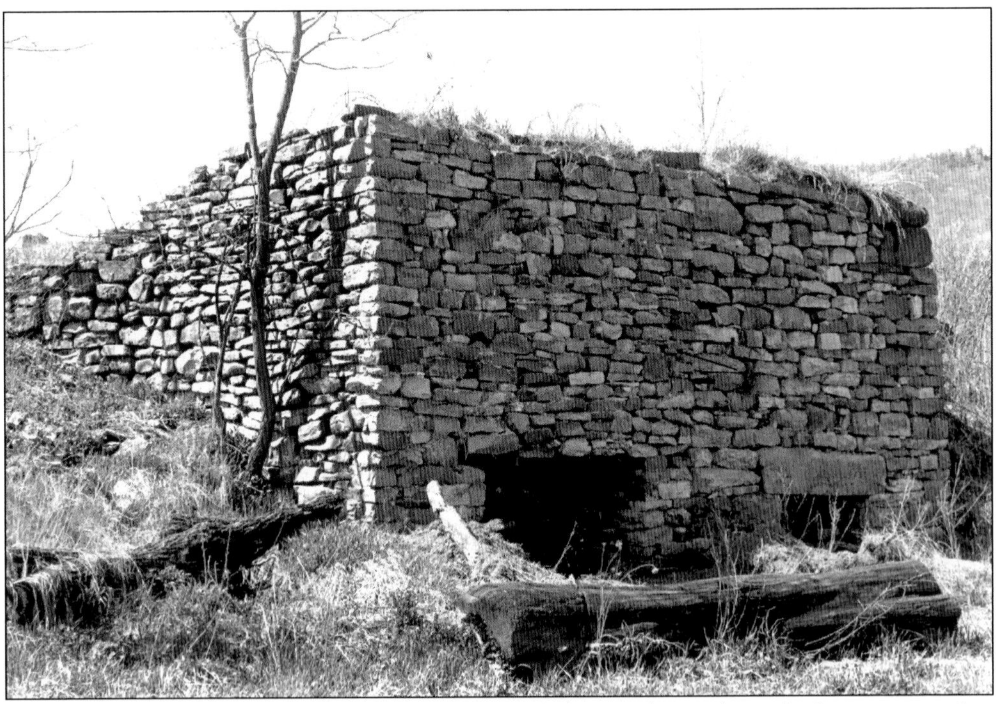

This limekiln was built on the Will Eck farm at Ecktown and is perhaps the best preserved in the valley. Such kilns were built into a hill so the alternating layers of wood and limestone could be loaded from the top. The whole thing was lit from below, with burning time from three to six days. The powdered lime gathered at the bottom and was wetted down, thus changing it from quick lime to slaked lime.

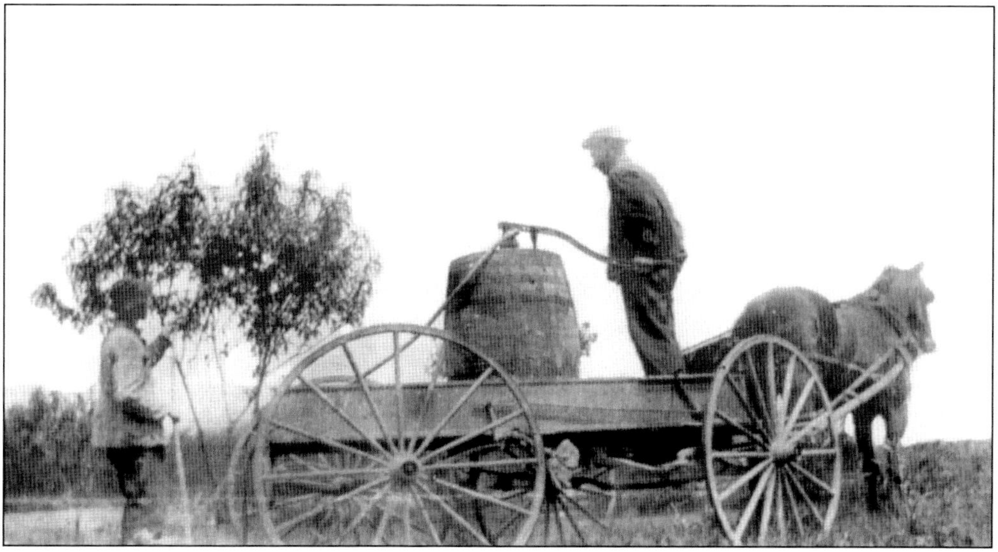

In the early days, every farm had its own orchard. There were well over 100 varieties of apples that were pretty well immune to endemic diseases. The spraying of fruit trees did not begin in Pennsylvania until 1889, and here are Al and Frank Bower spraying with equipment of the day. The first spray was London Purple, and the first spray calendar established by the state was issued in 1894.

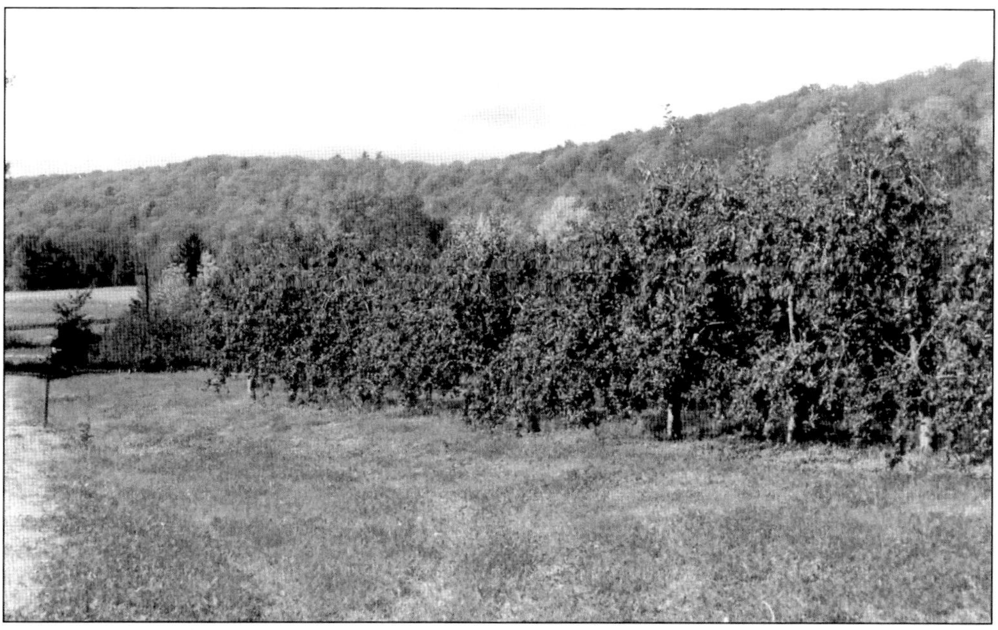

Fruit orchards in the valley were established by such families as Pearson, Kissel, Dietrich, Enders, Hampe, Lorson, Winter, Steinbacher, Haas, Schuler, Sheadle, Lehman, Welshans, and Thomas and Hurr. At one time, the latter mentioned was the largest in the county. Commercial orchards began about 1900. Old-time varieties included Baldwin, Spitzenberg, Rambo, King, Yellow Russet, Pippin, Northern Spy, Smokehouse, Winesap, and one known as the Nippenose apple.

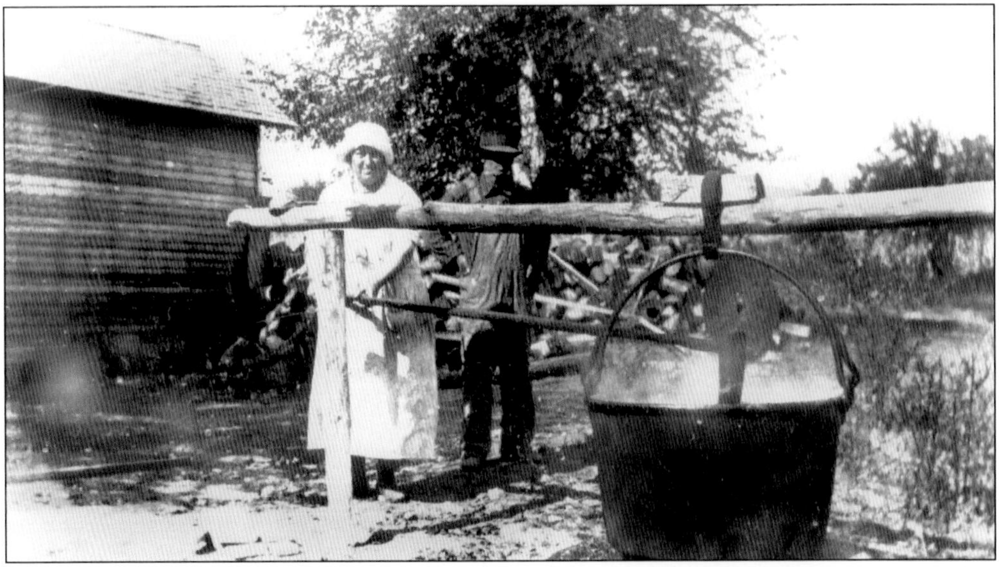

Farm families made apple butter in the fall, and here John and Edith Eck are seen doing just that in 1924. There were countless recipes and conditions for making the very best, including using a copper or brass kettle, selecting the apple varieties, and choosing the best wood for the fire and stir. It took about three bushels of apples to make a stir and about 50 pounds of sugar, and the whole process was made sweeter with good music, laughter, and lots of food.

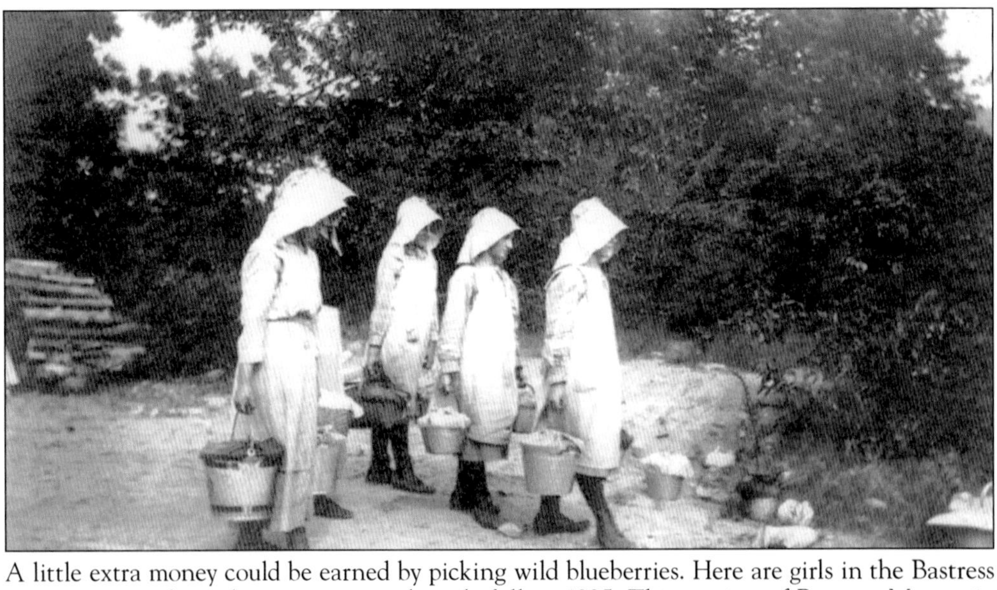

A little extra money could be earned by picking wild blueberries. Here are girls in the Bastress area returning from the mountain with pails full in 1925. This section of Bastress Mountain had recently burned off, making the picking good. "Picking along the stone rows was best," said Esther Stopper, but that is where the rattlesnakes were. The berries brought 8¢ a quart, and picking 1,000 quarts was not uncommon.

Byron Welshans had this to say about the Depression: "Well, people looked on folks like us as poor dirt farmers—we didn't have nothin. The Depression come and the main thing I noticed was—other people didn't have nothin either. We had our place and plenty to eat and the Depression kind of come and went and we didn't pay it much never-mind." In the early days, families ate what they were able to produce and preserve, and nothing went to waste.

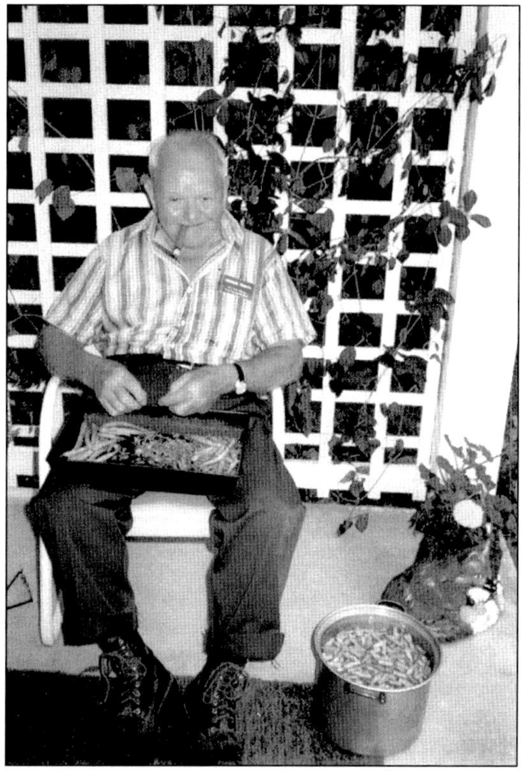

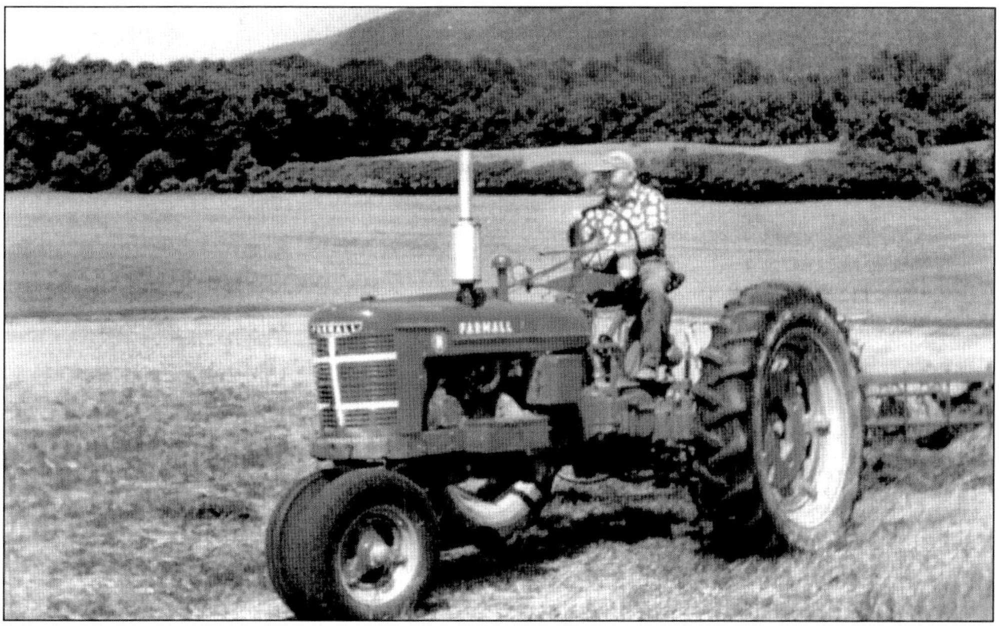

The gasoline-powered tractor played a more important role in mechanizing agriculture than did the reaper. Small farms and small fields held this advancement back a bit here in the valley. The first light general-purpose tractors became available in 1925. The power takeoff was introduced in 1924, and pneumatic tires were first used in 1934. Byron Welshans farmed for 70 years and only ever owned two such tractors, but he had a lot of cigars.

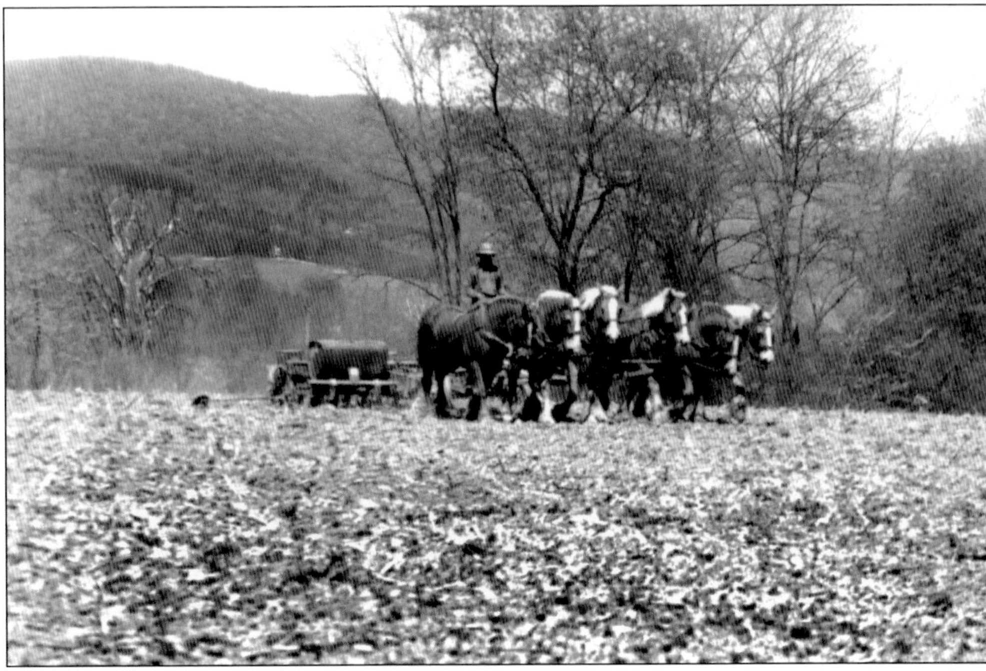

The old-timers who gave up their horses for tractors would likely not believe what they see here today—farming again with horses. The Amish began moving into the valley in 1985, and the first farm purchased was the original Welshans farm near Jamestown. The Beiler and Stoltzfus families were the first to come. Here is a man planting corn at the Upper End with a six-horse team. There are about 34 families here today.

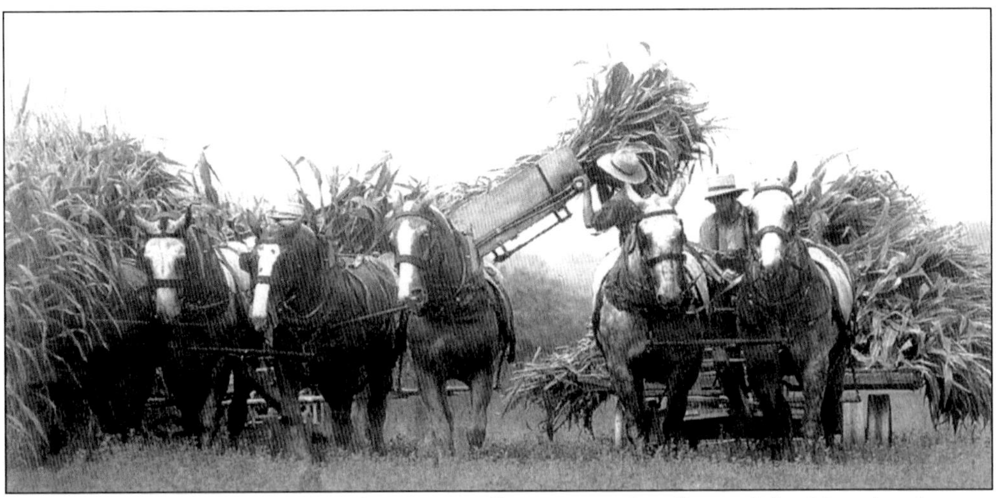

Farms the Amish have purchased are generally active and well cared for. New farmhouses, barns, and outbuildings were built, water systems were improved, and small businesses were established. There is more livestock in the valley than there has been for years. This picture of Amish working a corn binder was taken by the *Williamsport Sun-Gazette* a few years ago. Pennsylvania Dutch is spoken here again, and the sight of Amish schoolchildren and buggies is commonplace.

Four

The Upper End

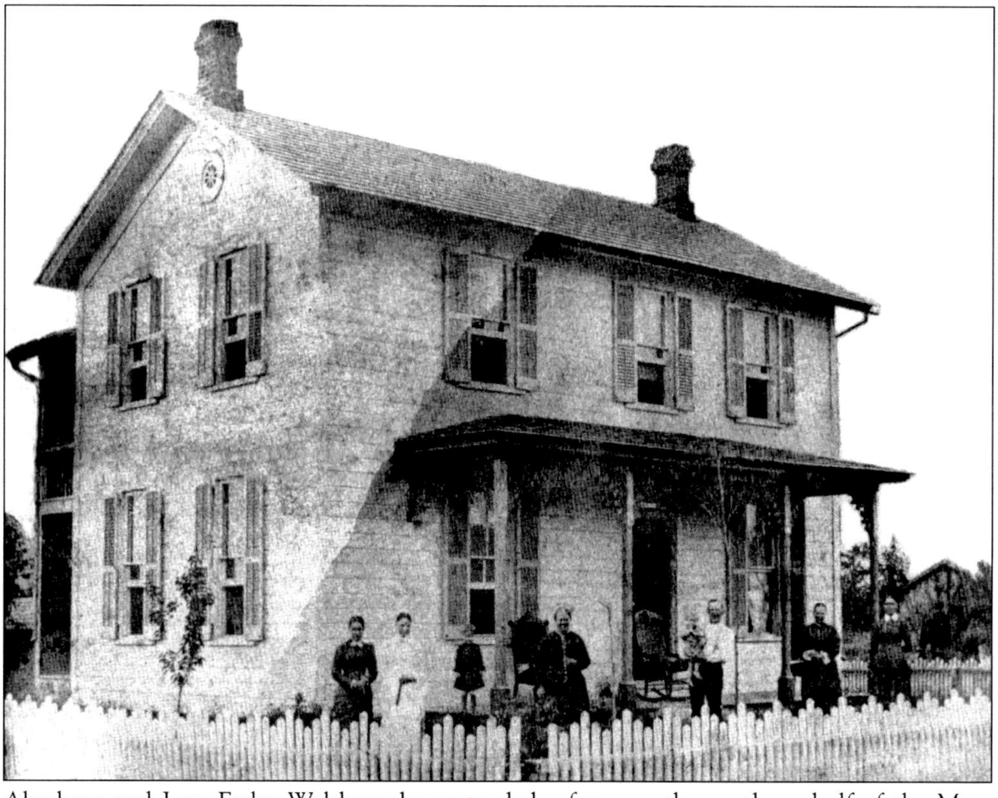

Abraham and Jane Farley Welshans homesteaded a farm on the southern half of the Mary Field warrant in 1850, and Elias Moore homesteaded the northern half. The big spring was part of this warrant until 1898. This was known as the Lower Place and was built new about 1870. The original Upper Place was built in 1850. The death of two girls, Lydia and Sarah Welshans, caused Abraham to build this place and move down. This is recognized as one of the valley's Century Farms.

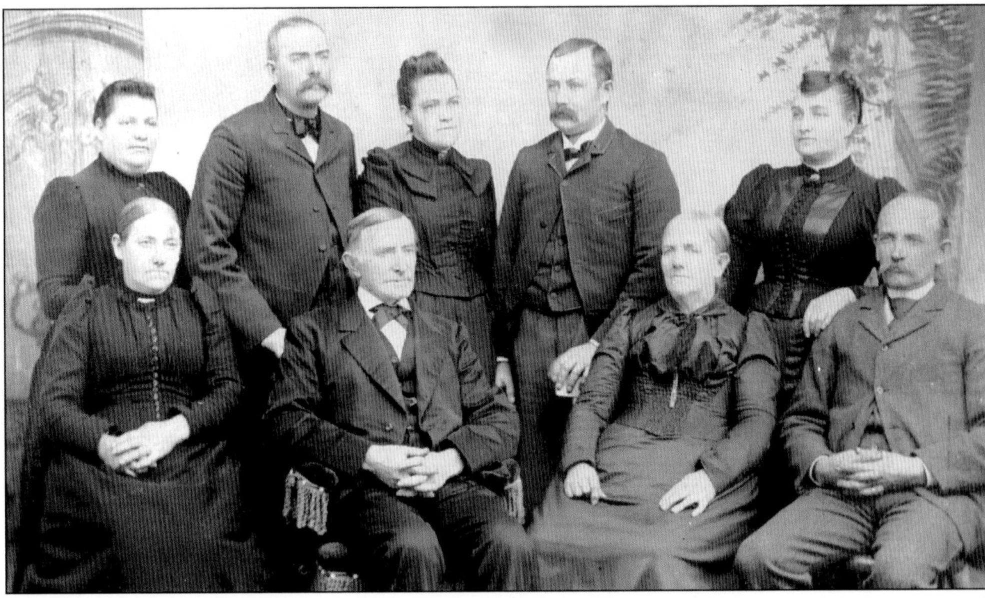

Abraham Welshans was one of 20 children born to William Welshans Sr. He and his wife Jane had nine children. From left to right are (first row) Mary Welshans (x Daniel Showers), Abraham (1821–1905), Jane (1826–1899), and Asher (x1 Eva Amelia Epler, x2 Susannah Voneida); (second row) Francis (x William Irvin), William Bigler (x Mary Stahl), Minnie (x George Fenstemaker), Ulysses Grant (x Mary Agnes Laubach), and Etta (x Thomas Dunlap). Lydia and Sarah died young.

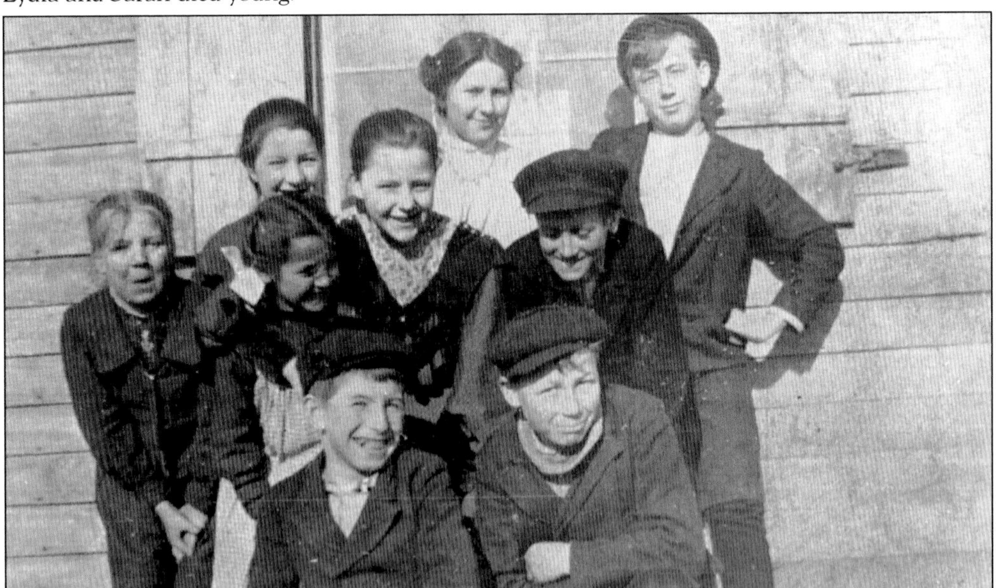

Above the Welshans farm stood the Moore School, apparently the second built on this site and named after the neighbor, Elias Moore. This school was built in 1896 and closed in 1915. From left to right are (first row) Hayes Laubach and Tom Weidler; (second row) Florence Bixel, Olive Bixel, and George Bixel; (third row) Mary Welshans, Fannie Welshans, Jane Welshans, and John Weidler. The Bixel farm was located high on the hillside and was formerly known as the Wensel and Shadle place.

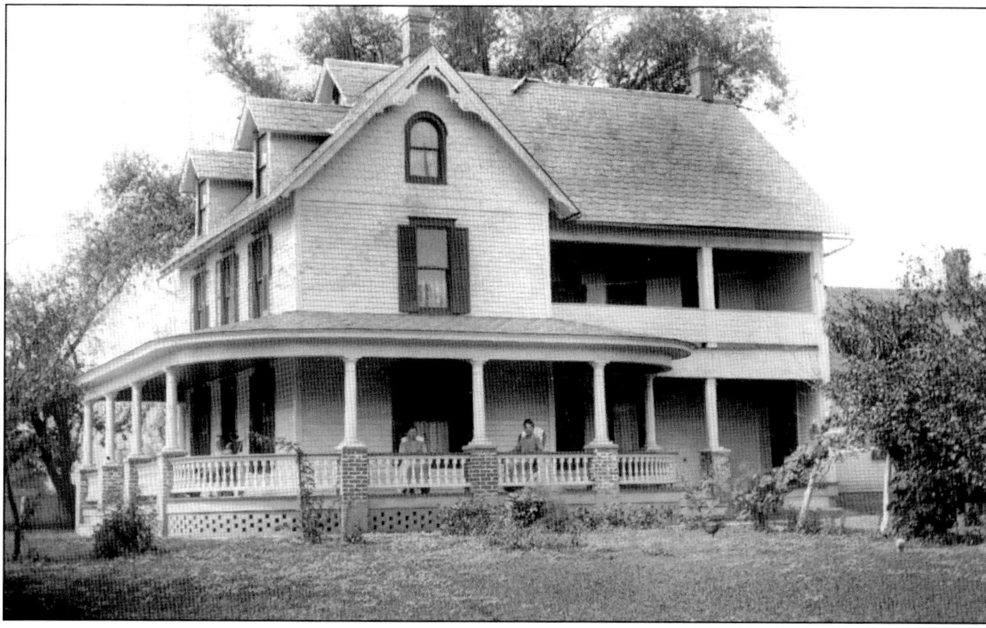

This was the Curtin Laubach farmhouse as it appeared in 1915. Three people are sitting on the porch. From left to right are George Gebhart (x Mary Grier), Mary Agnes Laubach (x Grant Welshans), and Fannie Gebhart (x Curt Laubach). This 117-acre farm had formerly belonged to the Stine, Rentz, and Lerch families and was later owned by Abram Welshans, Lester Wagner, and Glenn Pepperman. The new front porch was built by the Seewalds.

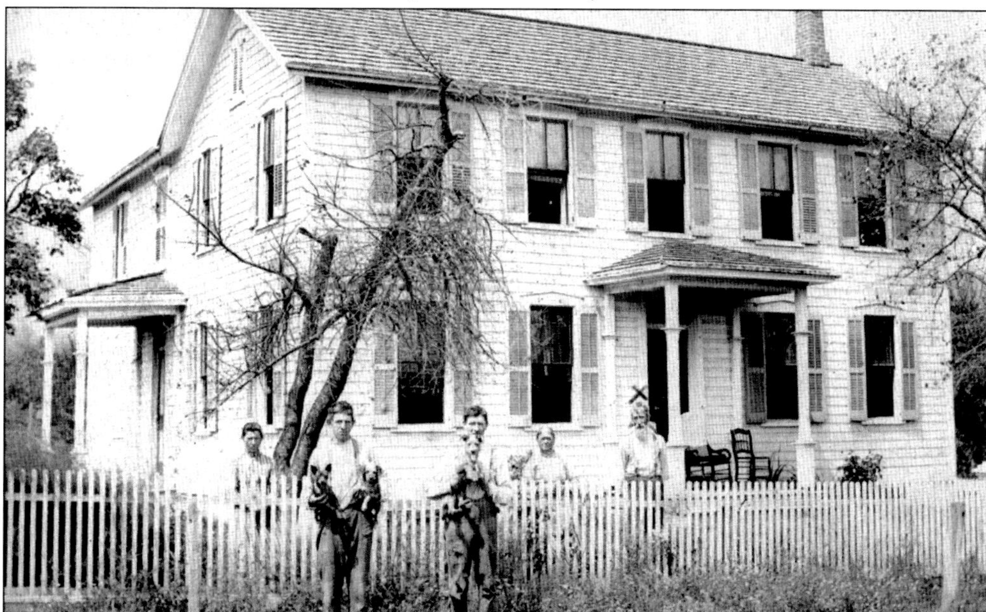

Stephen Laubach (born in 1827) moved to this place in 1889, having sold his farm to Jacob Overdorf in the Upper End. Here he built a new house and barn to replace the old log structures. At the time, Jacob Sallada owned it, and a John Fenstemaker was living here. In the front yard, from left to right, are Mary Agnes Laubach (born in 1864), Curt Laubach, Henry Laubach, Lydia Frantz, and her husband Stephen Laubach. The Laubachs came to the valley in 1846.

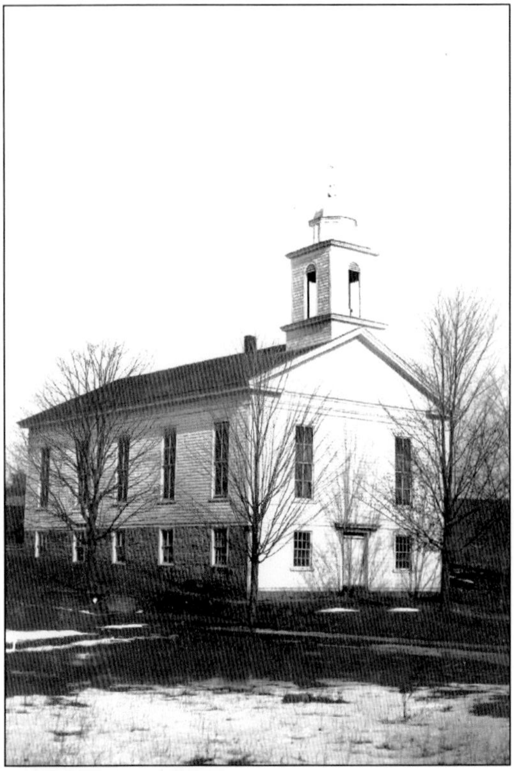

This is St. James Lutheran Church as it appeared in 1910. It was the third church built on this corner. The first, a Union church, was built in 1814 in the middle of today's cemetery, and the second church, for German Reformed and Lutherans, was built behind this one in 1842. The Sunday school class of 1910 included Naomi Fenstemaker, Winifred Brosius, Olive Bixel, Edna Laubach, Ella Sents, Phoebe Tomb, Ida Clark, Esther Getgen, Anna Dunlap, and Dora Osborne.

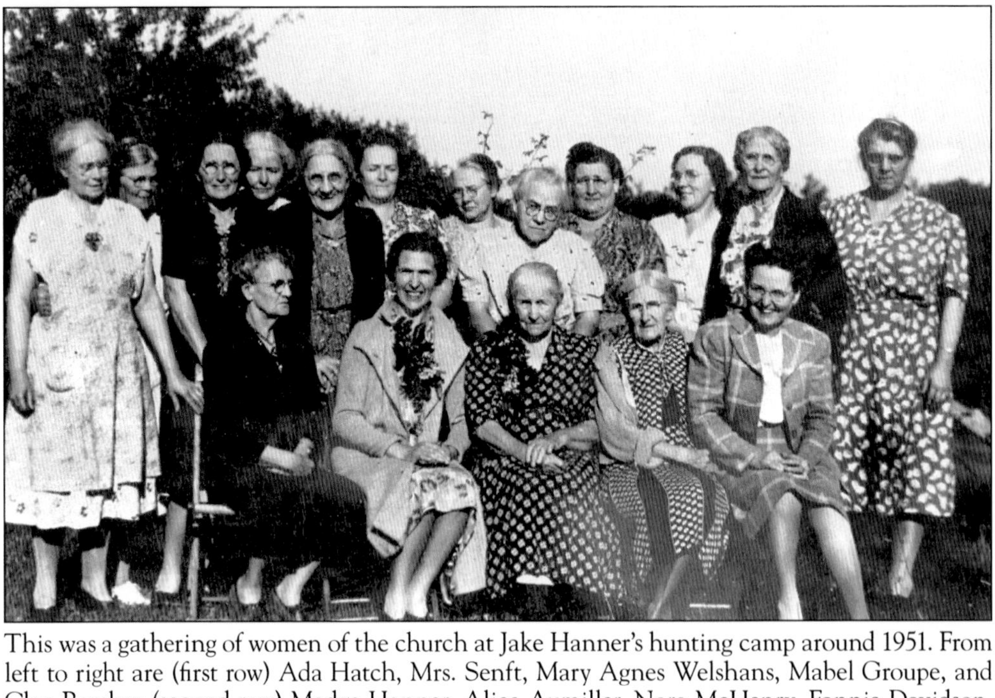

This was a gathering of women of the church at Jake Hanner's hunting camp around 1951. From left to right are (first row) Ada Hatch, Mrs. Senft, Mary Agnes Welshans, Mabel Groupe, and Cleo Barclay; (second row) Madge Hanner, Alice Aumiller, Nora McHenry, Fannie Davidson, Hattie Brosius, Lydia Fenstemaker, Edna Mantle, Carrie Smith, Hazel Lehman, Bea Welshans, Lizzie Tomb, and Lulu Sitler.

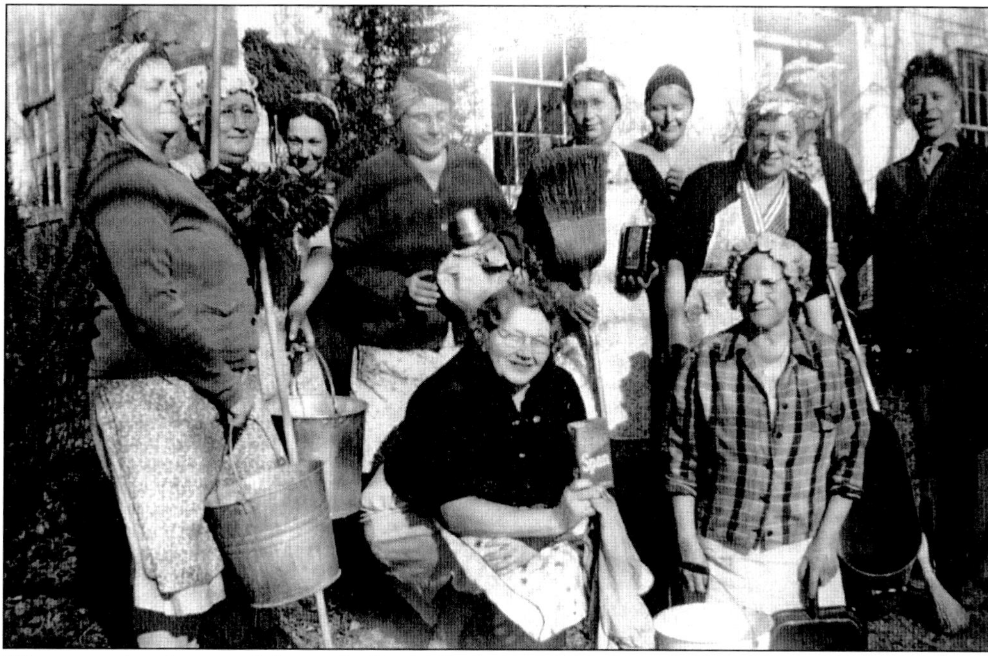

Women gather for a workday at St. James Lutheran Church around 1947. From left to right are (first row) Mrs. Raymond Gotshall and Ida Getgen; (second row) Lydia Fenstemaker, Hazel Lehman, Mary Getgen, Edna Mantle, Grace Welshans, Fannie Davidson, Bea Welshans, Madge Hanner, and Rev. Phillip Senft.

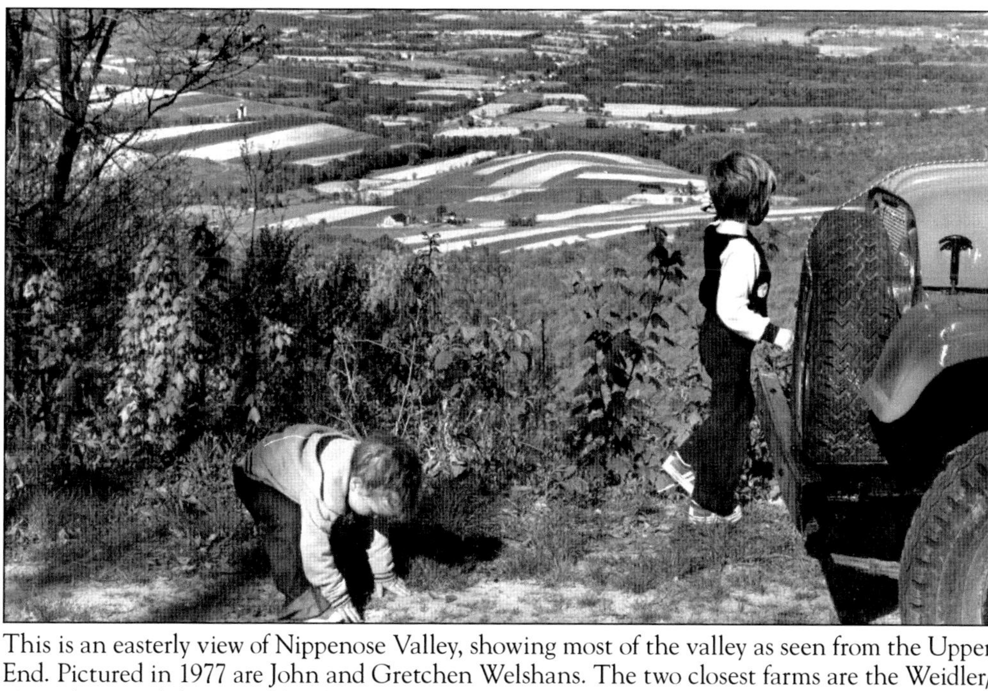

This is an easterly view of Nippenose Valley, showing most of the valley as seen from the Upper End. Pictured in 1977 are John and Gretchen Welshans. The two closest farms are the Weidler/Heim farm and the Forney/Welshans farm. The villages of Jamestown, Oval, and Collomsville are located down the center of the valley, and Bastress is farthest away on the side hill left of center.

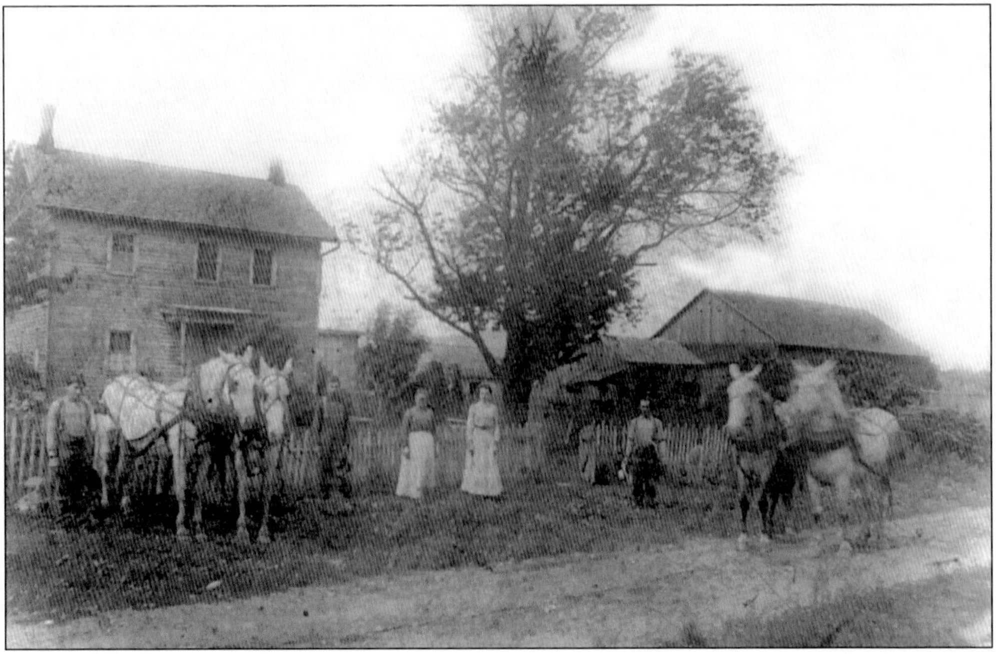

This image shows the Ulysses Grant Meixel farm and family members as they appeared in 1902. From left to right are Clarence Meixel, Floyd Meixel, Louisa Martz Meixel, Lenora Meixel, and Ulysses Grant Meixel. The farm was located just beyond the "pigs ear." Other owners of the farm included Harvey Laubach, Charlie Fenstemaker in 1923, Boyd Mantle (house burned), and William Heck. In 1994, Elam and Mary Jane Stoltzfus bought the farm and built a new house and barn back from the road.

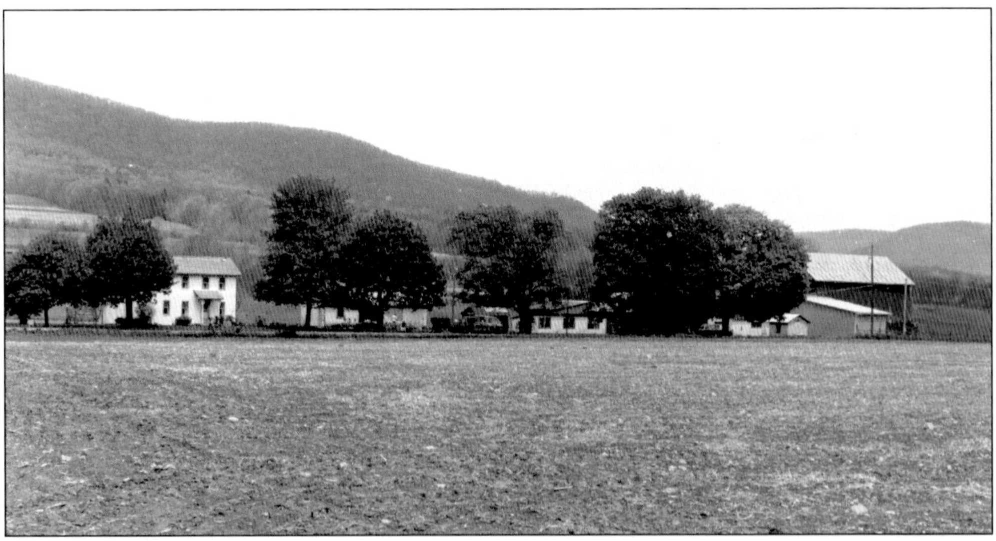

This is the McKeague/Mantle/Fox farm in the Upper End. Alfred William Mantle brought his family here in 1913 from Beech Creek. Their furniture was shipped by rail, and the family walked and traveled by covered wagon. The lead group and older children, with their father, drove the stock and laid over at Castanea. The mother, Eudora Adams Mantle, and youngest son, Wentworth, came by a second covered wagon. The second day, they made it over Pine Mountain to this place.

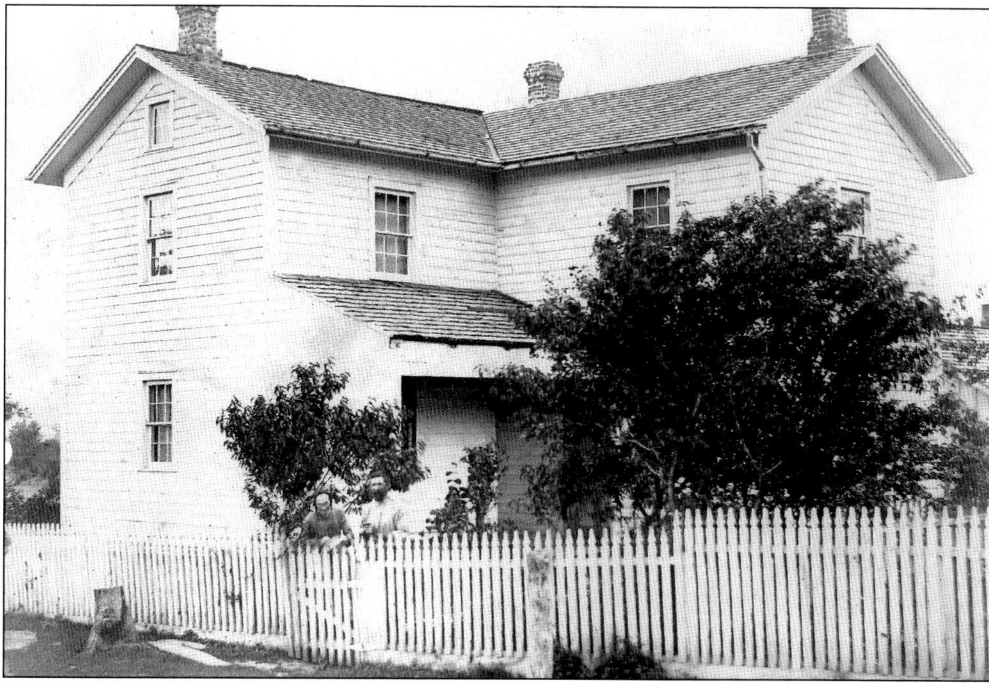

The Edward and Sarah Allison (1828–1892) Laubach place no longer exists. It stood near the fencerow halfway between the Mantle place and Pine Mountain Road. Edward (born in 1831) was one of four Laubachs, including Jesse, Stephen, and Charles, that moved to the valley with their father, Christian (born in 1772) in 1846. They purchased 305 acres on September 23, 1846. Stephen married Lydia Frantz, and Charles married Sarah Frantz. Mary was married to Conrad Lerch, and her sister Julia was married to Rudolf Kemmerer.

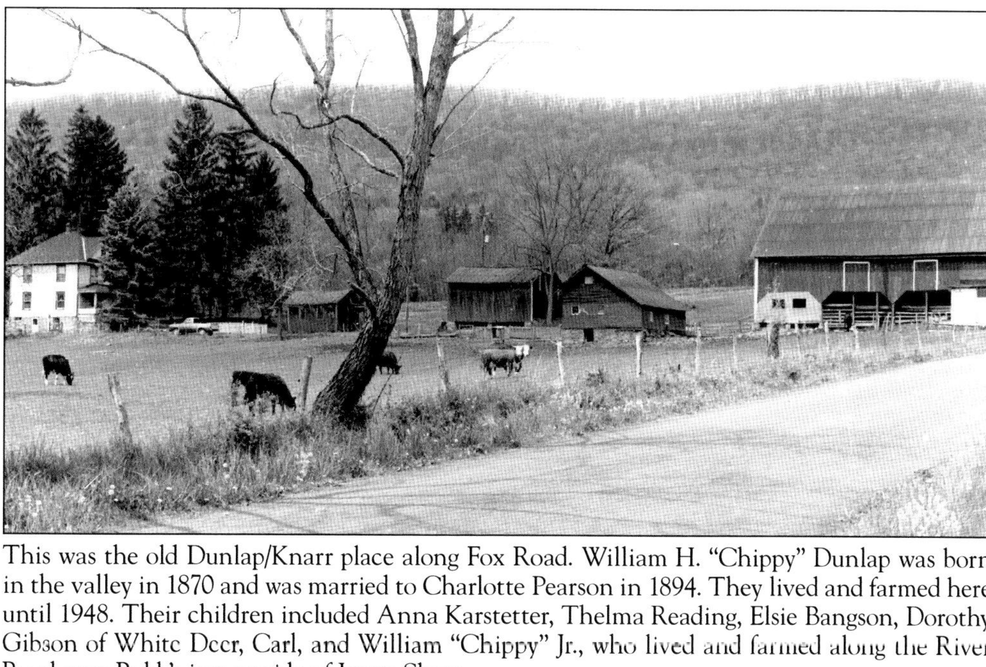

This was the old Dunlap/Knarr place along Fox Road. William H. "Chippy" Dunlap was born in the valley in 1870 and was married to Charlotte Pearson in 1894. They lived and farmed here until 1948. Their children included Anna Karstetter, Thelma Reading, Elsie Bangson, Dorothy Gibson of White Deer, Carl, and William "Chippy" Jr., who lived and farmed along the River Road near Bubb's just outside of Jersey Shore.

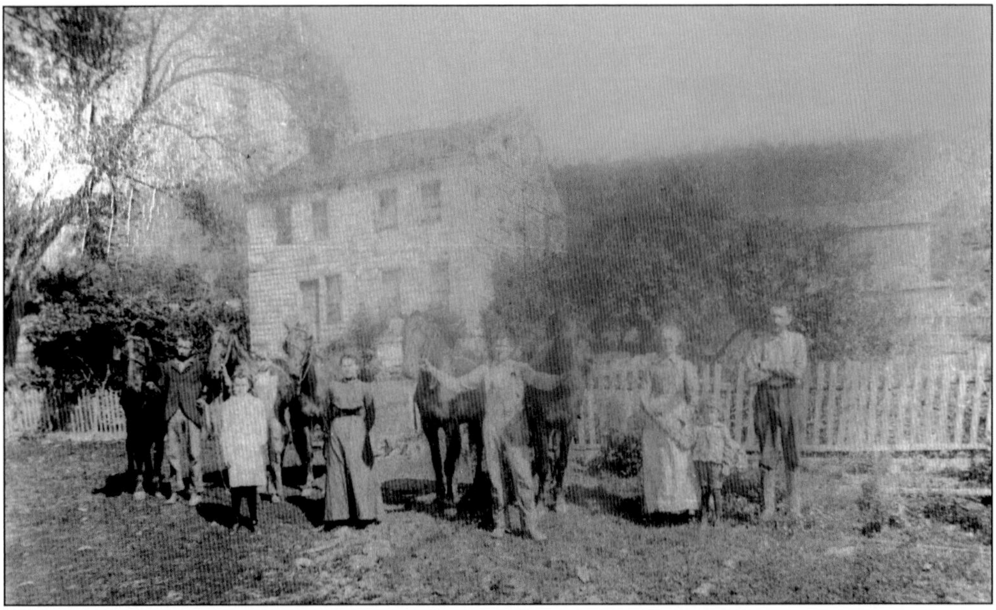

This log house stands at the junction of Fox and Thompson Roads. William H. Smith lived here during the Civil War and was followed by Jacob Nathan Smith (1843–1919) and his wife, Hanna Wensel (1851–1916), shown at right in the photograph. The Wensel farm neighbored this one. The family members, from left to right, are Tillman Smith, Margaret (Maggie) Smith, Oscar Smith (1886–1949), Aunt Annie Smith, and Jacob Smith. This farm also belonged to the Pence, Gheen, Poet, Fox, Bower, and Noll families.

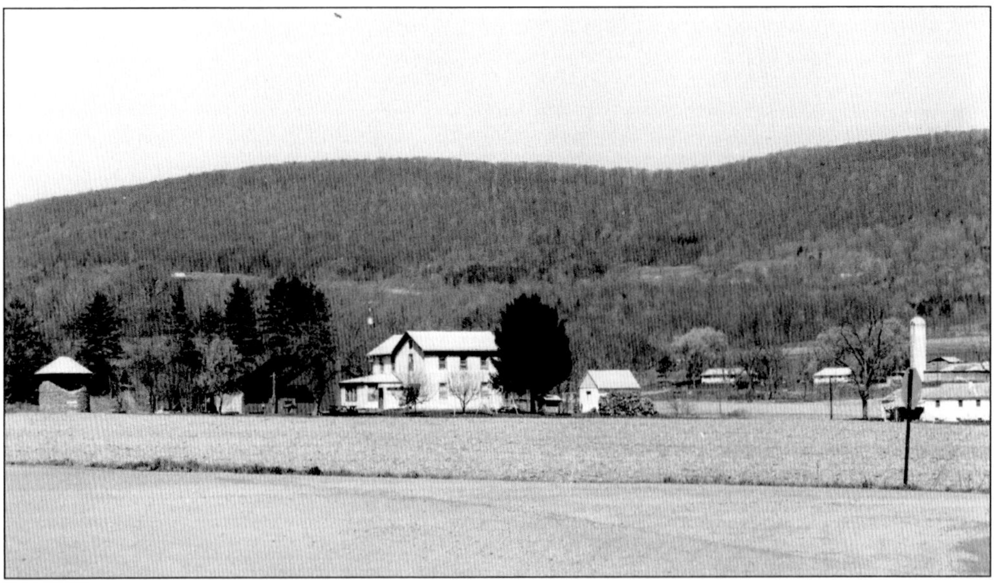

This land was issued to John Clark in 1802 and later acquired by Peter Pence. It then passed to his daughter Elizabeth Pence in 1825, to William Gebhart, and then to Jacob Getgen in 1854. During the Civil War, it belonged to John Getgen. Near this place stood the St. Elizabeth Church, a sawmill, and the Gebhart Cemetery. Joseph Welshans owned it in 1881 when a plaster mill operated here. More recent owners were Albert Laubach and Byron Sylvester "Brownie" Welshans.

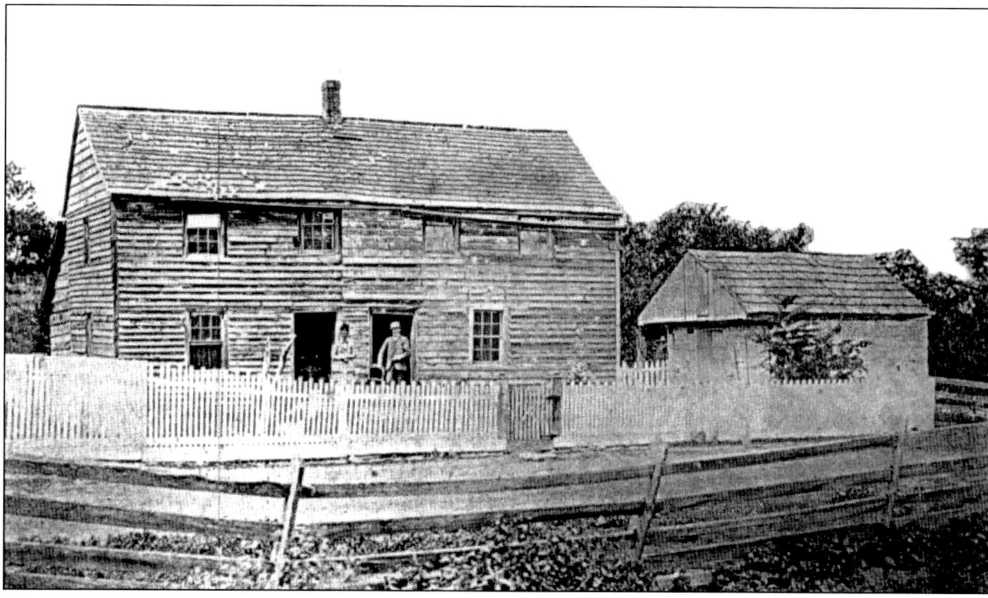

This was the log home of John Kissel (died in 1921) that was located across from the St. Elizabeth Church. Floyd Meixel bought it in 1923. Members of this family were quite enterprising and were involved with a lot of things, including farming, stone crushing, sawmill operation, the water company, the fire company, television, selling farm implements, operating a repair shop, and running a bar in town. Like a number of valley families, they worked with Prince Farrington during Prohibition.

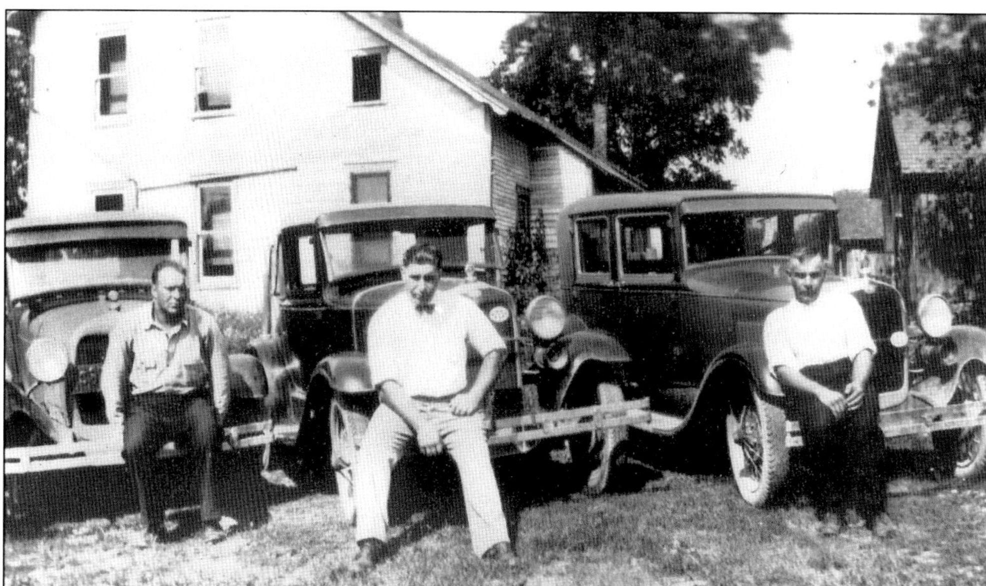

This image shows the Meixel place around 1928 and, from left to right, Ernest, Clyde, and Floyd with their three new Ford Model As. Under the basement of the outkitchen was a cellar that could hold up to 100 barrels of Prince Farrington whiskey. It was about 150 proof, but it was cut to 98 proof and transferred to 5- and 10-gallon kegs and hauled away 10 to 15 barrels at a time, often in the middle of the night.

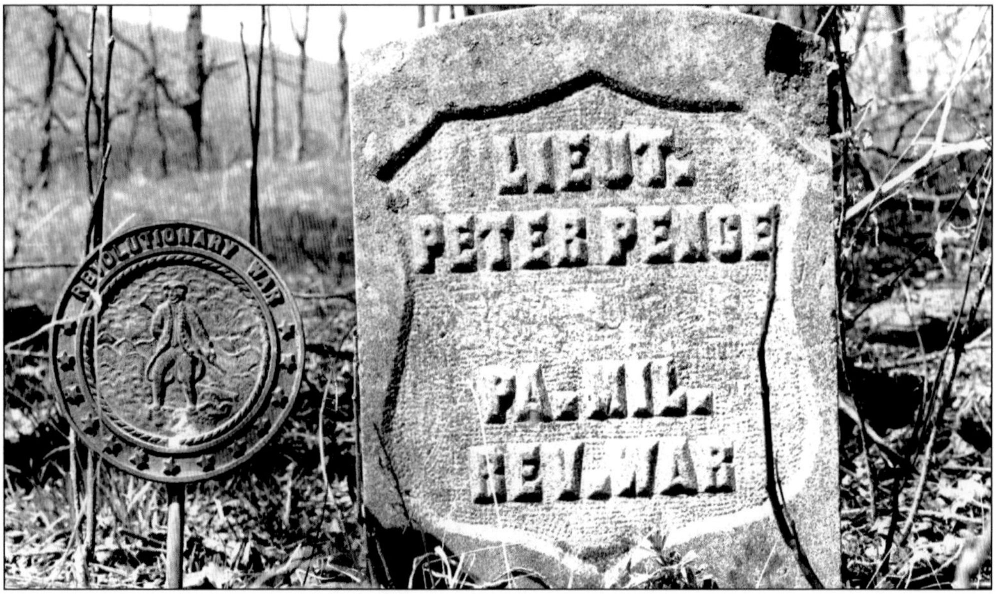

Peter Pence (1732–1812) was a pioneer, scout, Native American fighter, patriot, and farmer. He enlisted under Capt. John Lowden on June 25, 1775, and served until April 13, 1783. He began his military career by marching to Boston to fight the British. He retired to Nippenose Valley in 1797, acquired a lot of land, and received a military pension of $40 a year in 1810. This marker was placed in the Gebhart cemetery in 1911 by the Daughters of the American Revolution (DAR).

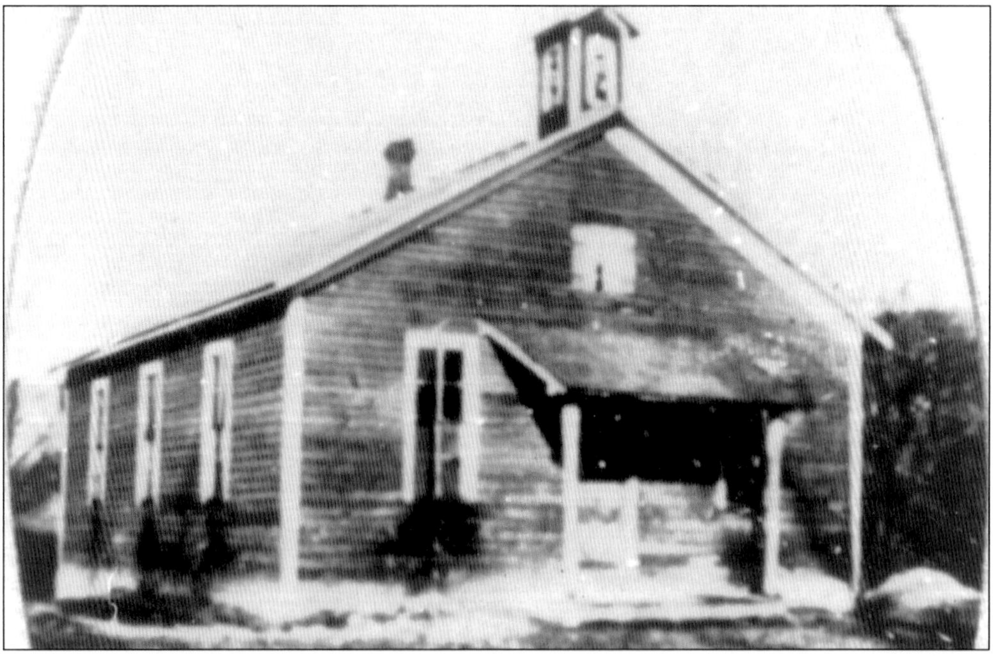

This is a rare photograph that was attached to Ernie Meixel's Upper End School pamphlet that was given to him in 1930. In 1874, there were four schools in this township, and they were not in the best condition. The school in Rauchtown was also open to religious services by various denominations. Before being torn down, this school was used as a township shed.

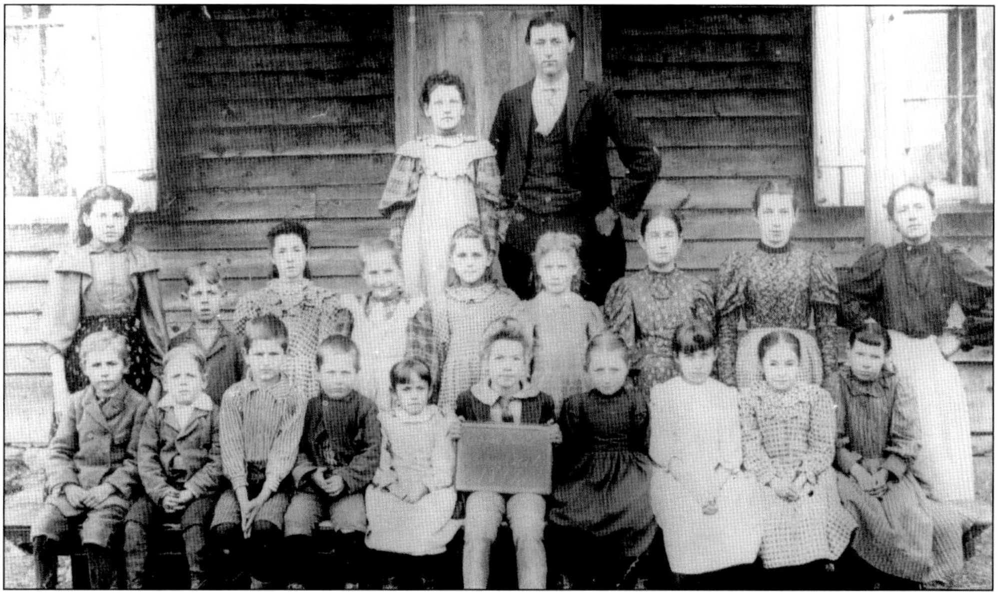

These students are standing in front of the Upper End School (Crawford Township School No. 1) in 1897 with their teacher Ernest B. Wentzel (1874–1950). His parents were Joseph (1839–1912) and Lydia C. Smith Wentzel (Wensel), and he was married to Daisy Rebecca Bowersox (1883–1953). He was a veteran forester of the Tiadaghton area for 30 years, and prior to that he taught school in Nippenose Valley and Williamsport for 25 years. He was a graduate of Lock Haven Normal School.

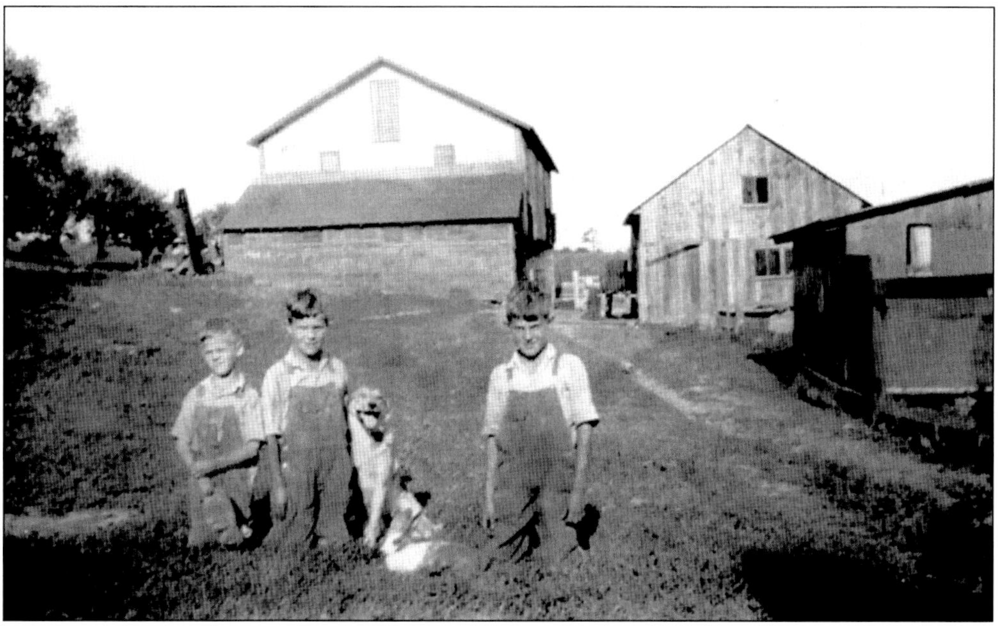

Here are Dale, Jack, and Harlan Kemmerer on the family farm on the north side of the Upper End. Their parents were Harry L. and Pearl Fetterhoof Kemmerer, who purchased the 123-acre farm from Cyrus and Mary Eoute Fetterhoof, Pearl's parents, in 1931. Cyrus bought it from George Gheen in 1914. It included two houses, a barn, and outbuildings. This was one of about three barns in the valley that was painted white.

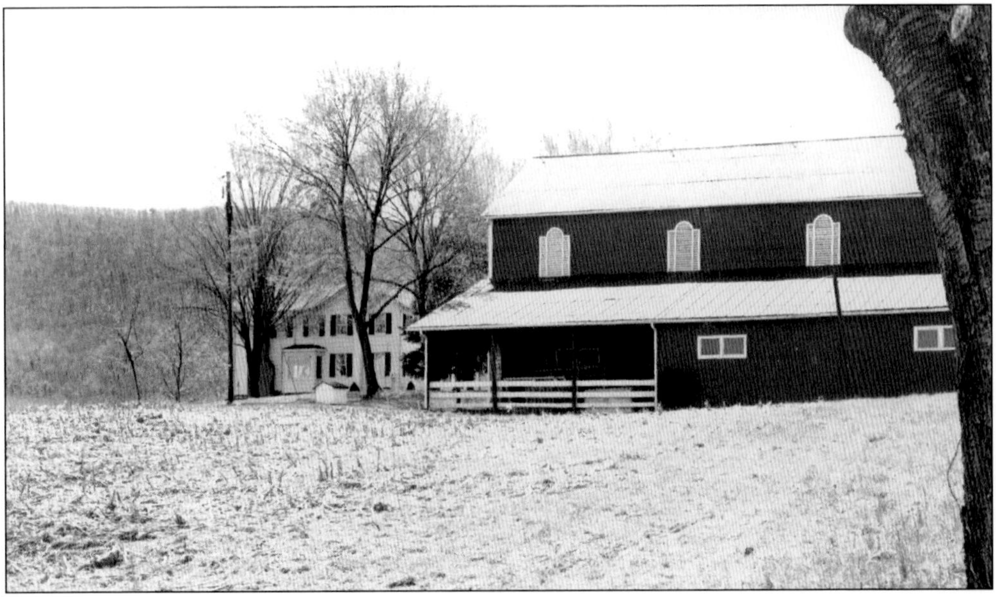

This farmstead was purchased by Christian (1818–1904) and Julia Ann Sallada Showers in 1854 from M. A. Steck and Philip Showers. The land was originally warranted to John Hatfield and Charles McElheny. Houston Weidler bought the Rauchtown gristmill in 1879 and ran it with his son Oliver until 1891, when he moved to town. Oliver acquired the farm in 1908. The farm did not leave the Weidler family until 1928, when it was sold to Ellery Fenstemaker, who in turn sold it to Kenneth Welshans in 1946.

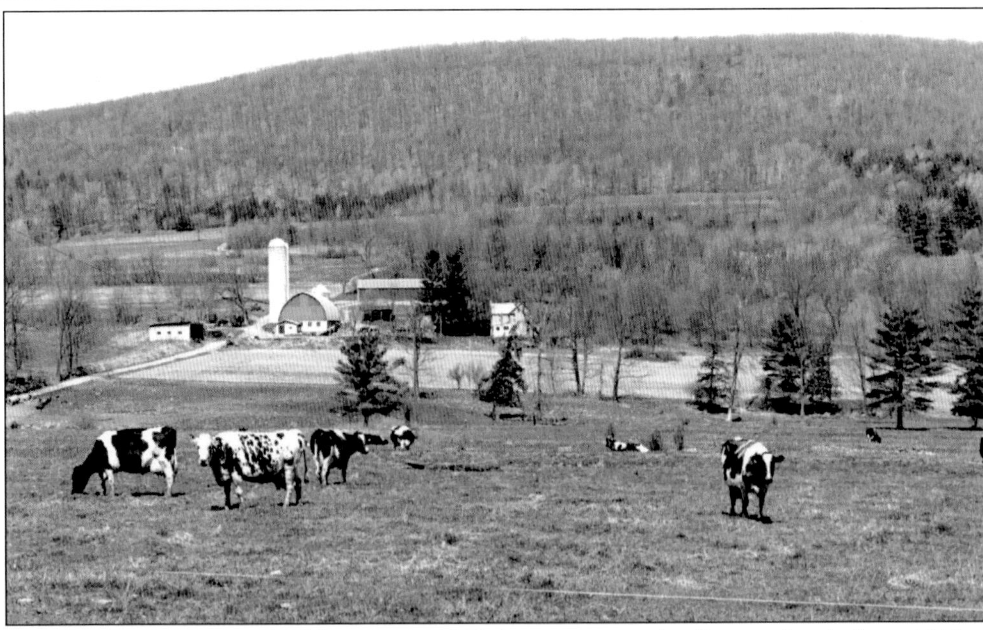

This has been the Overdorf farm since 1883, but it was in the Everett family from 1840 to 1856 and then was sold to Jacob Stine, Daniel Glenn, and Stephen Laubach. Jacob Overdorf purchased the farm in 1883 for $3,000, and it was sold to his son Rufus in 1903. Rufus was born in Logan Township in 1873. He was married to Minnie B. Lewis in 1900, and their sons Calvin and George acquired the farm next.

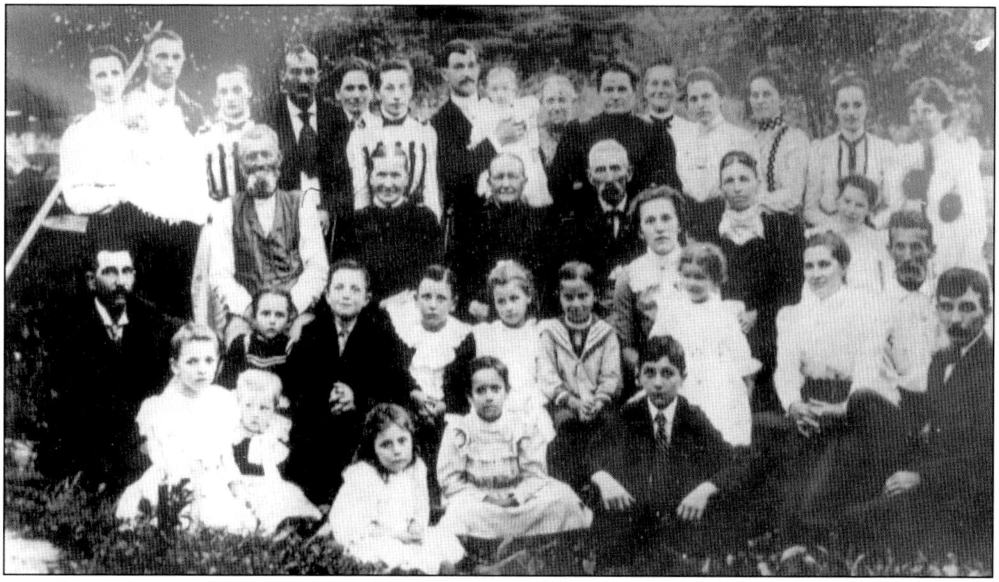

The Curts place was above the Overdorf farm and below the Shrader farm. This family reunion photograph shows Samuel Curts (1844–1902) and wife, Christina Hess Curts (1846–1912), in the third row, center right. Samuel was a Civil War veteran who signed up at Jersey Shore to fight in Company I, 131st Regiment of the Pennsylvania Volunteers. He signed up under Capt. Frank Wilson, and his enlistment paper is held by the Jersey Shore Historical Society. Jacob and Mary Ann Overdorf are to their left.

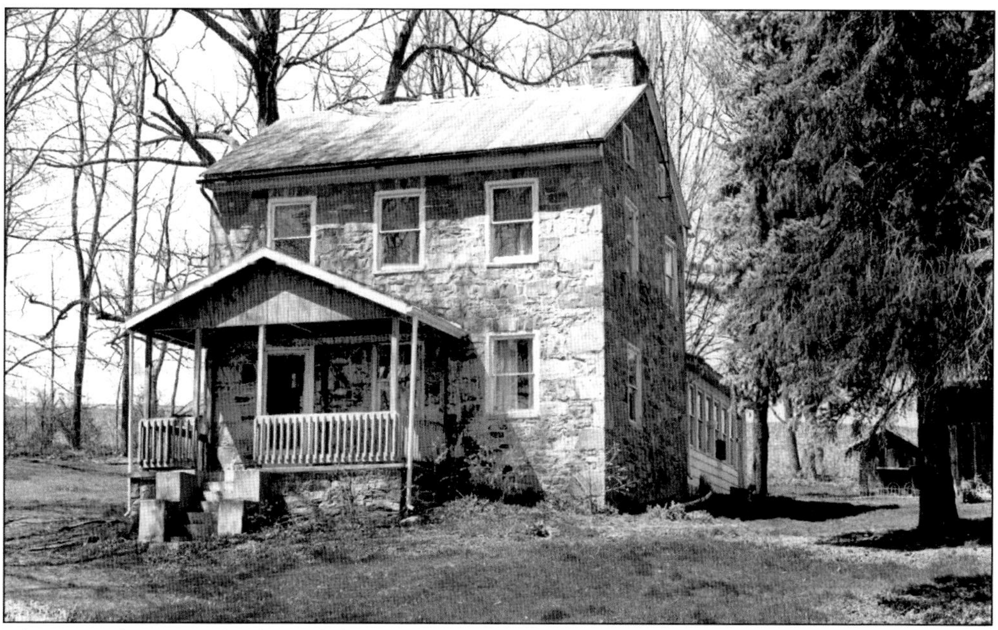

This stone house at the foot of Shaw Mountain is one of the oldest in the valley. It was built by Jacob Sallada as early as 1818 on land settled by John Clark in 1776. By 1800, this place belonged to Michael Showers (1748–1818), whose daughter Catherine (1792–1863) married Jacob Sallada in 1809. Other owners of this farm include David Shaw, Samuel Shadle, Ray Phleger, Howard "Pete" and Laura Weaver Eck, and Duane Wasson. It has been beautifully restored.

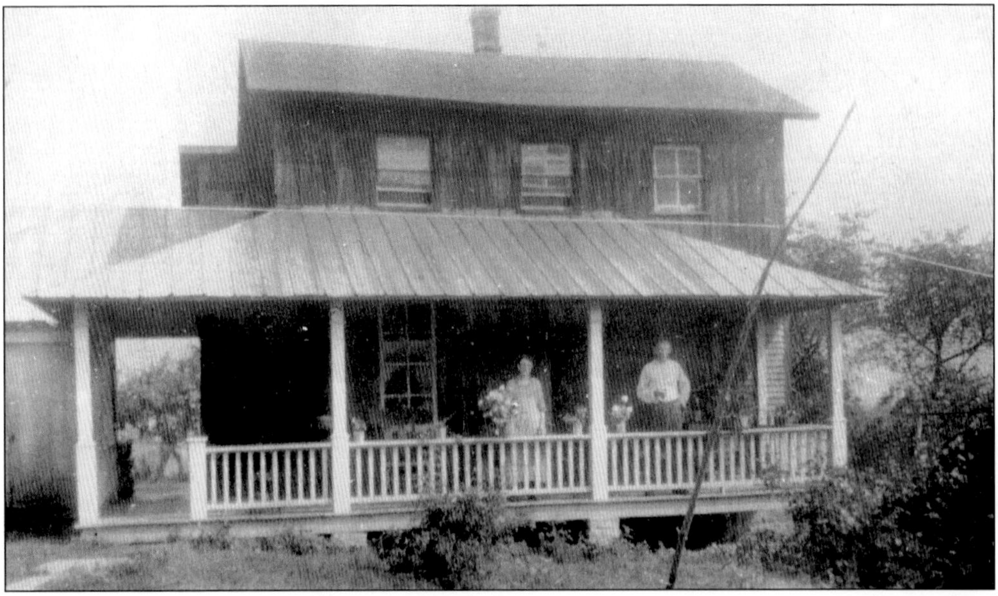

Here stand Henry (born in 1876) and Effie Miller (born in 1879) Karstetter on the porch of their home at the foot of Keiler Hollow. Henry was a carpenter by trade. Miles and Clara Karstetter Keiler lived above them. In 1911, Bea Karstetter and Minnie Keiler were attacked by a catamount after dark on their way home from the Lutheran church. The Karstetter children included Bea (x Jacob Sees Welshans), Florence (x Bill Weidler Sr.), Les (x Lois Barner), and Paul (x Martha Bower).

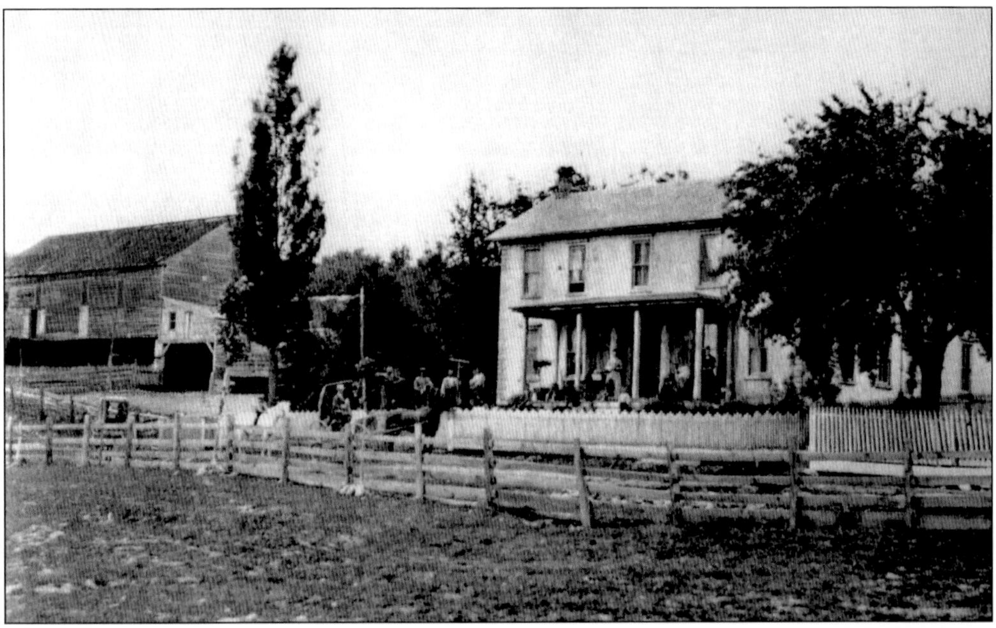

Years ago this old picture was sent from Chicago to Mike Moore in Oval. It is titled "Residence of Col. Jesse Shours, Nippenose Valley, Penna." Shours was the son of Christian Showers, who donated land for the Union church and cemetery and whose daughter Julianne was first to be buried there. Shours had this house built around 1870 to replace the old one. Charles and Edward Knarr also owned this farm.

Five

RAUCHTOWN

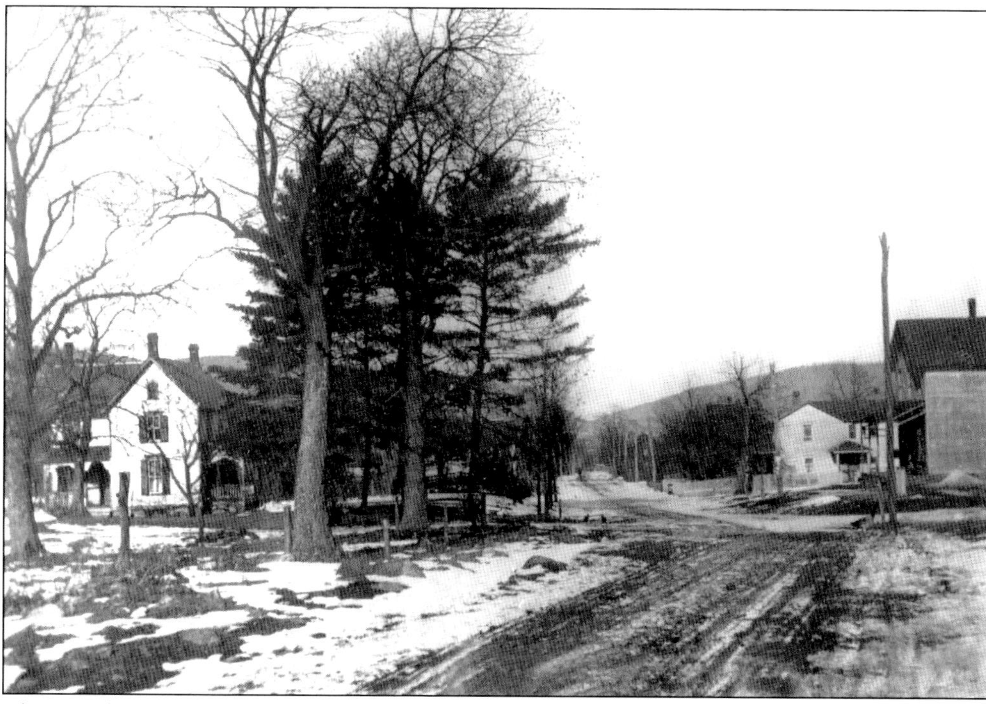

The Rauchtown crossroads looked like this 80 years ago. The Weidler/Welshans place was on the left with the schoolhouse visible through the trees. On the right was the road leading to the Groupe, Reading, and Welshans farms, and the place on the corner had been a store for a long time run by the Rauch, Sweitzer, and Reading families. Lulu Sweitzer ran the post office here for 25 years. This village was first named South Gap.

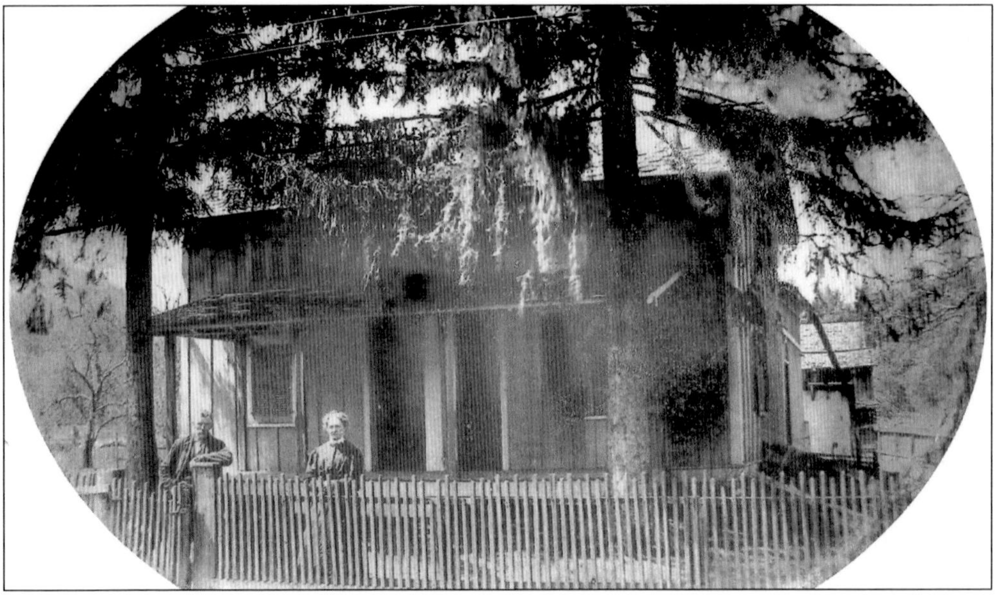

This was the home of William H. (born in 1855) and Vanetta Wensel Garrett. William's parents, Jacob (1828–1889) and Elmira Garrett, were listed on the 1860 census with four children, three of which were named Rebecca, William H., and John. Andrew Vincent "Bimp," Ambrose "Brose," and William T. "Doodle" Welshans lived in the house across the street and two others nearby. Ambrose was the village blacksmith, and the other two, William T. (father) and Vincent (son), were in the lumber business.

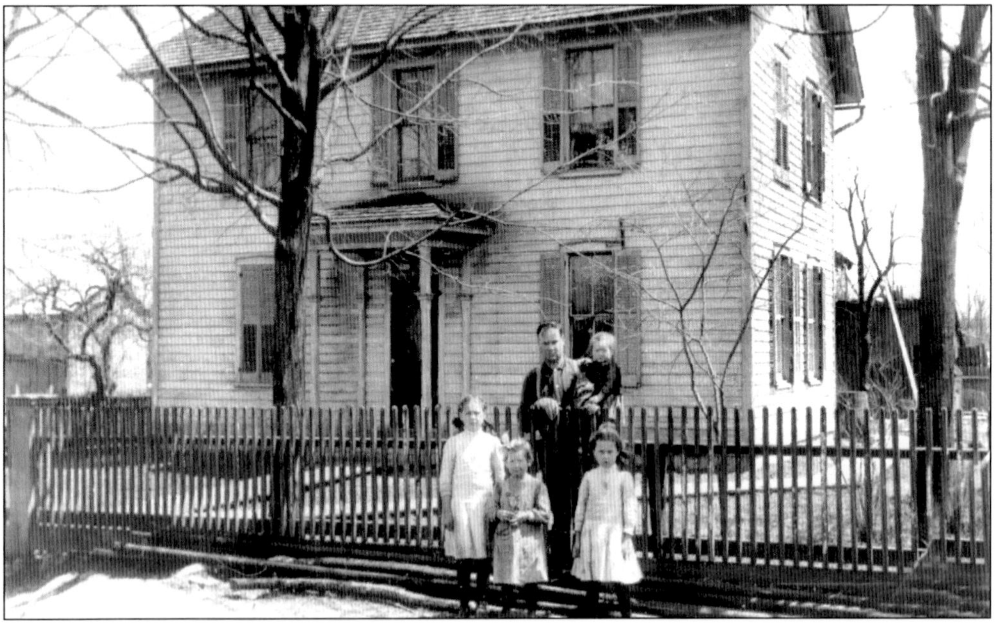

This was the Bimp Welshans place in Rauchtown. His parents were William T. (1850–1912) and Emma Group (1849–1931) Welshans. Andrew (1878–1933) was married to Nellie Getgen (1880–1954). From left to right are Cleta Dorothea (1902–1977, x Nathan Hampe), Mary Elizabeth (born in 1809, x Edward Fowler), and Henrietta Grace (born in 1904, x Edison Clark), and son Kenneth Vincent "Butt" Welshans is being held by his father.

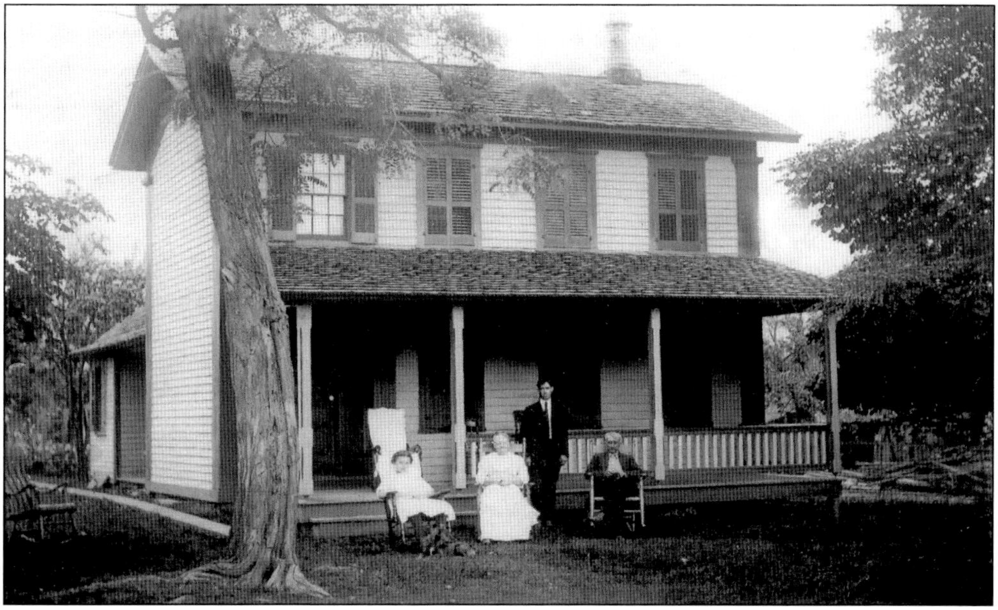

George (1852–1924) and Minnie Welshans (1858–1932) Fenstemaker lived here in the early 20th century. Their daughter Naomi Etta (1889–1930) sits on the rocker at left, and her brother Carl is standing between their parents. The name Etta came from Minnie's sister, Etta Welshans (x Tom Dunlap). Naomi was married to Samuel Frederick Garrett in 1915. Other members of the Fenstemaker family included Elmer, Harry, Ellery "Dutch," Roy, and Earl.

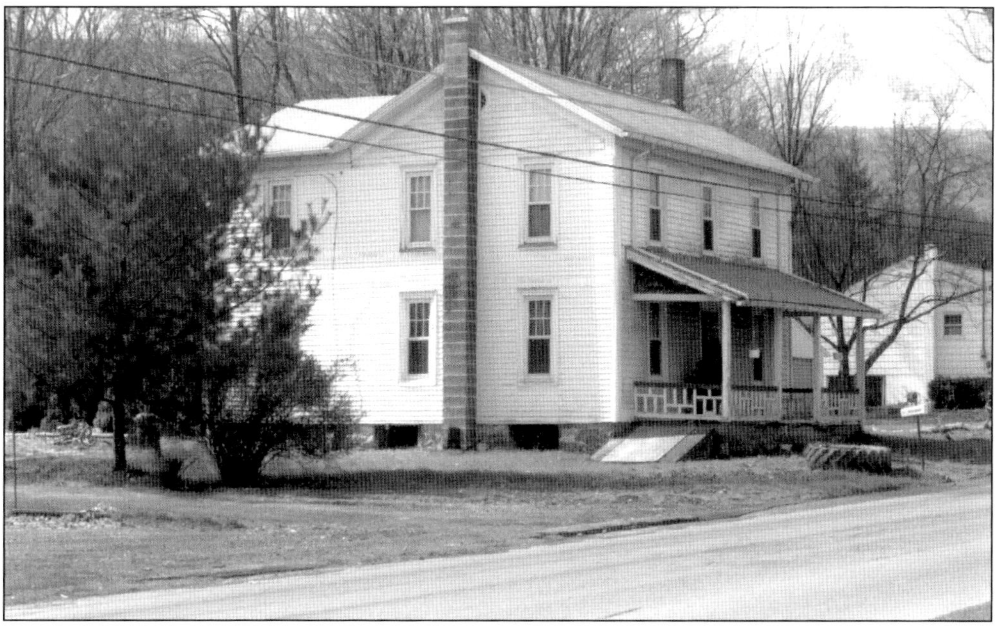

The Crawford House was located at the junction of Pine Mountain Road and the main road through Rauchtown. People from Sugar Valley going to market in Williamsport stopped at the hotel, as it was a two-day journey each way. The hotel was opened by John and Phoebe Metzger in 1873. Israel Fravel also ran a hotel here and used a neck yoke to carry pails of water from the creek.

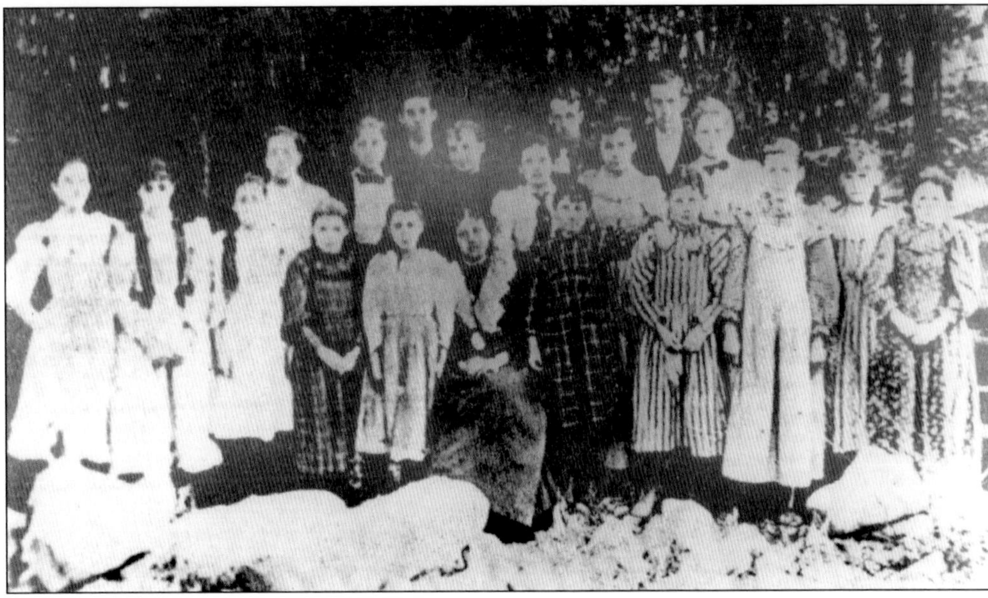

This class of students attended the old Rauchtown School about 1895. It was located on the creek side of the road. Included in this photograph are Nora Welshans (Gheen), Nora Sallada (Hughes), Jenny Fenstemaker (Mowery), Bessie Getgen, Bernice Fravel, teacher Miss Sweeley, Pearl Gheen, Lulu Welshans (Sweitzer), Alda Metzger (Smith), Stella Brosius (Jenkins), Clarence Gheen, Nora Rauch, Ethel Arnot, Sheridan Fravel, Alice Fenstemaker (Bastian), Landis Allen, and Nellie Getgen (Welshans).

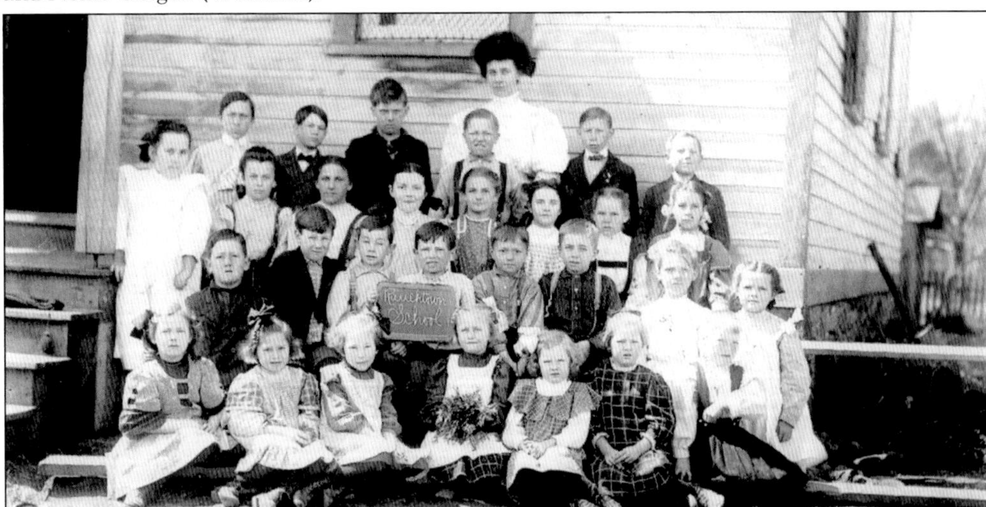

These Rauchtown School students are pictured with their teacher, Lulu Welshans, the daughter of Ambrose and Harriet Keiler Welshans, around 1909. Lulu married David Sweitzer. From left to right are (first row) Winifred Brosius, Helen Getgen, Margaret Wentzel, Edna Curts, Mabel Welshans, Cleta Welshans, and Claire Group; (second row) Bob Garrett, Bill Welshans, Arden Curts, Charles Wentzel, Bob Getgen, unidentified, Dora Osborne, and Naomi Fenstemaker; (third row) Jennie Showers, Phronie Shively, May Baysore, Edith Groupe, Mae Knarr, Myrtle Curts, Helen Groupe, and Ruth Bower; (fourth row) Stuart Groupe, Guy Gheen, Charles Groupe, Glen Getgen, Bill Weidler, and Fred Garrett.

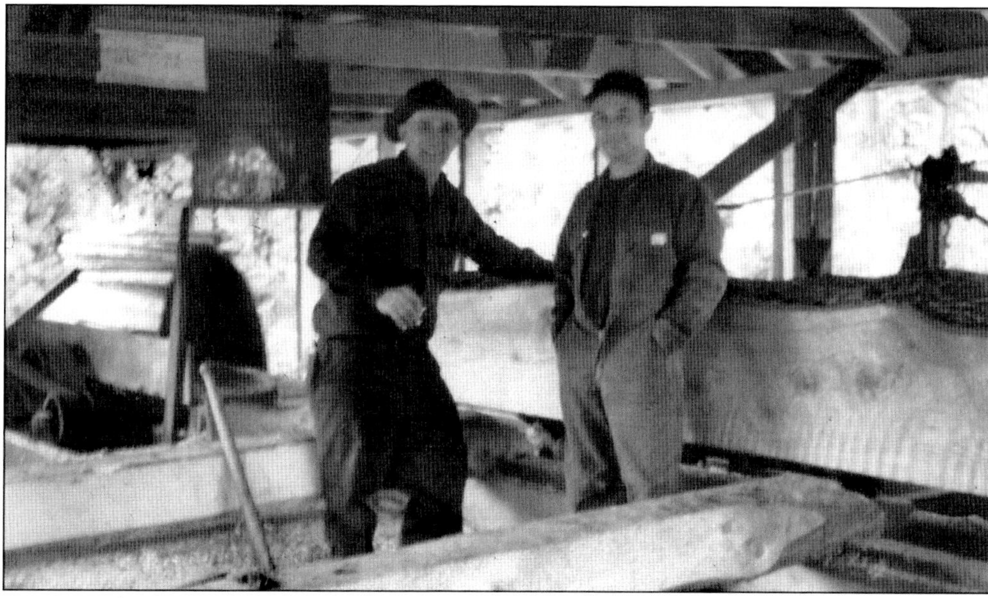

Stewart Eck's sawmill at Rauchtown is shown here with Joe Winter (right) in 1972. Over the years, there have been many in or near the valley. Waterpower was needed until steam power was available. Along Antes Creek in 1873 were the McMicken and Youngman mills followed later by the Plankenhorn and Welshans mills. There was the John Getgen mill in the Upper End (1861), and mills on Sweitzer Stream were run at various times by Elijah Williamson, Nathan Sweitzer, Brady Gower, and Harry Myers.

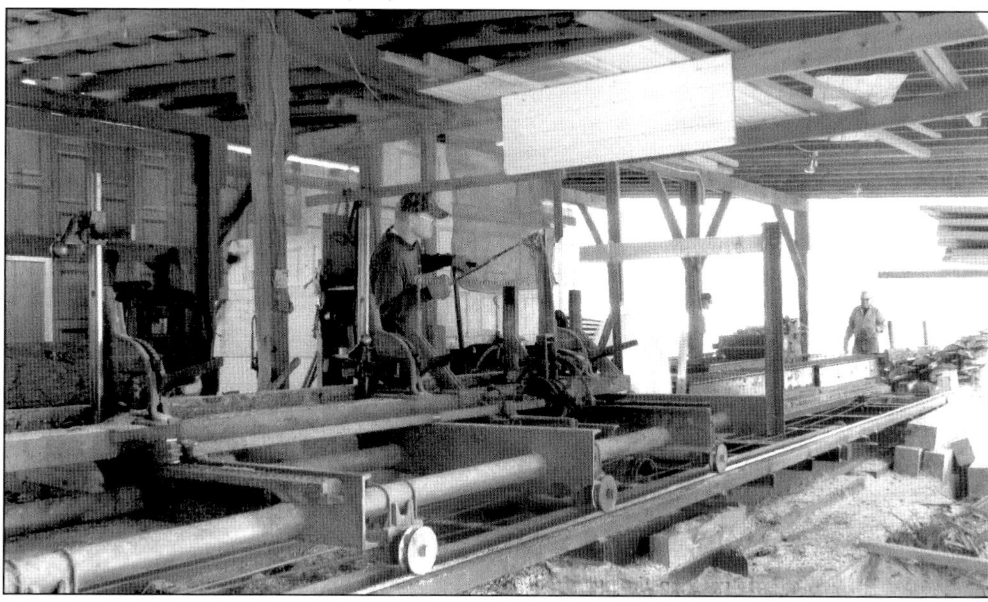

Bob Mundrick bought the mill from Eck in 1984 and ran it until 2007. Mundrick is shown running the mill in 2005 with Charles Welshans catching the boards. Other temporary mill sites included Reeser and Gauger in Morgan Valley. Also Boaz Geyer ran one in Winter's woods, Jacob Clark ran a lumber and shingle mill near Collomsville, the White Deer Lumber Company was in Denworth Gap along with their narrow-gauge railroad, and the mill just removed from Lehman's had been at work on the Kissel and Thompson farms.

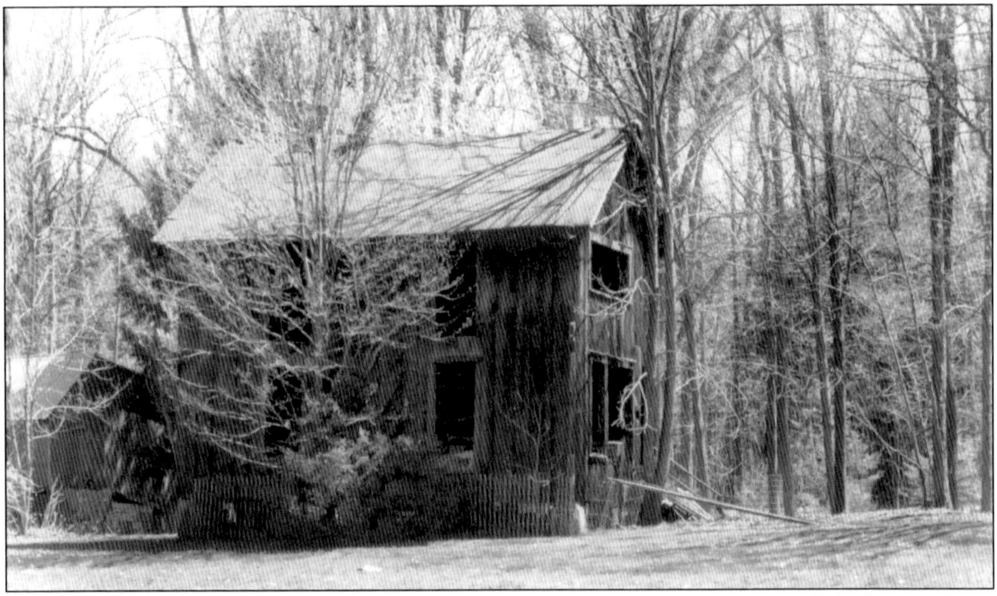

This was the old water-powered gristmill built on the Peter Group property in Rauchtown. Peter (1807–1877) and Elizabeth (1811–1891) Group came to the valley from Adams County at a very early time. He was likely the first blacksmith to settle in Rauchtown. His son John Wesley Group became a lawyer in 1874, receiving his degree from the University of Michigan. His sister Emma married William T. Welshans. The Groups owned 200 acres that included most of today's lower Rauchtown.

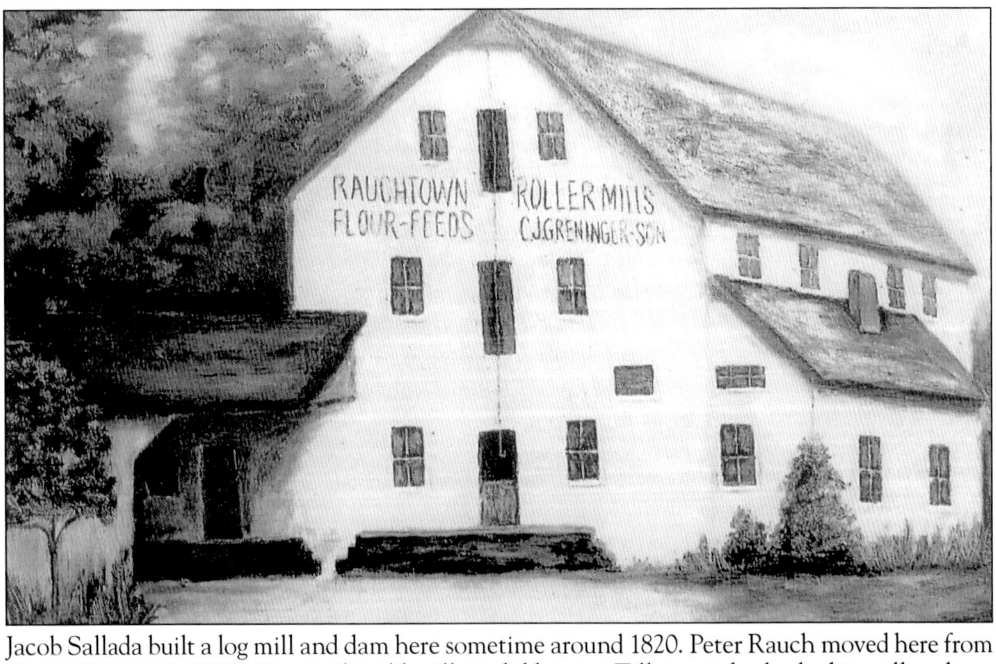

Jacob Sallada built a log mill and dam here sometime around 1820. Peter Rauch moved here from Union County in 1836. He ran the old mill, as did his son Tillman, who built this mill and ran it until 1879, when he sold it to Christian Weidler. In 1892, Houston Weidler joined his father in the business. Later D. H. Shale ran it for a time, followed by Nathan Homler. Clayton Joel Greninger (1875–1956) bought the mill in November 1915, and it stood until 1964.

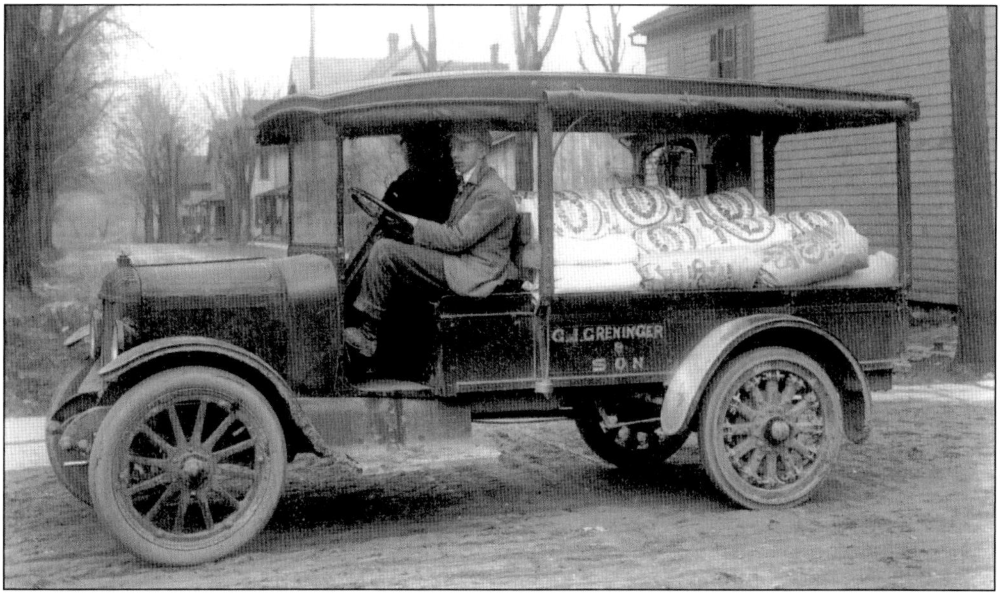

Upon buying the mill in 1915, Greninger refurbished it and had it in full operation by May 1919. In 1918, he purchased this Republic truck to better handle business. These trucks were made in Alma, Michigan, between 1913 and 1929, and this company was a major supplier of "Liberty" trucks used by soldiers during World War I. He later bought a larger truck made by Kearns. His son was William Forrest Greninger (1896–1964), who owned the business next. The Greningers were from Sugar Valley.

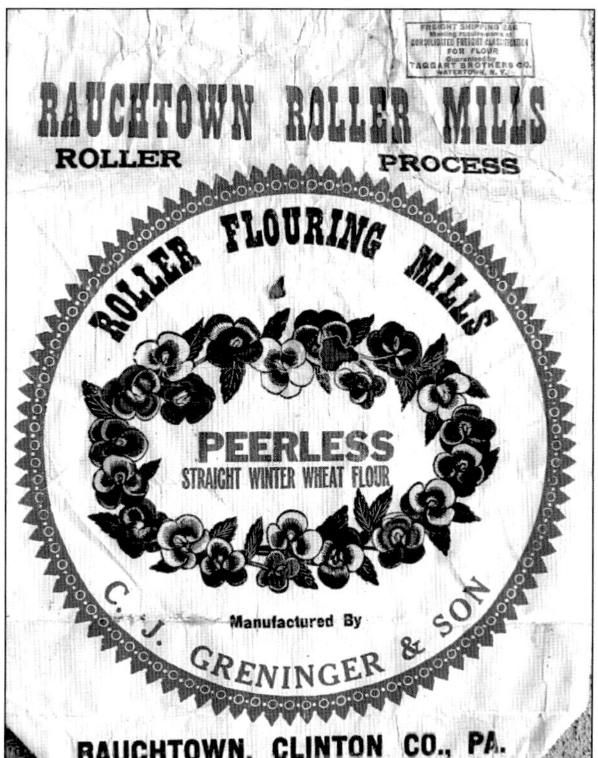

During Colonial days, Pennsylvania farmers grew more wheat than any other colony, and milling was a major industry. The state was known as the breadbasket of the 13 colonies. European immigrants brought wheat, rye, barley, oat, and buckwheat seed with them. Swedish immigrants built the first water-powered gristmill in the state in 1643. The milldam and race delivered water to the old wooden-geared turbine until it was replaced by a one-cylinder diesel engine around 1937.

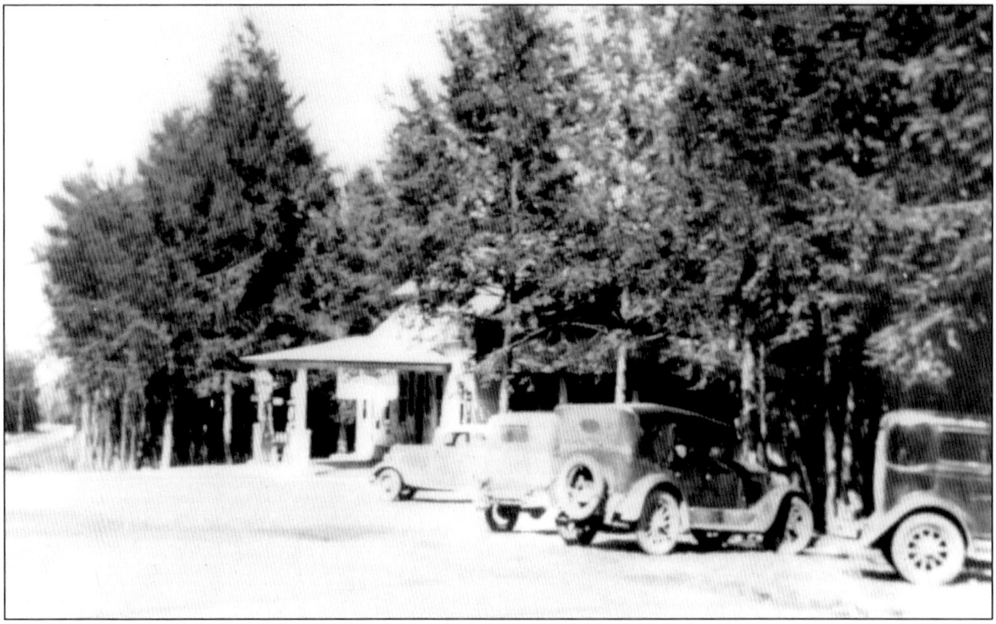

Floyd Meixel built this establishment, Raven's Rest, in 1933 and acquired a liquor license for it. He ran it until just before World War II, when his son Ernie Meixel took over the business. The land belonged to Ernie's grandfather William Bower, who also ran the Bower House in Rauchtown. In 1948, Ernie moved the business to the red house at the corner of Pine Mountain Road, tore it down, built a bar, and operated Meixel's Tavern until 1964.

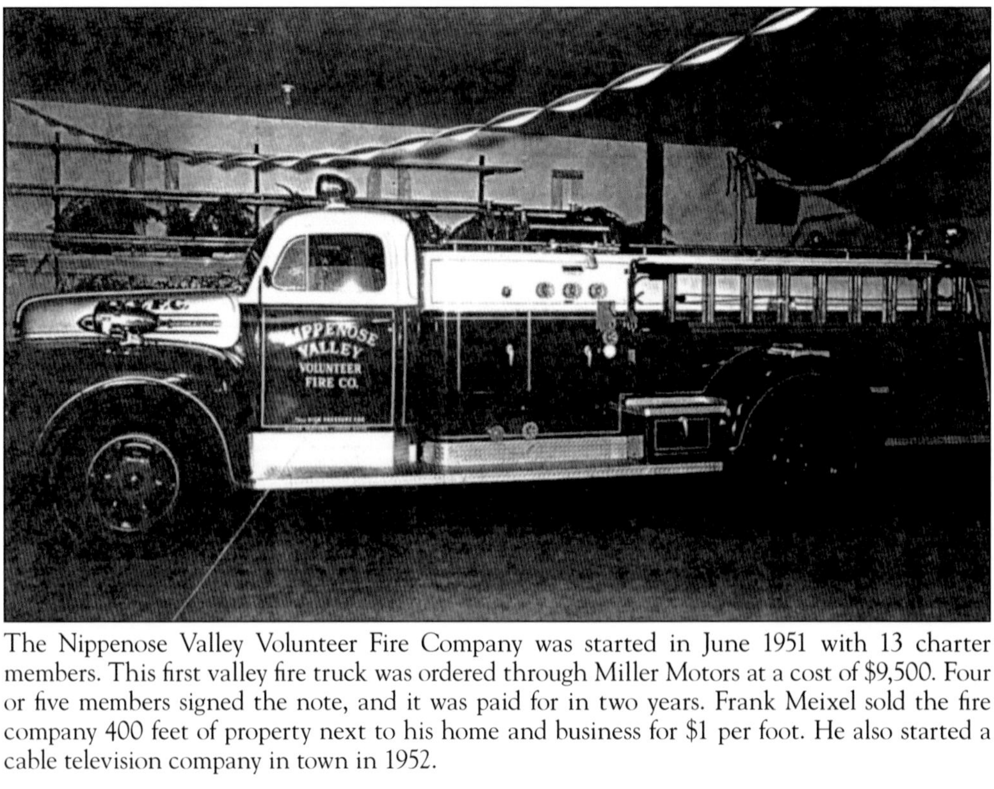

The Nippenose Valley Volunteer Fire Company was started in June 1951 with 13 charter members. This first valley fire truck was ordered through Miller Motors at a cost of $9,500. Four or five members signed the note, and it was paid for in two years. Frank Meixel sold the fire company 400 feet of property next to his home and business for $1 per foot. He also started a cable television company in town in 1952.

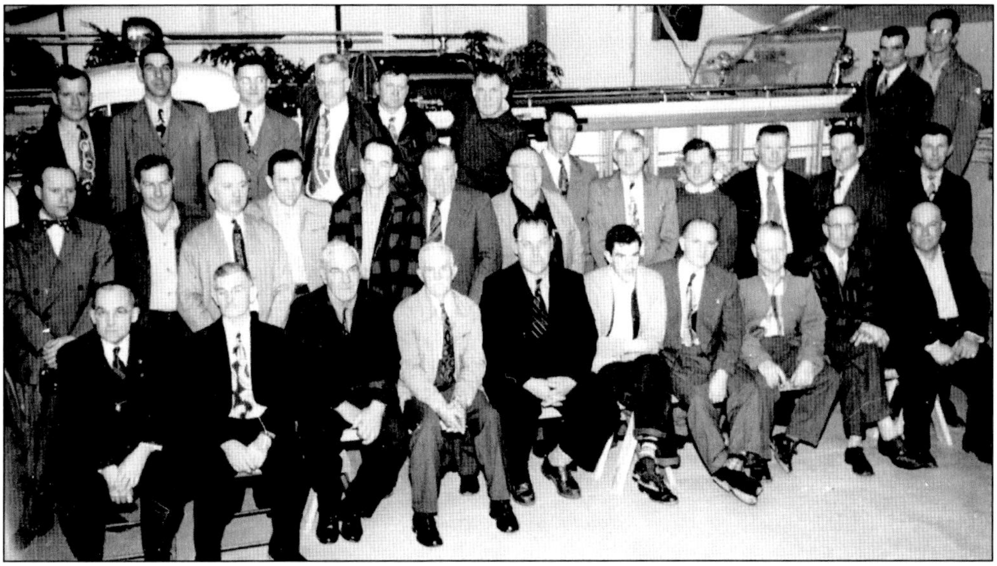

These men were members of the fire company in 1953. From left to right are (first row) Sam LeFever, Ercel Ramsey, Floyd Meixel, Charles Getgen, Stewart Meixel, unidentified, Larue Getgen, Byron S. Welshans, Orie Reading, and Ernest Meixel; (second row) John Jenkins, Art Meixel, Robert Getgen, Bill Getgen, Ernest Welshans, Victor Lehman, Leonard Mercer, George Lehman, Elmer Rell, Rudi Sweitzer, Verus Lehman, Sam Lehman, and Kenneth Welshans; (third row) Ted Getgen, Frank Meixel, Ed Shadle, Lorraine Davidson, Earl Schrack, Brownie Welshans, Joe Welshans, and Gordon Snook.

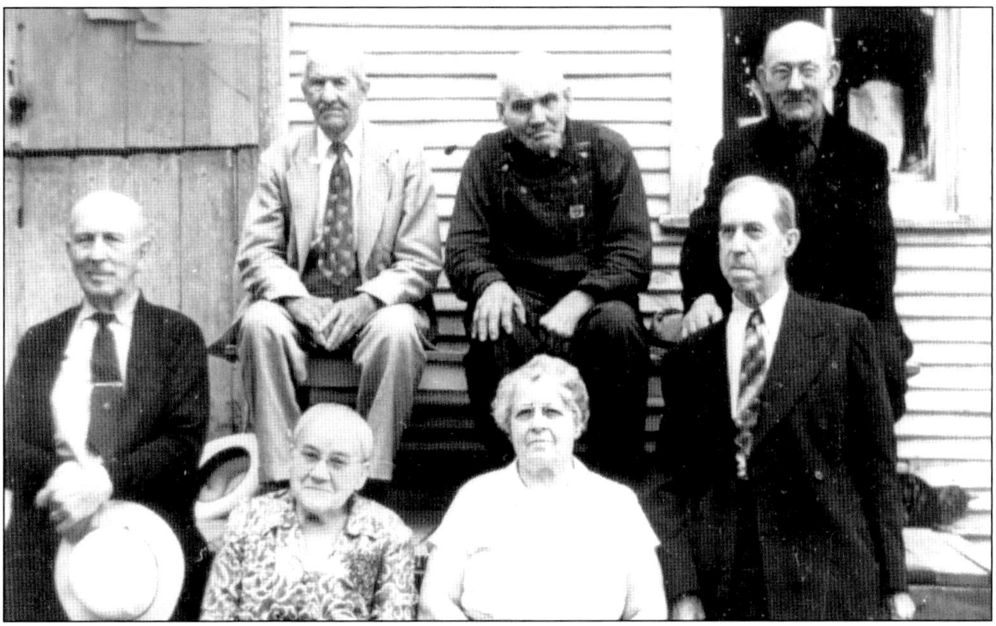

This picture was taken during the 100th anniversary celebration of the founding of Rauchtown in 1950. It was headed by Frank Meixel and was a major event in this small community, with fire trucks, bands, floats, food, speeches, and the crowning of a Miss Rauchtown. From left to right are (first row) Harry Smith, Carrie Showers Smith, Genevieve Yarrison, and John Sents; (second row) Henry Laubach, Jesse Poet, and John Bixel.

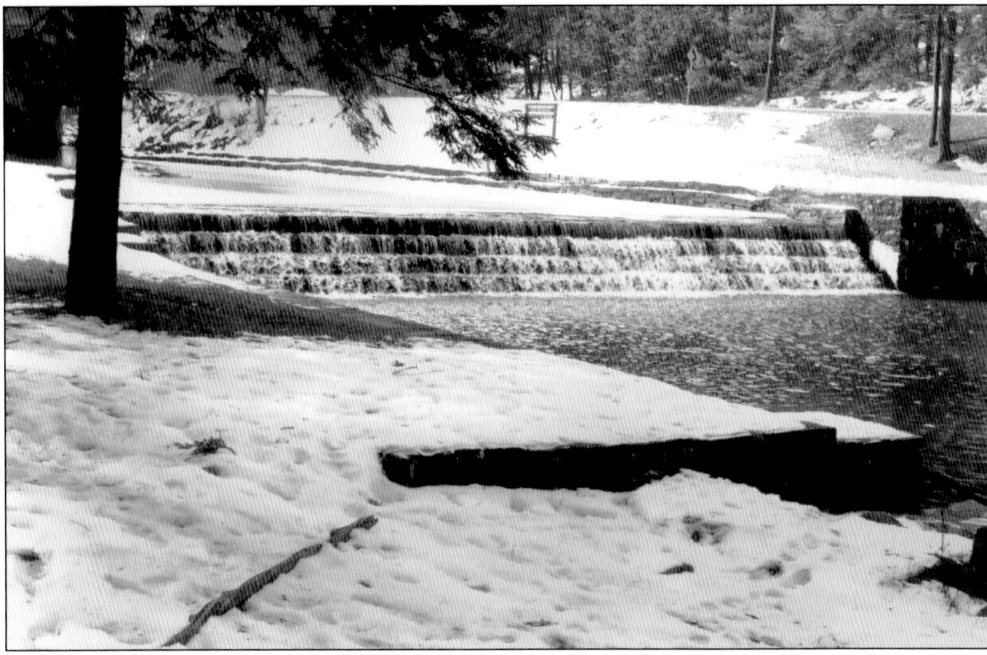

This dam was built by the Civilian Conservation Corps (CCC) in 1935, the year Ravensburg State Park was established. The park was dedicated to the CCC and was under control of the state forest service until 1971 when the Pennsylvania Department of Environmental Resources (DER) was established.

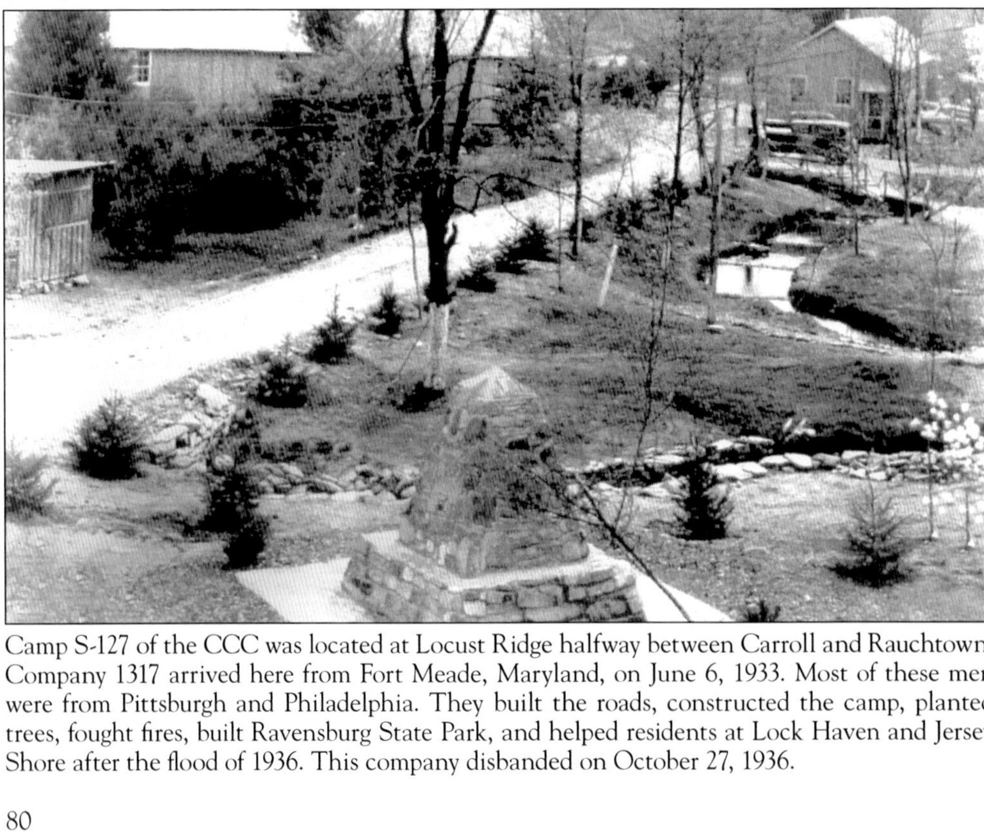

Camp S-127 of the CCC was located at Locust Ridge halfway between Carroll and Rauchtown. Company 1317 arrived here from Fort Meade, Maryland, on June 6, 1933. Most of these men were from Pittsburgh and Philadelphia. They built the roads, constructed the camp, planted trees, fought fires, built Ravensburg State Park, and helped residents at Lock Haven and Jersey Shore after the flood of 1936. This company disbanded on October 27, 1936.

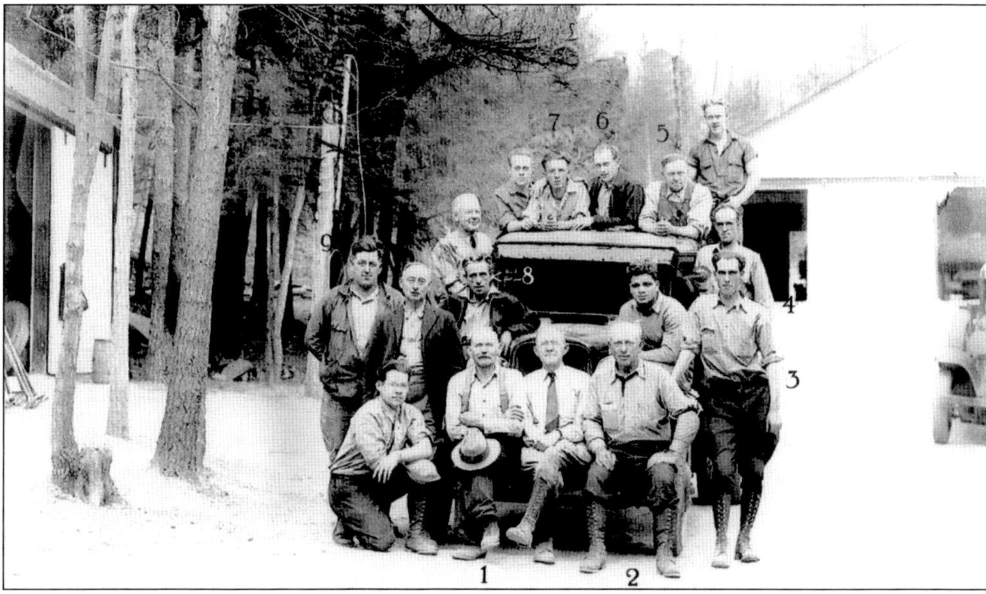

Company 5475 arrived from North Carolina and South Carolina on October 27, 1936. This company consisted of 140 men plus 23 leaders and technical personnel. Here is a supervisory group of Local Experienced Men (LEM). Pictured are John Bixel (1), Harry Smith (2), Pete Welshans (3), Art Welshans (4), Calvin Bowersox (5), Verus Smith (6), Ralph A. Rauch (7), Walter Keeler (8), and Robert Garrett (9). There were as many as 113 camps in the state, and there were nine camps in the Tiadaghton District.

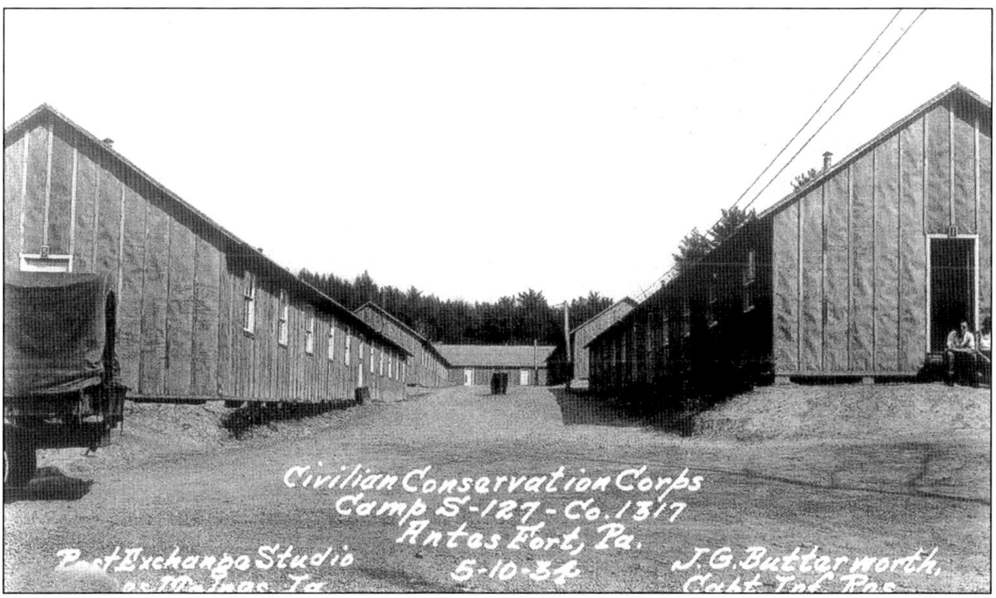

The barracks at Camp S-127 housed 40 to 50 men per building with about 200 in the camp. Enlistment was for six months, and a new man was called a Peavey. The camp newspaper was called *Echo of the Pines*. In 1934, there were 4,500 camps in the nation, and a few were established for women in New York and New Hampshire, which was Eleanor Roosevelt's idea. Lyman Run and Bark Shanty camps were used as German prisoner of war camps and held about 280 men in all.

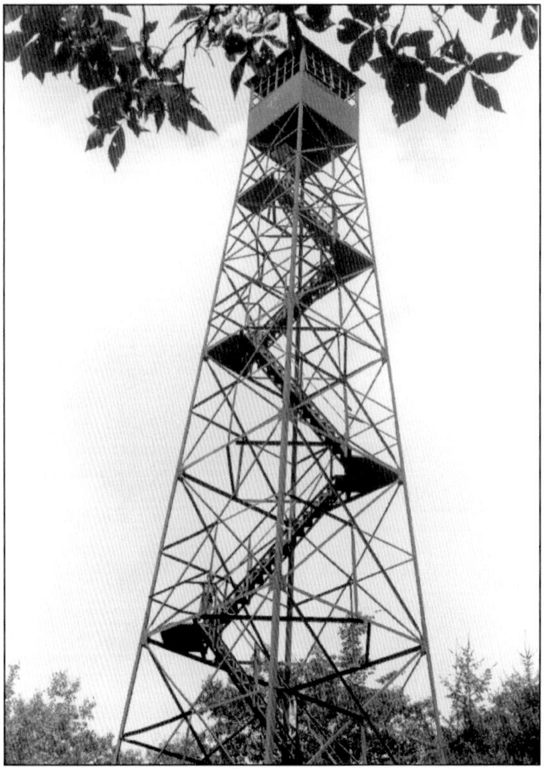

The Rauchtown Fire Tower on top of North White Deer Ridge was built in 1933 by the CCC and was dismantled in 1974. Changes in civil service hiring requirements made it difficult to hire local, knowledgeable men, and a change in the law made the state liable for accidents on these towers. The first fire tower was built in 1905, and it was made of wood. Towers made of steel were first constructed in 1914, and by 1948, some 150 towers had radio communication.

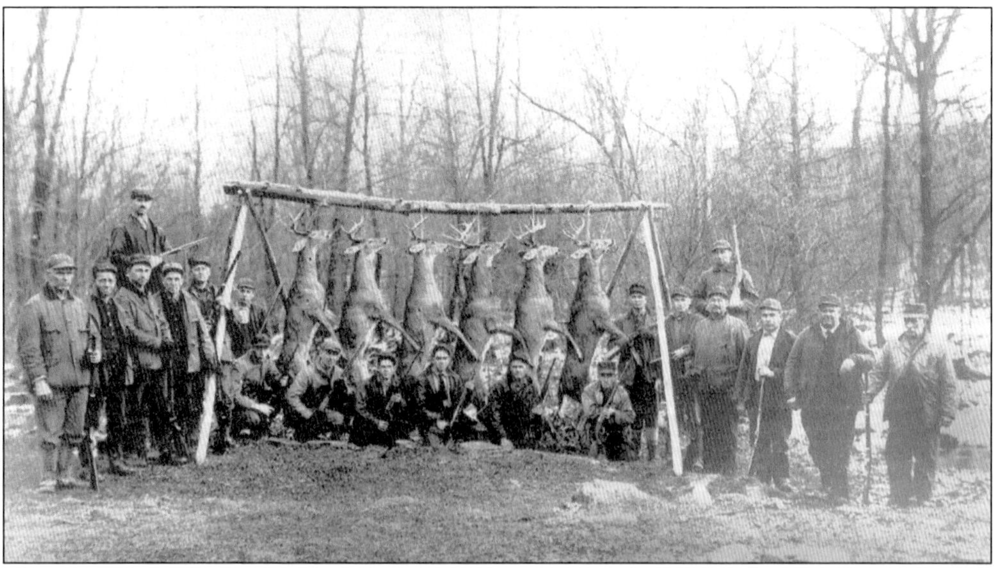

Members of the Rauchtown Rod and Gun Club posed with their kill in 1921 at the Charles Harbach farm at the east end of Sugar Valley. Pictured are (standing at left) Charles Hinkle, Newton Smith, Herb Tobias, Clarence Gheen (with gun), Charles Beechert, Raymond Shadle, and Ernest Meixel; (kneeling) Harry Harbach, Abe Killian, Brownie Welshans, Tim Groupe, Ernest Welshans, and Mike Fenstemaker; (standing at right) Charles Williams, Charles Wensel, Charles Lang, J. Stuart Groupe (with a gun on his shoulder), Floyd Meixel, Harry Hubler, and Billy Bower (camp cook).

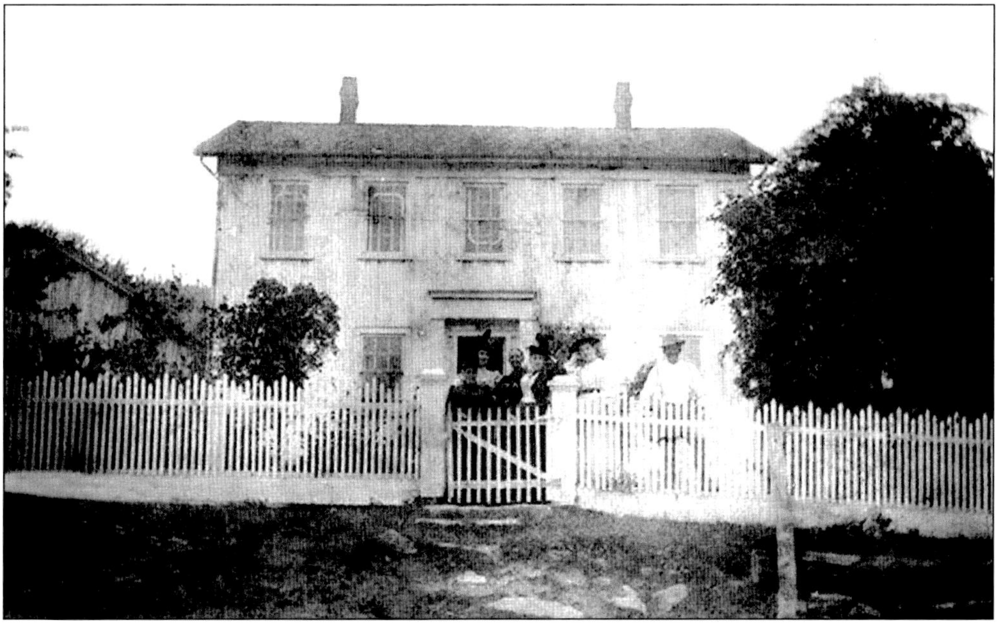

John (1820–1878) and Rebecca Welshans (1820–1894) Sallada lived here in 1861. The original house had burned and was replaced with this one. One of the Sallada's seven children, Martha Jane (born in 1849), married Andrew Groupe, and the next owner of this farm was their son John Stuart Groupe. The farm contained 215 acres plus 52 acres that had previously been owned by William Bigler Welshans. The farm was called Valley View.

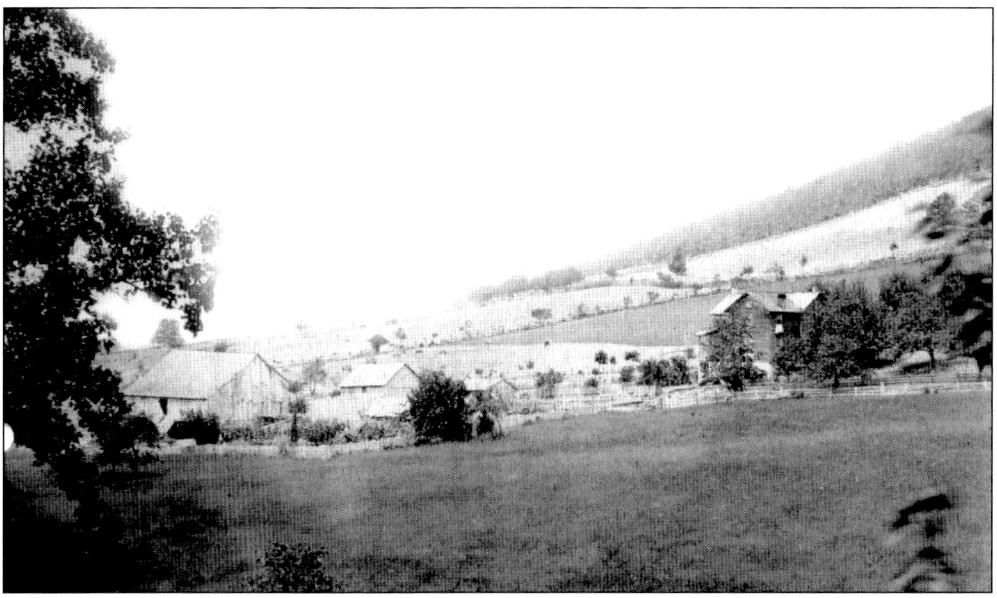

This was the old place on the Reading farm that sat above the new one, which was built around 1892. The 1862 map shows it belonged to John "Fligger" (misspelling of Phleger). The Garrett family lived here afterward, and the farm was next owned by Leonard Wright. The Clark Reading family moved to the valley from West Virginia and bought it in 1914, and later the farm was owned by Orrie and Edith Fenstemaker Reading, who sold it to Paul and Margaret Barner Reading in 1964.

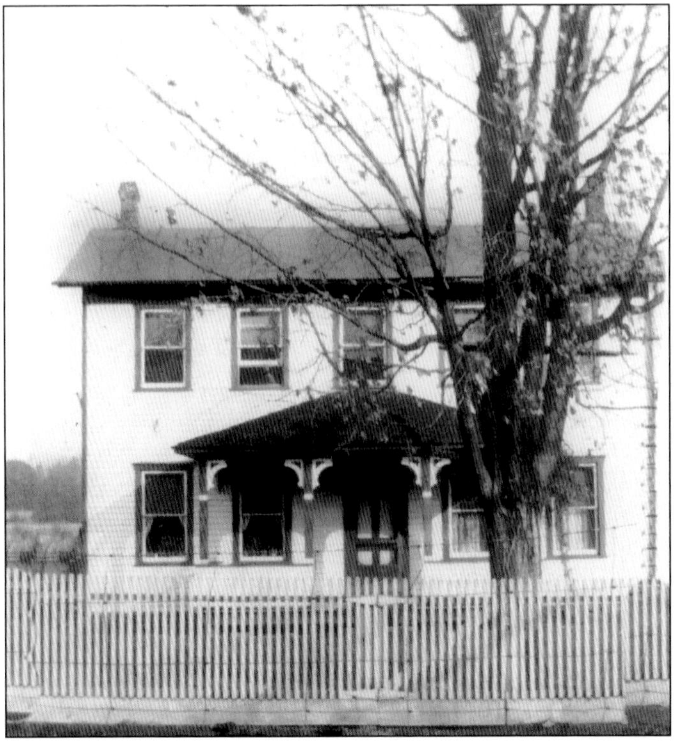

The Samuel Smeck family lived here in the 1860s, followed by William Welshans in the 1870s. This is the farmhouse as it appeared in the 1920s when owned by Wilbert Lehman, and it has remained in the Lehman family through Sam and Dean Lehman. Wilbert (born in 1881) was married to Susan Amelia Eck (born in 1884), and their children included Elias Joseph, Verus Franklin, Glenn A., Samuel Sylvester, Dale, and Margaret Elizabeth.

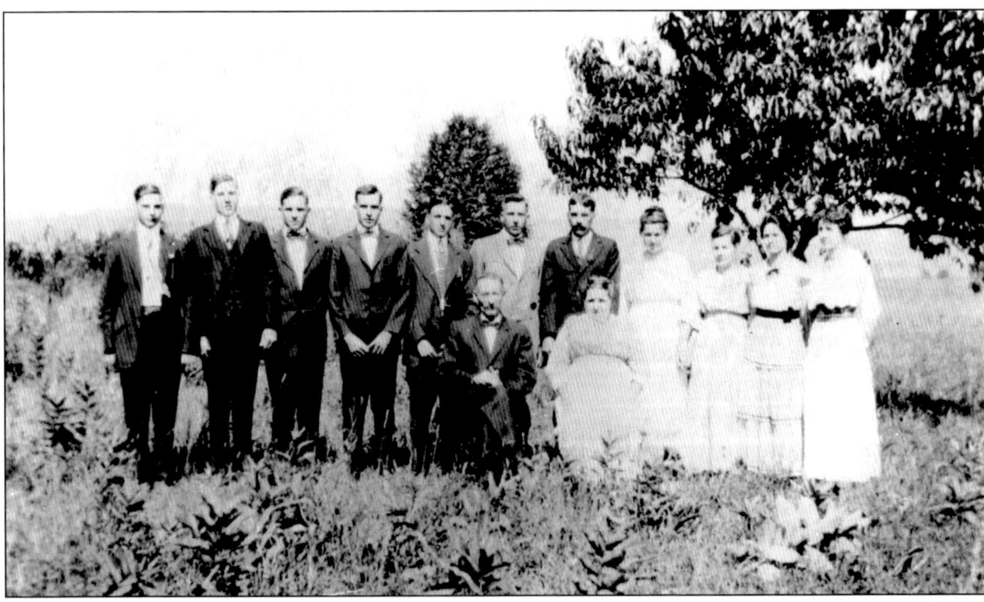

This was the Alexander Lehman family as photographed in the 1920s. From left to right are Chester (born in 1900, x Sophie Becker), Ernest (born in 1898, x Catherine Eck), Victor (born in 1896, x Hazel Phleger), Milford (born in 1892, x Bessie Wolmer), Daniel (born in 1896, x Catherine White), Charles (born in 1888, x Mabel Brownlee), Wilbert (born in 1881, x Susan Eck), Nora (born in 1882, x Harvey Embick), Elizabeth (born in 1880, x James Gamble), Ellen (born in 1884, x Clarence Quiggle), Emma (born in 1894, x George Heller), and parents Alexander (1855–1939) and Margaret Miller (1861–1928). Missing are Harvey, Howard, and Guy.

Six

JAMESTOWN

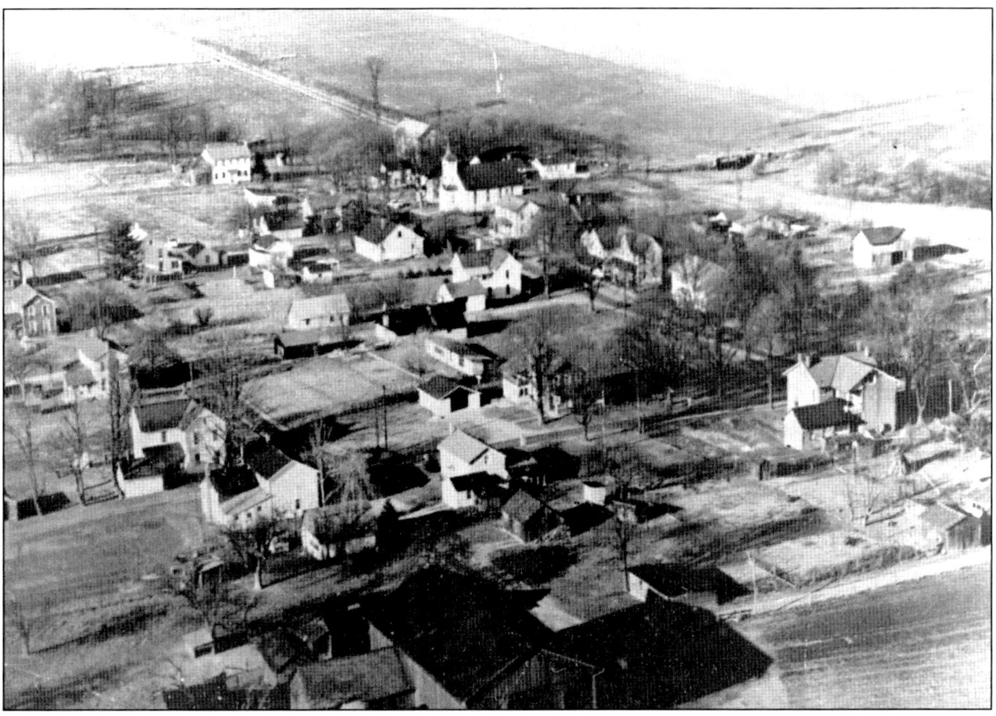

The village was laid out and named by James Gamble in 1838 on a land warrant issued to James Wilson in 1782. A post office was established here in 1872 and was named Oriole. During the early years, there was a doctor living in the village, two blacksmith shops, a cabinetmaker's shop (where valley caskets were built), a cigar factory, a shoe shop, a general store, and a print shop.

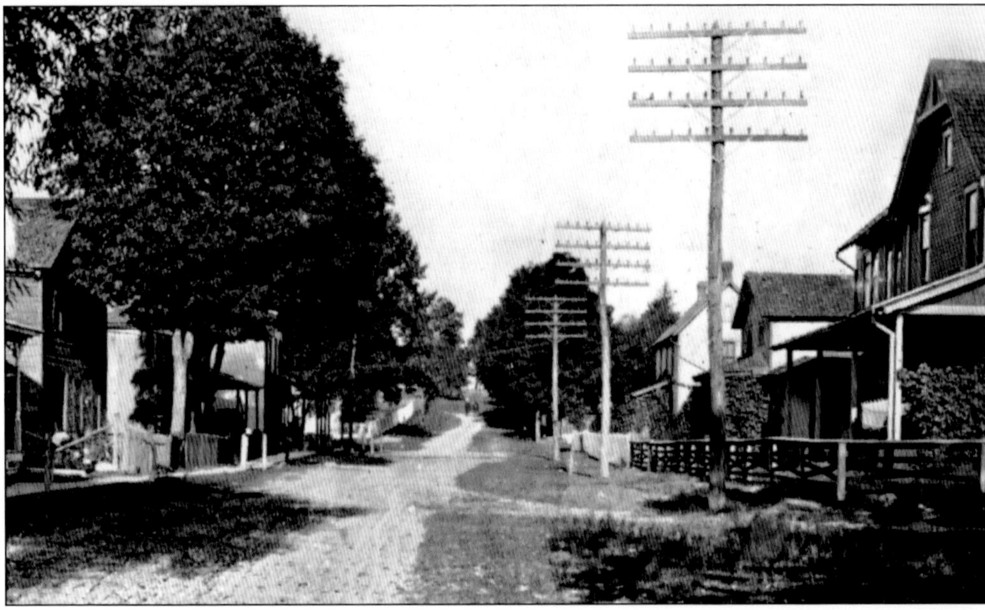

This is a view of Main Street about 1930. The telephone poles carried messages through the switchboard that was located at Henry York's store and did so until 1945 when the telephone company moved to Oval. The Union Telephone Company began a three-year contract in 1903, but the price of $36 a year was considered very high. At this time, operators worked three eight-hour shifts at 75¢ a shift.

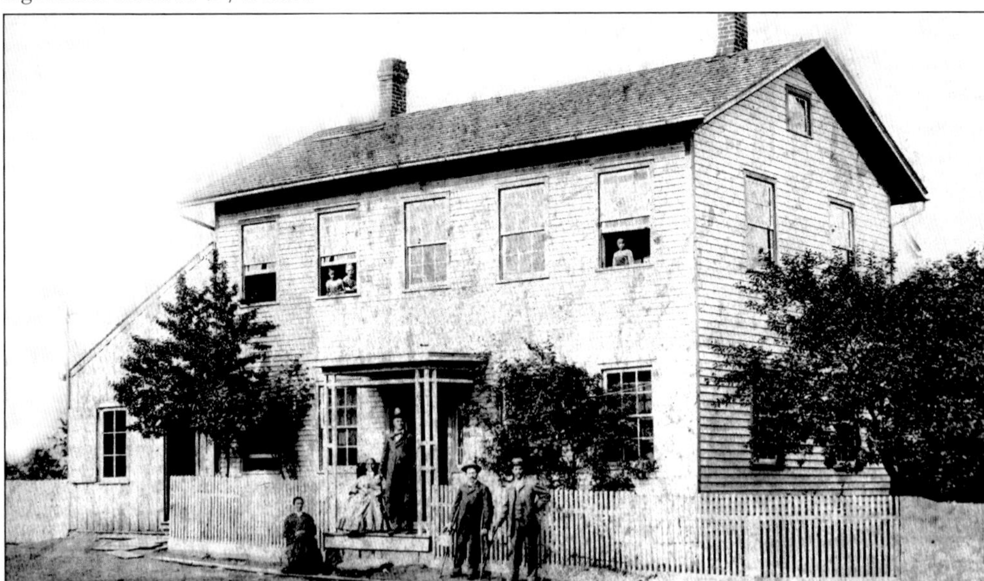

Dr. John Hays Grier's home and office was located on Nippenose Street. He graduated from Jefferson College in 1840 and moved to the valley in 1859. Dr. Grier (1813–1894) was the oldest son of Rev. John Hays Grier, the Presbyterian minister in Jersey Shore from 1814 to 1851. The doctor and his wife, Amanda Malvina Quiggle (1816–1894), are seen on the porch along with three children, (from left to right) Mary, Bobby, and John. The doctor's office was on the left side of the second floor.

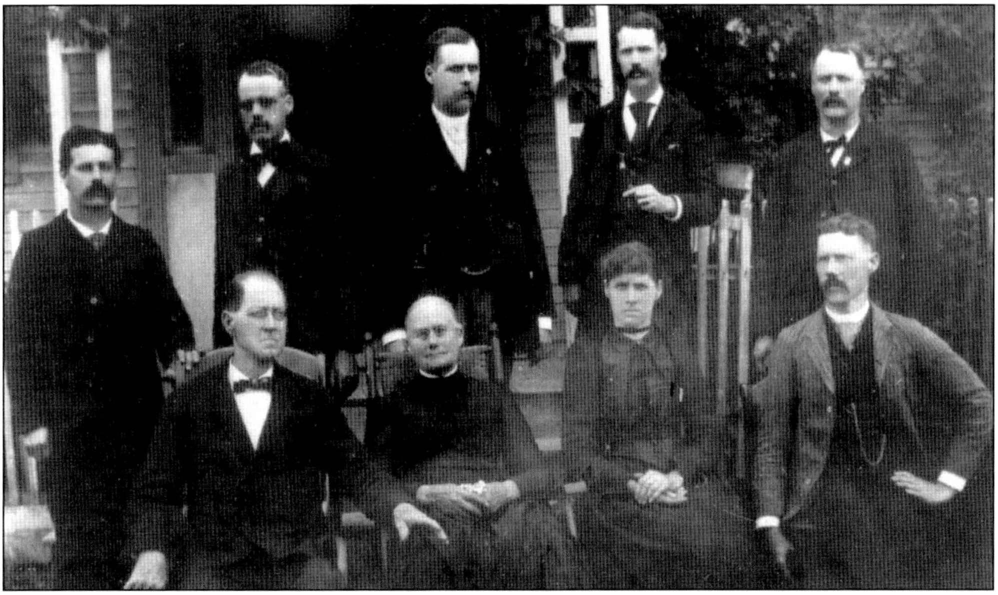

This photograph shows the doctor's family around 1900. From left to right are (first row) Dr. John Hays Grier, Amanda Grier, Mary E. Gebhart Grier (1845–1905), and Robert H. Grier (1854–1934); (second row) James Dougal Grier (1847–1926), Albert C. Grier (1843–1901), William Hays Grier (1841–1915), John W. Grier (1850–1935), and Samuel M. Grier (1852–1934). Dougal was a valley tinsmith. Robert H. ran a store and post office on Main Street, and in 1877, he and John W. became editors and proprietors of a newspaper called *Jersey Shore Vidette*.

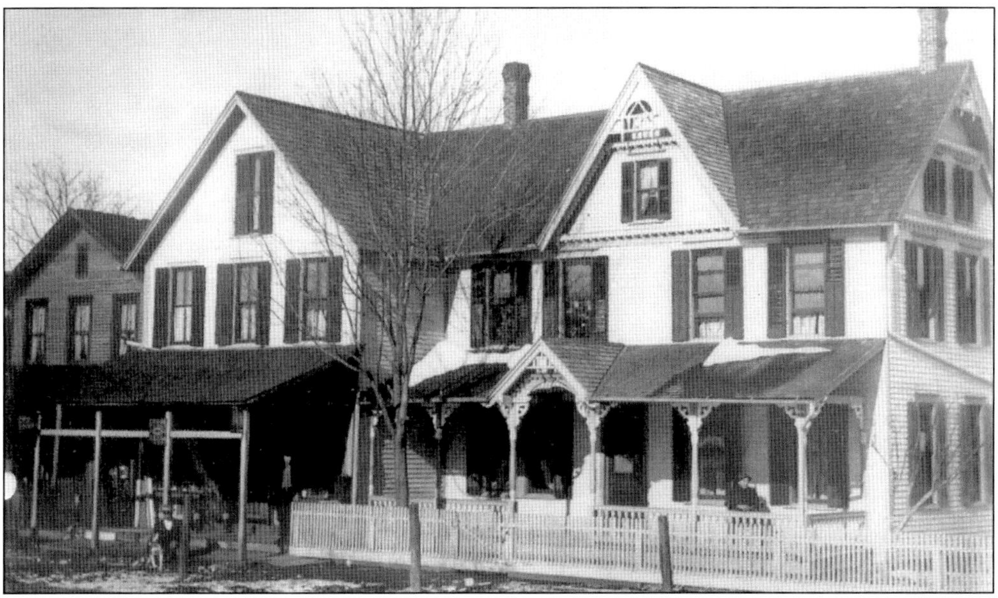

This was the home and store of Henry E. Yorks. It was built on Main Street about 1905. The store and telephone switchboard were located in the left half of the building. Yorks was born on February 14, 1864, in Columbia County and got his teaching degree from Muncy State Normal School. He taught for a few years and moved to Jamestown in 1889. He married Ella Grier, the daughter of Albert C. Grier, on October 21, 1890. Their three children were Hays, Gertrude, and Joseph.

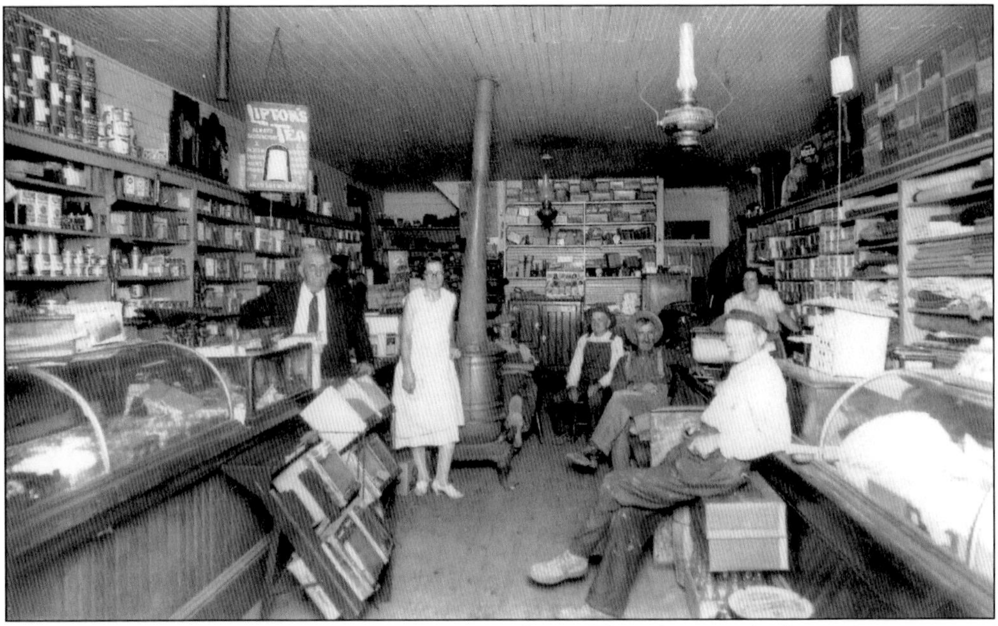

General stores have always been great meeting places. This photograph shows the interior of Yorks General Store about 1934. Henry E. Yorks served as superintendent of the Methodist Sunday school for 48 years and was a justice of the peace for 45 years. In the store, from left to right, are Henry E. Yorks, Nora McHenry, Lamar Thompson (by stove), George Pearson, John Fenstemaker, Dora Yorks, and Mike Tomb.

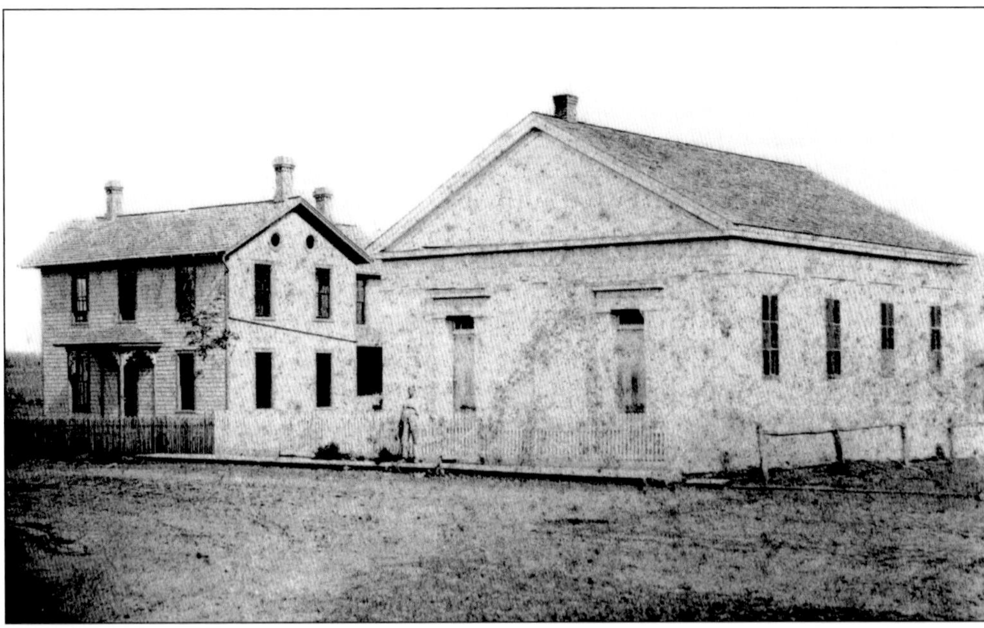

This photograph shows the new parsonage that was built for the Jamestown Methodist Church in 1880. The church was built in 1851 under the direction of the trustees. Those from Lycoming County were John Clark, James Clark, Thomas Clark, Lewis Gann, Jonas Rauch, and Hugh Purcel. Trustees from Clinton County were Peter Group, Tillman Rauch, and Thomas Perry. This church burned on the night of January 31, 1915, and nearly took the parsonage with it.

John Wise was one of the best-known hunters in this section of the country and the last professional hunter in Jamestown. He was born in 1844 and was married to Jane Clark on August 26, 1869. For 30 years after her death in 1884, he lived the life of a hermit and supported himself by hunting and trapping. He lived on the corner of Addition and Chestnut Streets and died in 1914, two years after this photograph was taken.

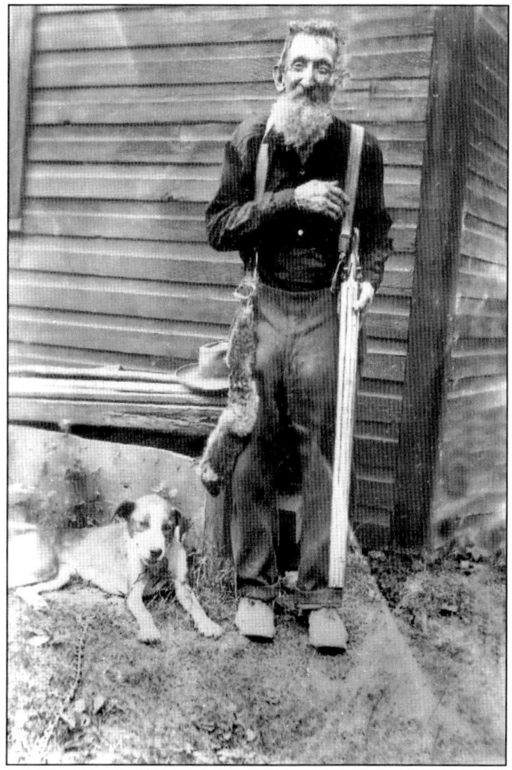

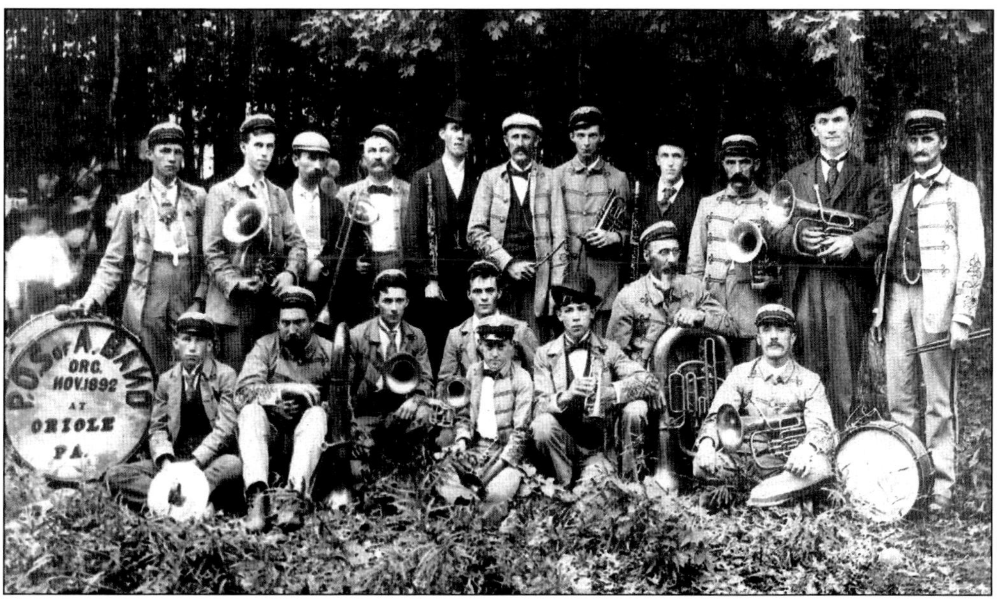

These 19 men were members of the Patriotic Order Sons of America that formed in Jamestown on January 11, 1890, as Washington Camp No. 501. The band formed in 1892. Pictured in front is Gordon Phillips. From left to right are (first row) George Hanner, William Showers, Philip Welshans, Charles Getgen, Hayes Keiler, Houston Weidler, and Ambrose Welshans; (second row) Lester Zerbe, Frank Weidler, Harry Barner, Jacob Hanner, Mr. Flanagan, John Phillips, William Sweeley, George Marcus, James Allen, Roger Clark, and Edward Cutler.

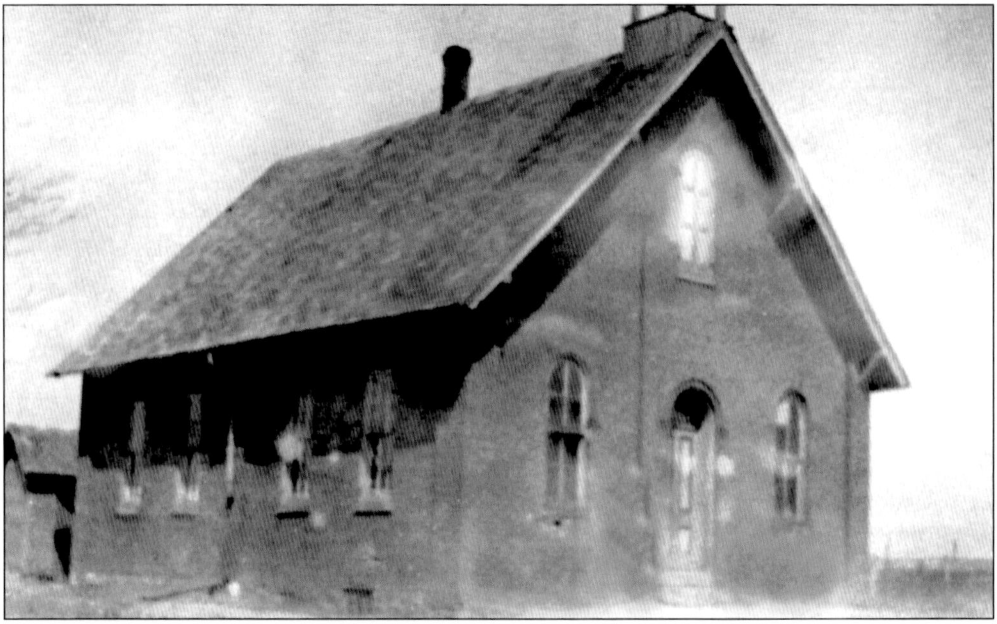

Both the 1861 and 1873 landowner maps show a schoolhouse just south of Jamestown, but like others in the valley, this was likely the second one at this location and was built bigger and better than the first. In 1892, there were nine schools in the valley and the school year was six months long. Six of the nine teachers were men. They were paid $35 per month, and the women were paid $30.

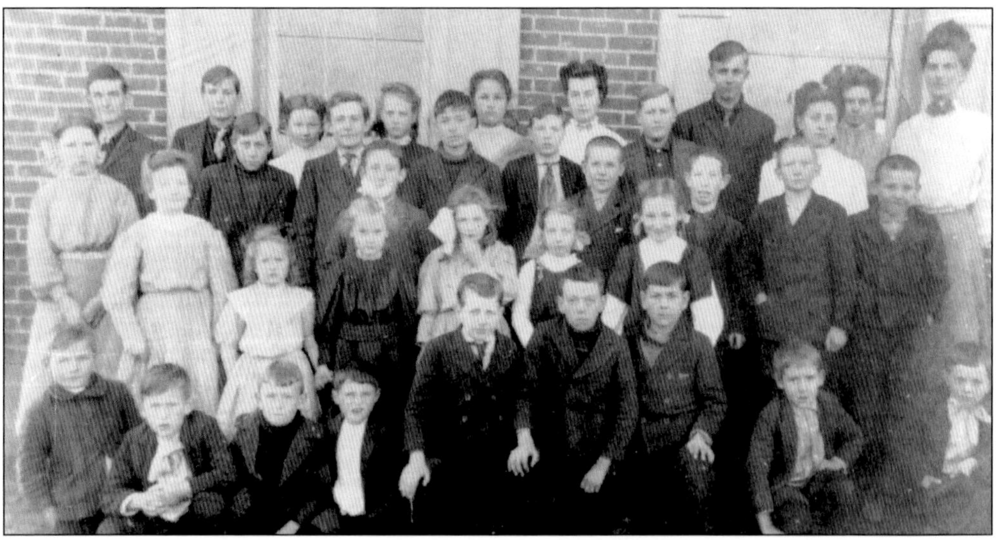

These were Jamestown School students for the year 1906. From left to right are (first row) Stuart Welshans, Carlton Tomb, Lawrence Eoute, John Sents, Bob Pearson, Fred Eoute, Charles Fenstemaker, Joe Yorks, and unidentified; (second row) Phoebe Tomb, Mae Knarr, Ella Sents, Bertha Pearson, and Hazel Phleger; (third row) Bertha Koons, Hays Yorks, Victor Lehman, Max Pearson, Deloss Ramsey, and Millford Lehman; (fourth row) Effie Pearson, Sees Welshans, Jim Bangson, Verus Fenstemaker, Harry Pearson, Raymond Shadle, and Helen Tomb; (fifth row) Ercel Ramsey, Harry Reading, Nellie Osborne, Erma Pearson, Bea Stout, Edith Fenstemaker, Frank Fulliner, Madge Welshans, and teacher Romana Reading.

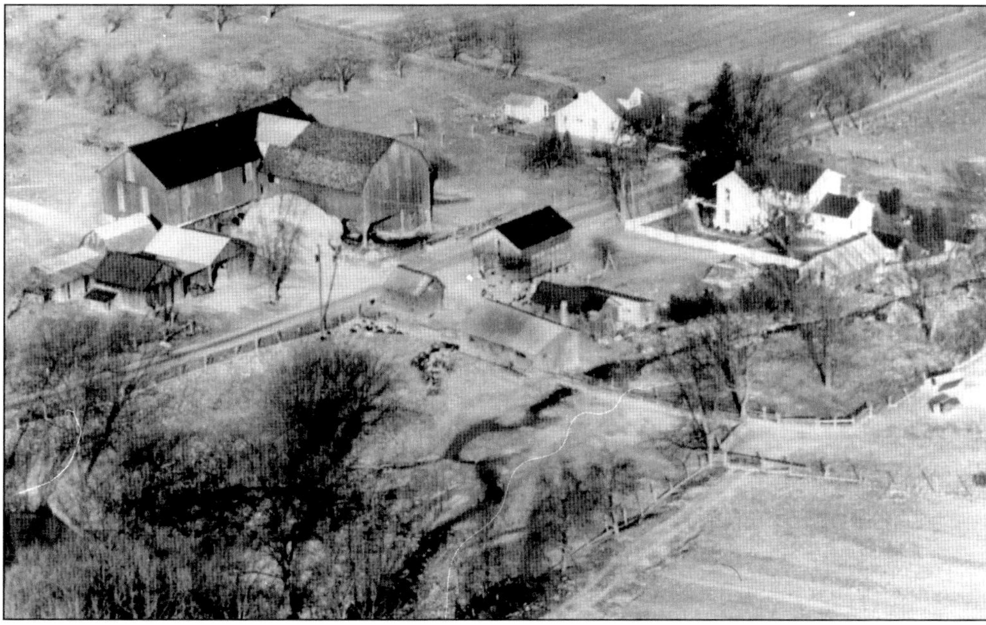

William Welshans Sr. (1792–1871) was the first of his family to move into the valley in 1837. He bought 391 acres at a sheriff's sale with a high bid of $738. This land was the William Gray warrant of 1793 and, at the time of the sale, it belonged to Francis Clark. The family lived in Clark's log house but over time built this farm complex. Welshans had 20 children by two wives, and the extended family grew to be quite large. This farm stayed in the family until 1985.

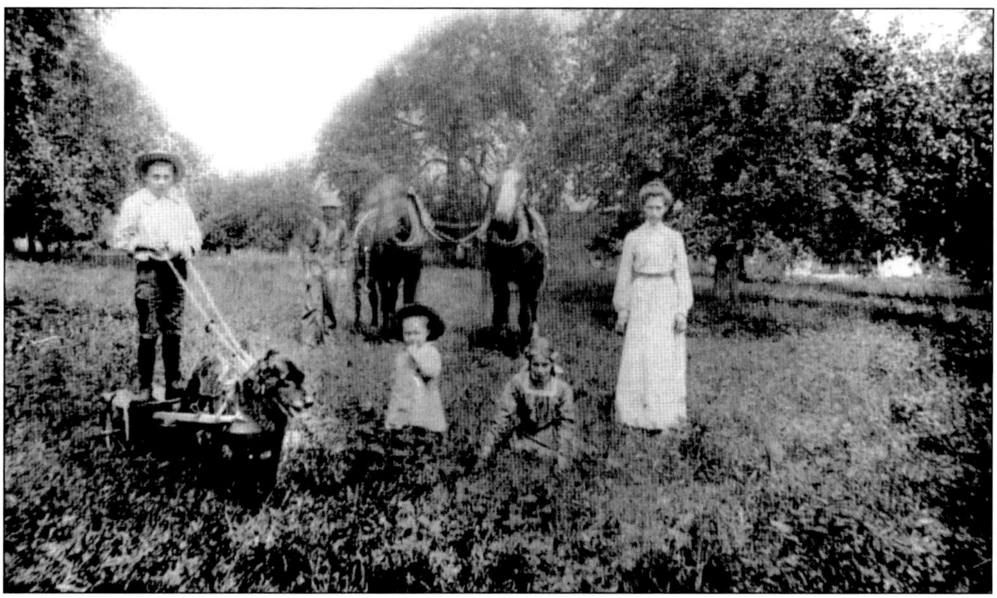

The original Welshans farm passed from William Welshans Sr. to his son William Jr. (1819–1894) to David Nelson (1856–1931) to Jacob Sees (1895–1973) to Leonard Cliff (1918–1983) and to Henry and Anna Beiler in 1985 with 56 more acres going to Sam Beiler in 1987. This picture, taken around 1905, shows Nelson Welshans and his wife, Carrie Sees, along with Sees (x Bea Karstetter) standing on a cart with the dog, either Torrance (x Margaret Snyder) or Stuart, and Madge (x Jacob Hanner).

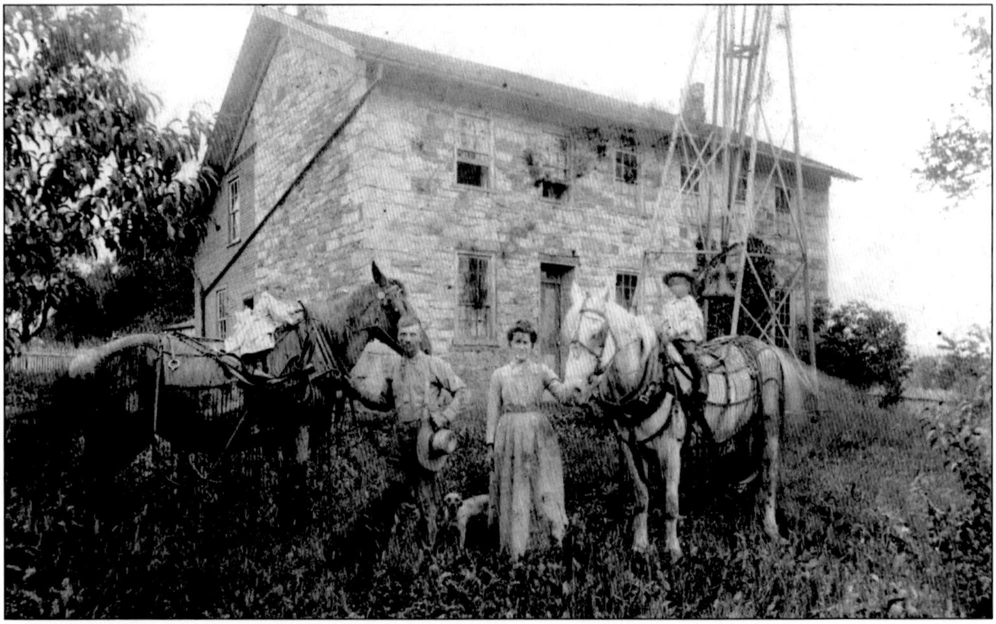

John and Edith Laubach Eck stand in front of the stone house on the farm they bought from Abraham Welshans in 1902. Their son Howard is on the horse to the left, and Foster is on the horse to the right. This land was warranted to Grace Little in 1776, surveyed in 1779, and warranted to William Hill in 1805. The property went through five owners until Matthew Gamble bought it in 1865. The stone house was built by Gamble between 1865 and 1873.

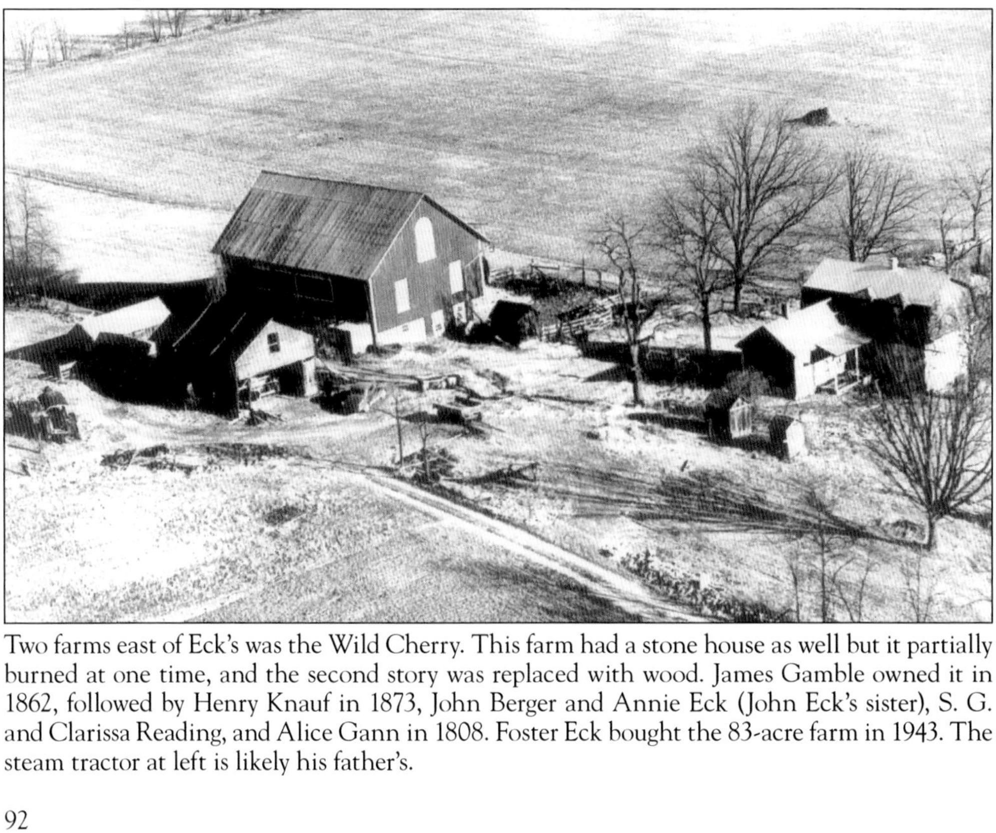

Two farms east of Eck's was the Wild Cherry. This farm had a stone house as well but it partially burned at one time, and the second story was replaced with wood. James Gamble owned it in 1862, followed by Henry Knauf in 1873, John Berger and Annie Eck (John Eck's sister), S. G. and Clarissa Reading, and Alice Gann in 1808. Foster Eck bought the 83-acre farm in 1943. The steam tractor at left is likely his father's.

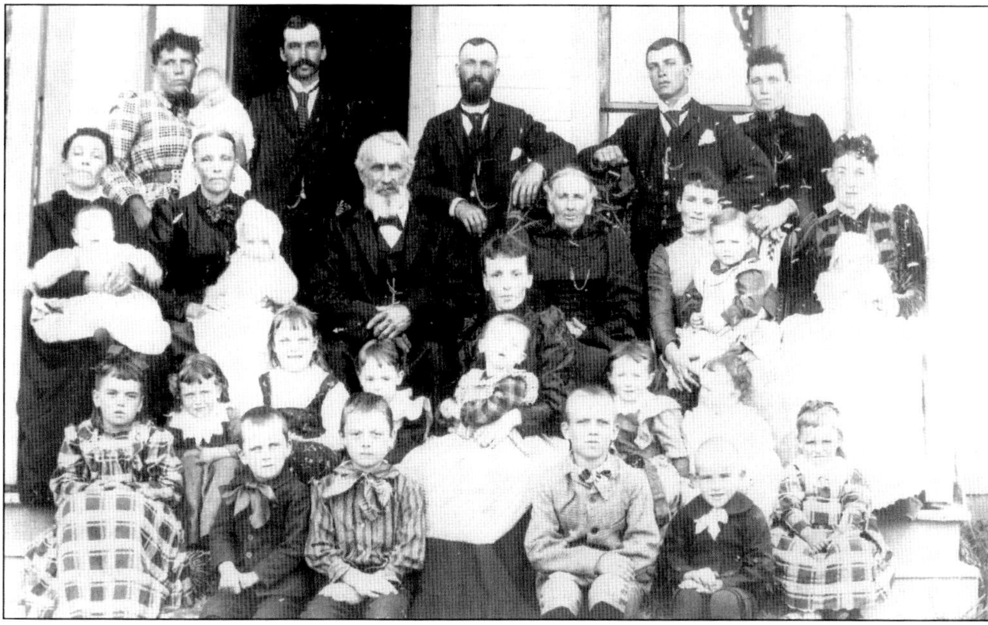

This is a photograph of the James A. Eck family taken at the Wild Cherry around 1890. The adults, from left to right, are (third row) Sarah "Jenny" Eck Kelley; Mary Ellen Eck Snyder; the parents James Eck (born in 1824) and Mary Ann Swoyer Eck (born in 1830), who were married in 1849 and had 12 children; Caroline Eck Clinger (in front of the parents); Elizabeth Eck Heiser, and Martha Jane Stambach Eck; (fourth row) Agnes Miller Eck, Robert Eck, James Eck Jr., John O. Eck (born in 1869), and MaryAnn Eck Berger.

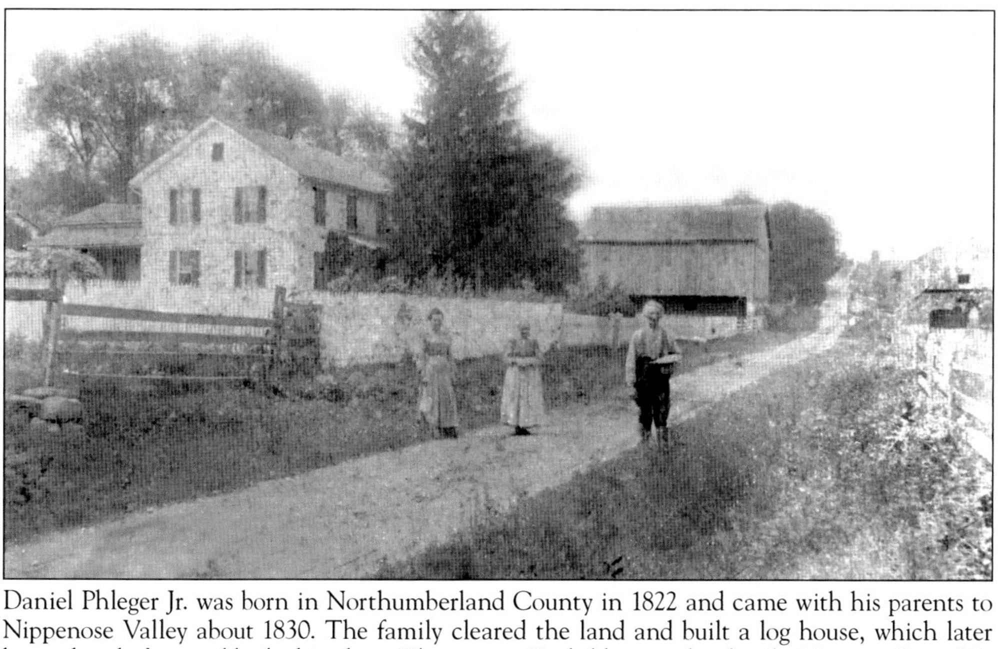

Daniel Phleger Jr. was born in Northumberland County in 1822 and came with his parents to Nippenose Valley about 1830. The family cleared the land and built a log house, which later burned and afterward built this place. There were 12 children in this family. Here are Daniel Jr. and his wife, Angeline Gheen, and likely their daughter Alice (x George Seifrit). Other marriages to this family included the Epler, Sypher, Barner, Welshans, Shaw, and Stahl families.

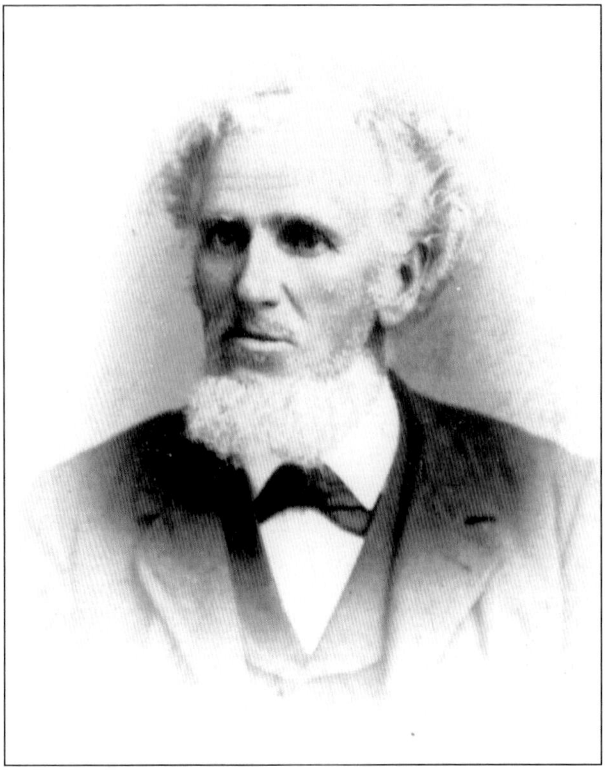

George Washington (Wash) Clark (1833–1895) was the son of John Clark, one of the first settlers in the valley. George was one of the pioneers that witnessed the transformation of the valley from a wild place to a beautiful and rich agricultural land. A story of his life was published in the September 6, 1895, issue of the *Nippenose News*, a valley newspaper published by Leonard Wright of Jamestown. The subscription price was 75¢ a year.

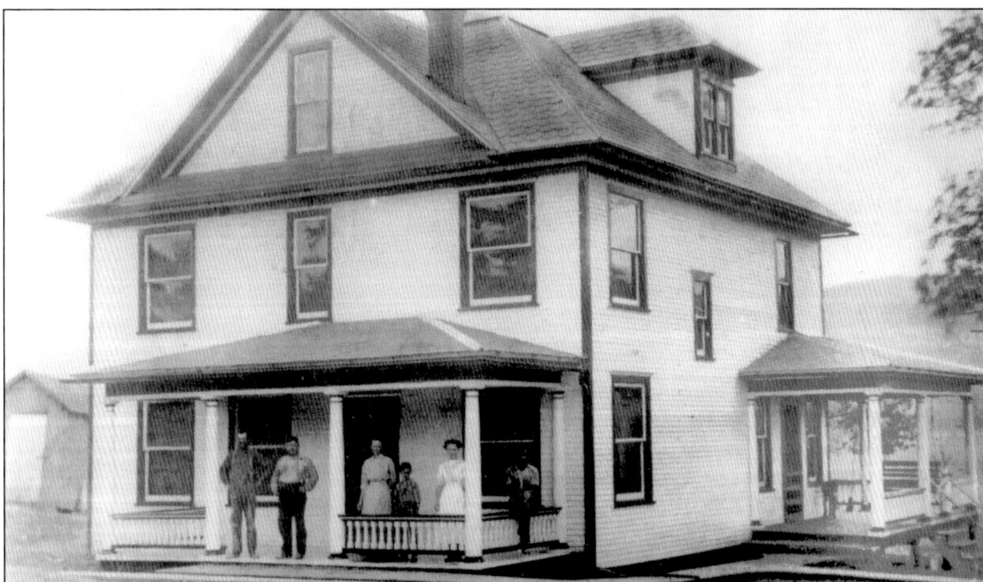

Another farm close to Jamestown was the Newton Phleger place, shown here when it was new. On the porch, from left to right, are Lawrence Wolfe, Newton Phleger, Margaret Rockey, John Phleger, Hazel Phleger, and unidentified. Jeremiah Meixel owned the place before Newton, and Newton's daughter Hazel (x Victor Lehman) owned it next, followed by her daughter Evelyn, who was married to Joe Welshans. In 1863, 16 acres of trees were cut from this land and used to build the barn.

Seven

OVAL

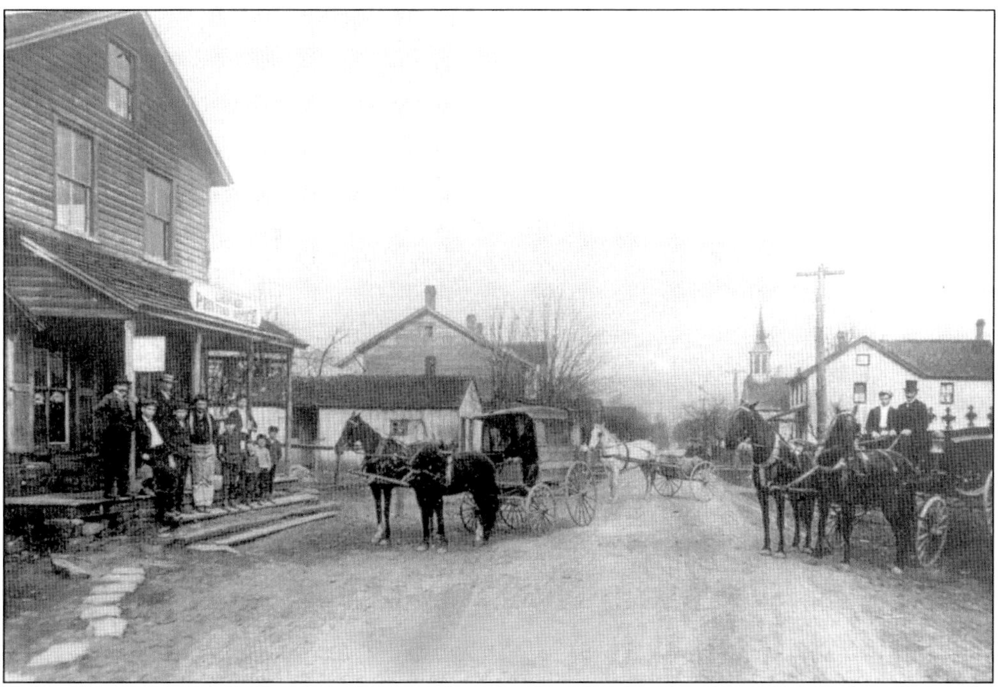

This photograph was taken on the main road through Oval in 1909. H. J. Moore's general store, pharmacy, and post office are at left, with the editor of the *Oval Ledger* newspaper shown leaning against the post. Fred and Warren Hampe are at the end of the line. Bill Brownlee's meat wagon is parked in the road, as is the carriage of Adam Eck. The valley hearse is at right with undertaker George Seifrit in the driver's seat alongside Lester Koons.

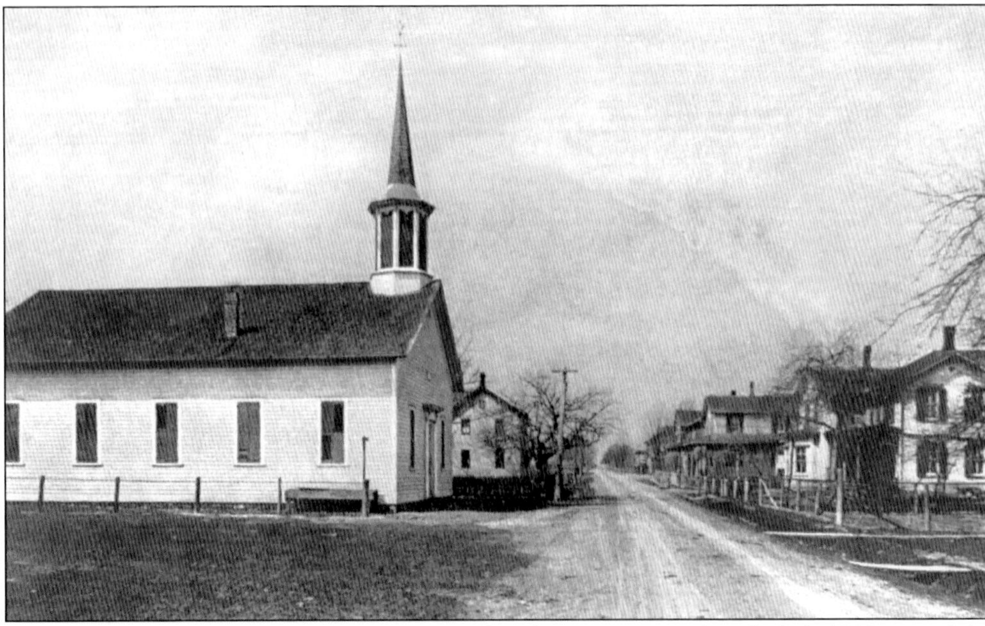

Few pictures were printed in early newspapers, but this one appeared in the July 1916 issue of the *Oval Ledger*. It was taken in front of Hepburn Clark's house across the street from his blacksmith shop. The Methodist church was built in 1876, and the house beyond belonged to Civil War veteran Hurst Clark. The first settlers here were Hugh Baty Tate, William R. Moore (also spelled Mohr), and Adam Epler.

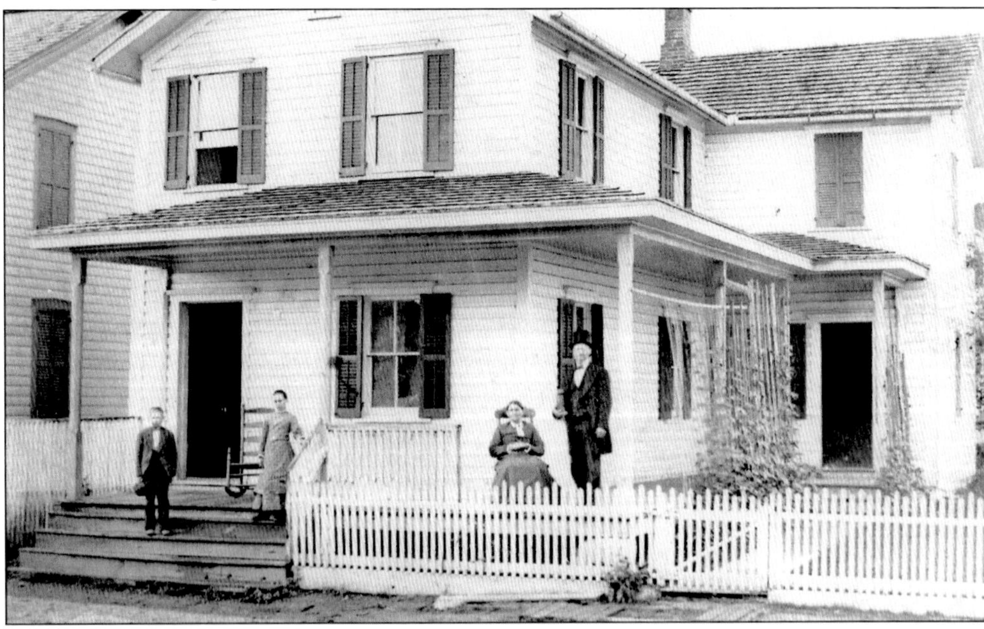

This house is located along the main road in Oval. The 1861 landowner map indicates a John Fenstemaker was living here and the place was associated with a shoe shop. The 1873 map has an Eck living here (perhaps when this picture was taken), and Nathan Sweitzer bought it in 1919, moved off his farm on the south side, and sold it to his son E. Wilson Sweitzer. Merrill Sweitzer lived here next, and the house to the left was the Moore (also spelled Mohr) home.

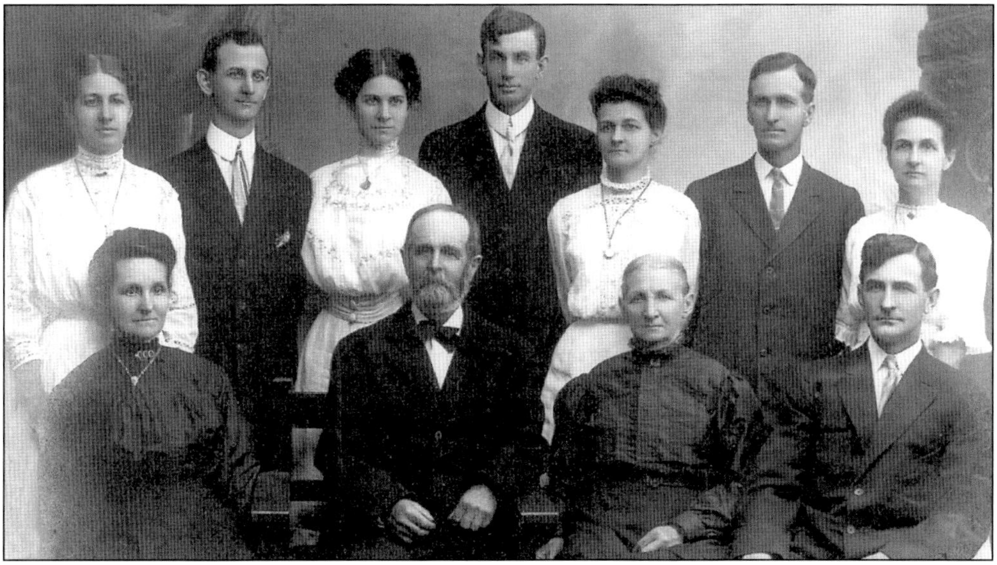

The Sweitzer (also spelled Schweitzer) family emigrated from Wurttemberg, Germany, about 1740 and settled near Reading. Five generations later, Nathan Sweitzer moved to Nippenose Valley and married Catharine Williamson in 1864. They lived on her father Elijah Williamson's farm at the foot of what was later called Sweitzer Gap. From left to right are (first row) Carrie (x James Gamble), Nathan, Catharine, and David (x Lulu Welshans); (second row) Savilla (x Paul Morris), Samuel (x Maud Wagner), Luella, Aaron, Mary, Wilson (x Catharine Koons), and Elsie (x George Hampe).

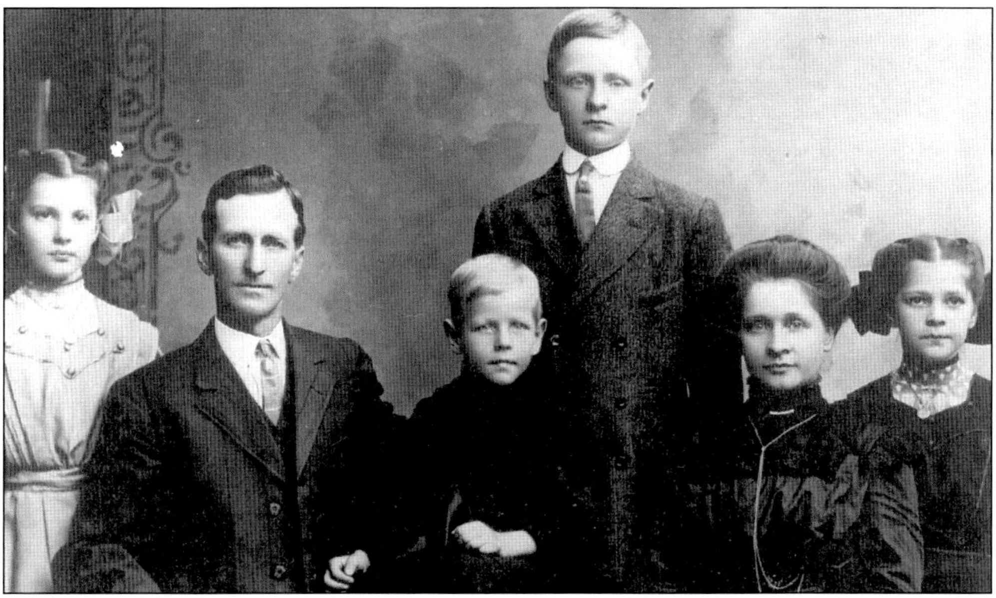

The Earnest Wilson Sweitzer family lived on the farm south of Oval that Nathan Welshans owns today. This photograph was taken about 1915. From left to right are Bessie (x1 Lincoln Cox, x2 Frank Forcey), Wilson (1877–1965), Nathan U. (x Mildred Ruths), Merrill (x Helen Mantle), Sarah Catharine Koons (1879–1932), and Mary Evelyn (x Byron Welshans). Mary Evelyn's grandparents were Joseph Koons (1840–1898), a Civil War veteran, and Mary Jane Tate (1843–1915). They had nine sons and one daughter.

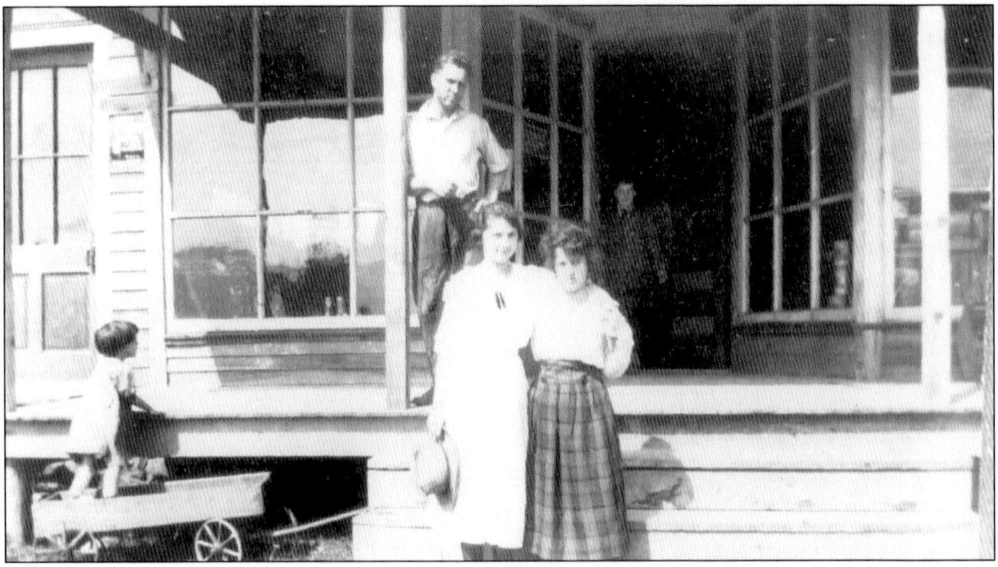

After the Koons family, a store was added to this home and run by John Welshans (1896–1944), who married Mabel Snyder in 1914. John is standing on the porch of the store, and Evelyn Sweitzer and Fay Bicksler (right) are in front. They were friends all through school. John's parents, James "Bucky" Welshans and Nancy Ellen Tate, lived next door. His brother Hugh was the first valley boy to die in service during World War I, and his sister Alice was married to George DeFrain.

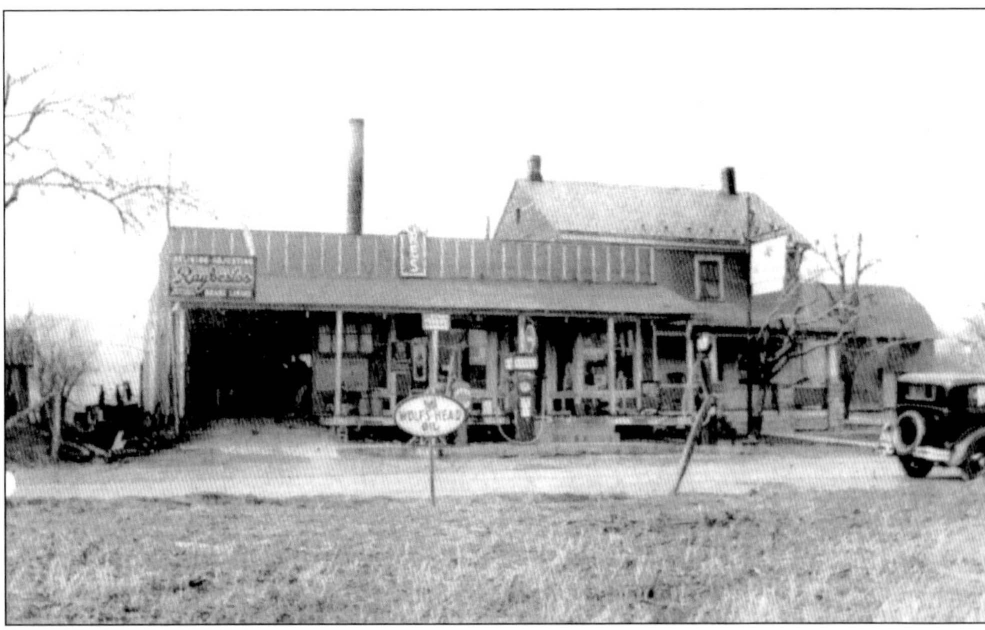

About 1930, Samuel Frederick Garrett bought the old Koons/Welshans place and ran a store, service station, and garage. He married Naomi Etta Fenstemaker on September 1, 1915. She died in 1930, and he married Elizabeth "Peg" Beaver in 1938. Bill and Margaret Lehman Garrett lived next door, and Bob Winter runs a photography business here today. This photograph shows Garrett's service station and store around 1930.

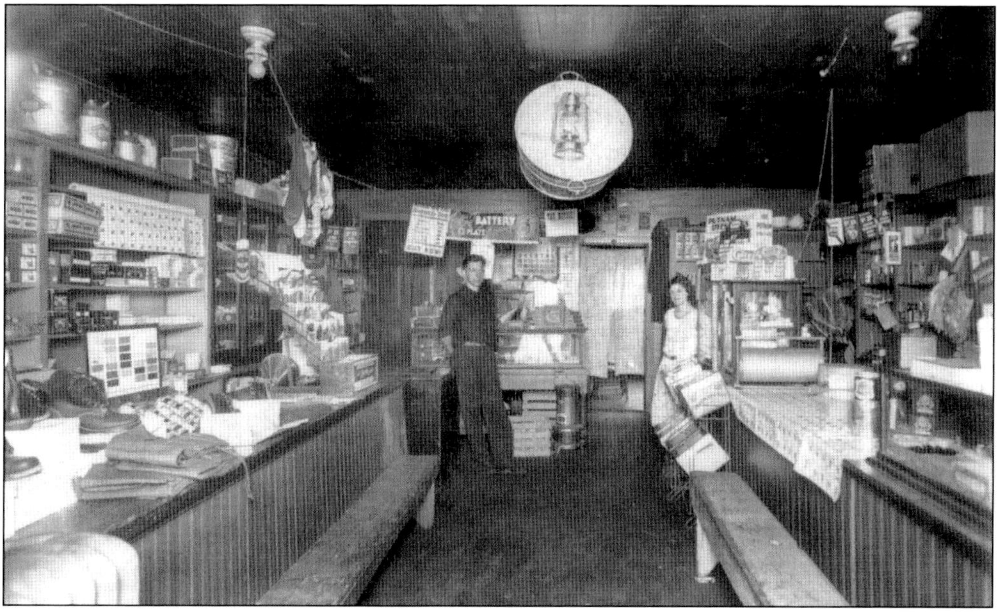

This photograph shows the interior of Garret's store in Oval around 1931. Electricity had just arrived in the valley, and the bare bulbs that lit the store can be seen attached to the ceiling. A look around the store shows work boots, gasoline cans, socks, a calendar and tax notice, a kerosene heater, loafing benches, and a radiator indicating central heat. About 1950, Garrett bought land across the street and built a new garage and farm store. He sold Massey Harris and Gale farm machinery.

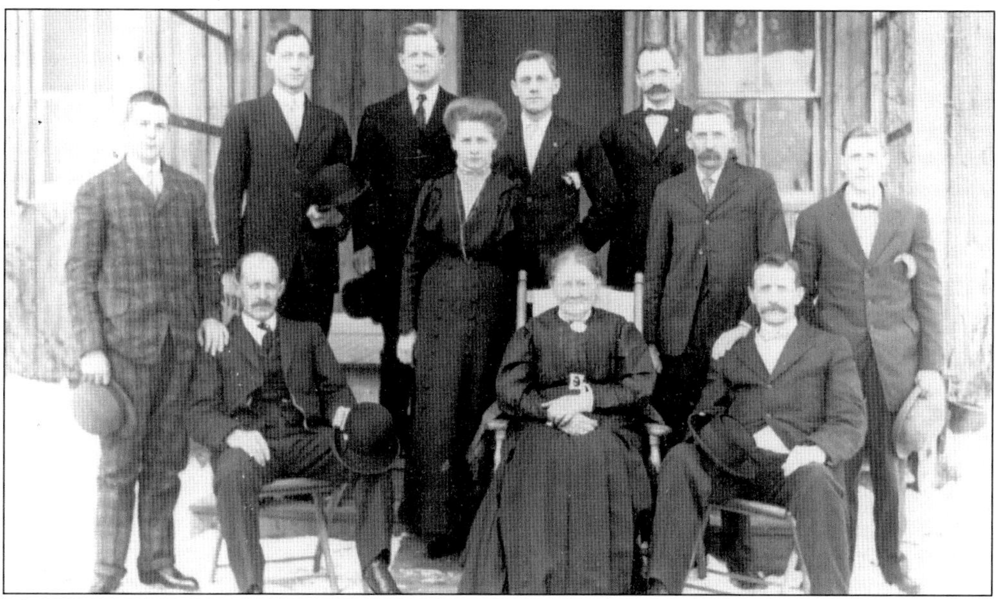

This was the front of the Joseph Koons home about 1900. From left to right are (first row) John Wilber Koons (born in 1867), Mary Jane Tate Koons (born in 1848), and Abram Miles Koons (born in 1872); (second row) Samuel Carson "Dick" Koons (born in 1885), Sarah Catharine Koons (born in 1879), Baty Ulysses Koons (born in 1866), and Joseph Oakland (born in 1880); (third row) Vaughn Rue "Larue" Koons (born in 1877), Merrill Tate Koons (born in 1873), George Washington Koons (born in 1875), and Harry Kryder Koons (born in 1870).

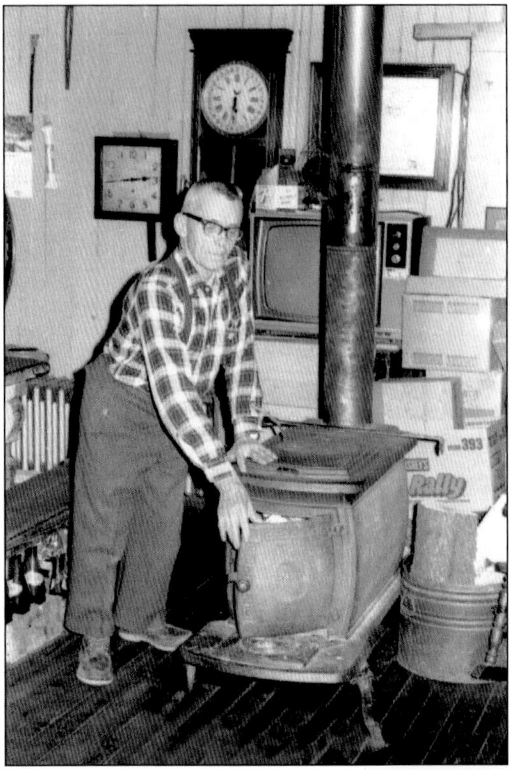

Joe Moore's general store opened on January 16, 1936. He rented the building at first but bought it in 1940 and constructed living quarters in the rear. He was one of the first in the valley to replace the icebox with a refrigerator. Bread was sold in wrappers but was not sliced. Soft drinks were a big seller in the summer, as was ice cream that was sold from May 1 to October 31. At first, he did not sell milk because there were about 70 dairy farmers nearby.

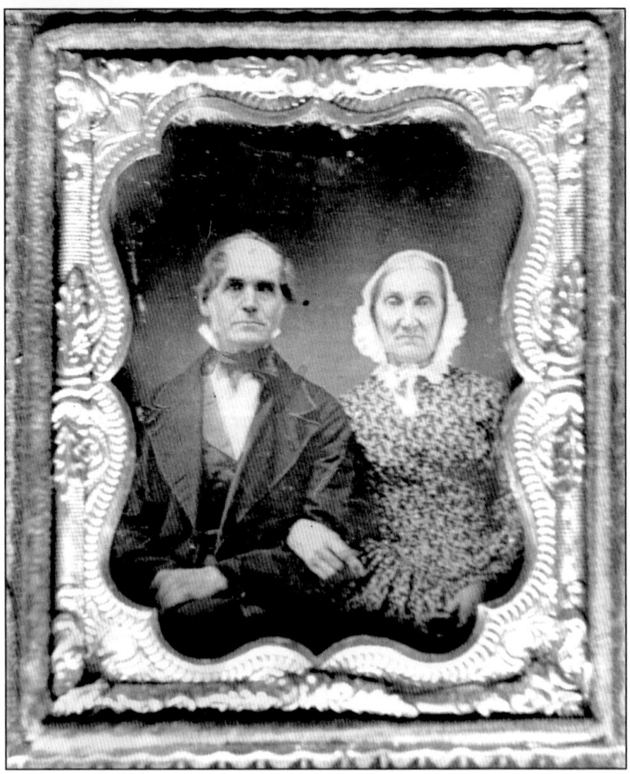

There are no Vandykes in the valley today, but the name is carried on by way of the Vandyke Road that follows the ridge of North White Deer Mountain. This tintype shows James C. (1786–1858) and Jane Elisabeth Clark Vandyke (1795–1872). Their farm was along the south side of the valley where Nathan Welshans lives today. Their daughter Margaret was married to Solomon Kaufman, and Esther was married to Jacob Voneida. Jane Elisabeth's parents were Thomas Clark (1756–1822) and Christina (1768–1833).

Voneida was the grandfather of this Nippenose Valley family. He was born on April 16, 1820, at Vicksburg in Union County. He came with his parents when he was still a young boy and helped build the family's log house and barn on their farm just south of Oval. He was married four times and outlived all his wives. His parents were Peter Voneida (born in 1780) and Esther Kauffman. They were married in 1810 and had 13 children.

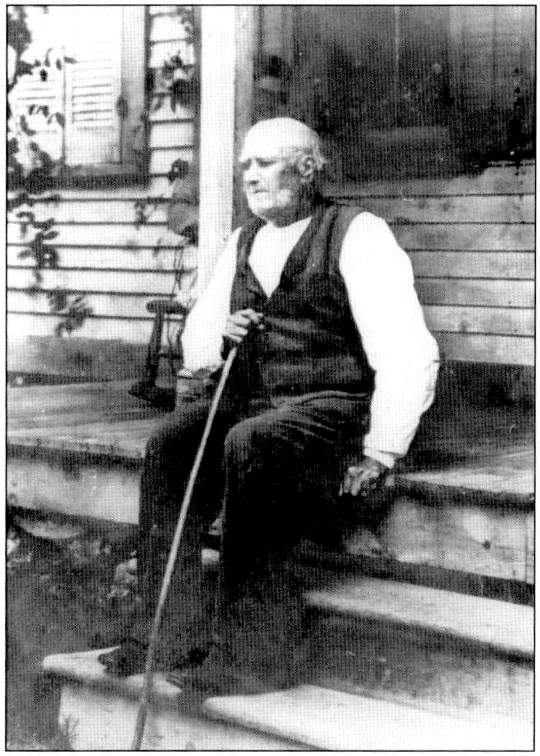

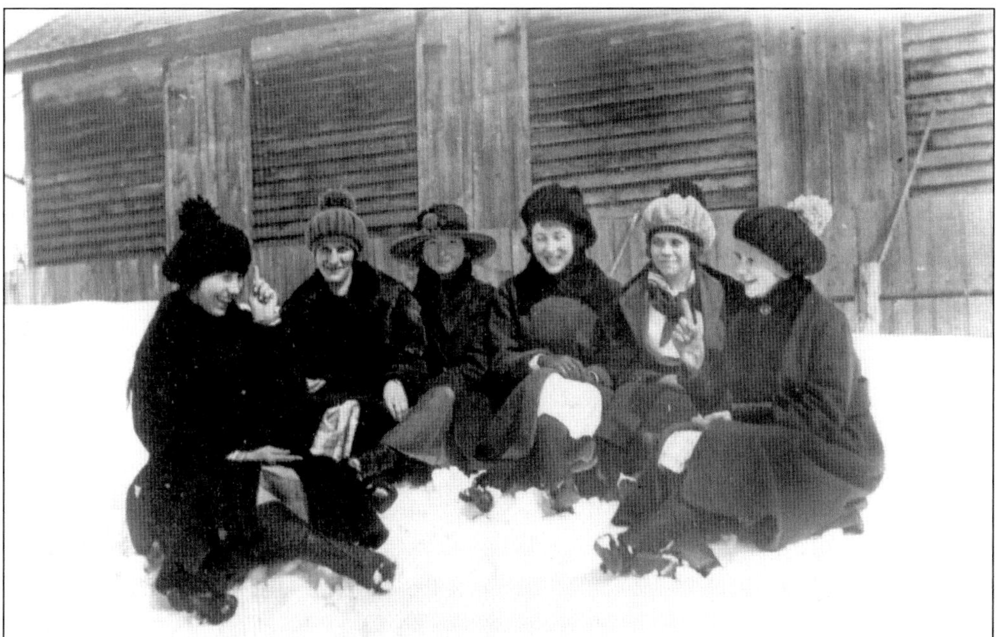

This group of high school students is sitting next to the old 1857 wooden schoolhouse in Oval in 1920. At the time, the 1891 school had burned, and the fourth school in Oval had been built in 1918 on the John Barner farm on the other side of the road. From left to right are unidentified, Pearl Dougherty, Olive Sheats, Evelyn Hill, Margaret Snyder, and Evelyn Sweitzer.

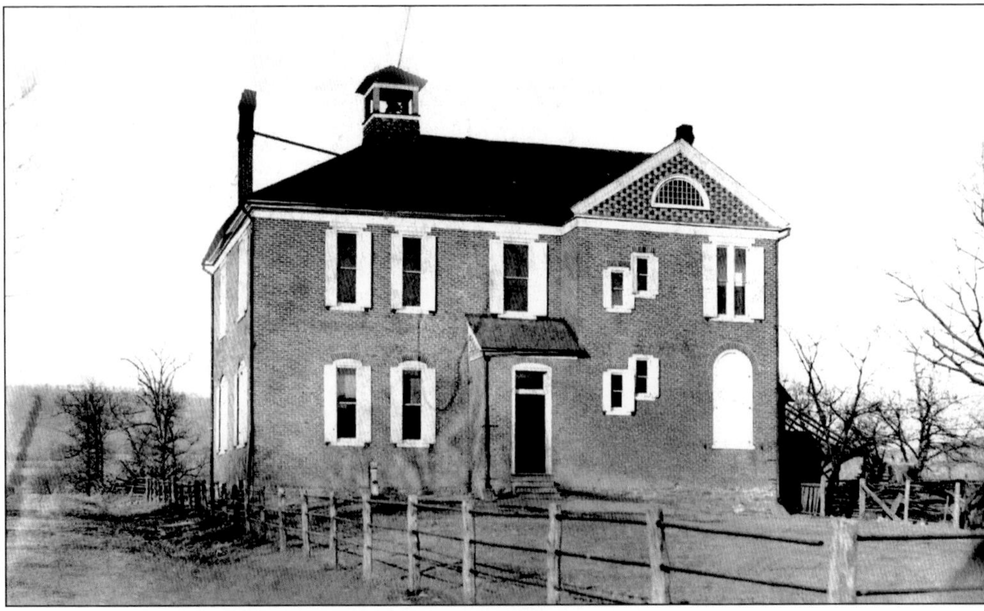

This two-story brick school building was built in 1891 at a cost of $5,000, and the 200-pound bell rang for the first time in January 1892. It was built as an elementary school, but a high school curriculum was established in 1907, with the first class graduating in 1909 and the last in 1928. This building burned on Monday evening, February 12, 1917. All was lost, including the township's supply of school materials.

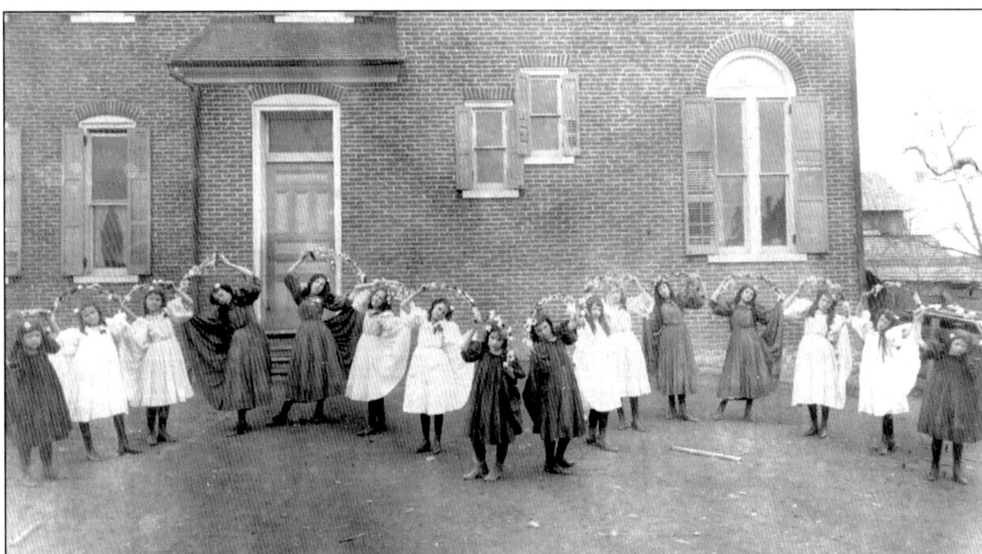

This is the same view of the school as the last picture but with a group of 16 girls holding arches of flowers. Maybe this was part of a May Day celebration? The building of this school in 1891 and a new brick school at Collomsville in 1905 prompted school directors to begin thinking about centralizing their many schools. By 1915, serious thought was given to closing the Moore, Reidy, Eck, and Mountain schools. Enough money could be saved to offer a four-year high school term.

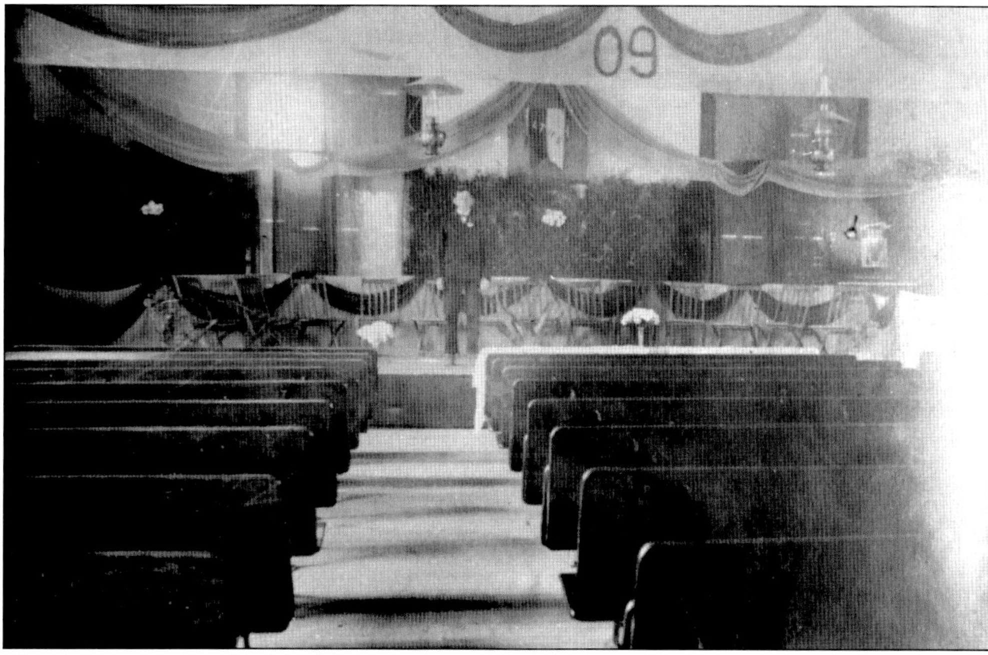

The 1891 two-story school had four rooms—two for the elementary grades on the first floor and one on the second for high school students plus this large auditorium, which was decorated for the first high school graduating class of 1909. A high school education at this time took only two years. Kerosene lamps hung from the ceiling and a large "LTHS" banner hung from the front wall.

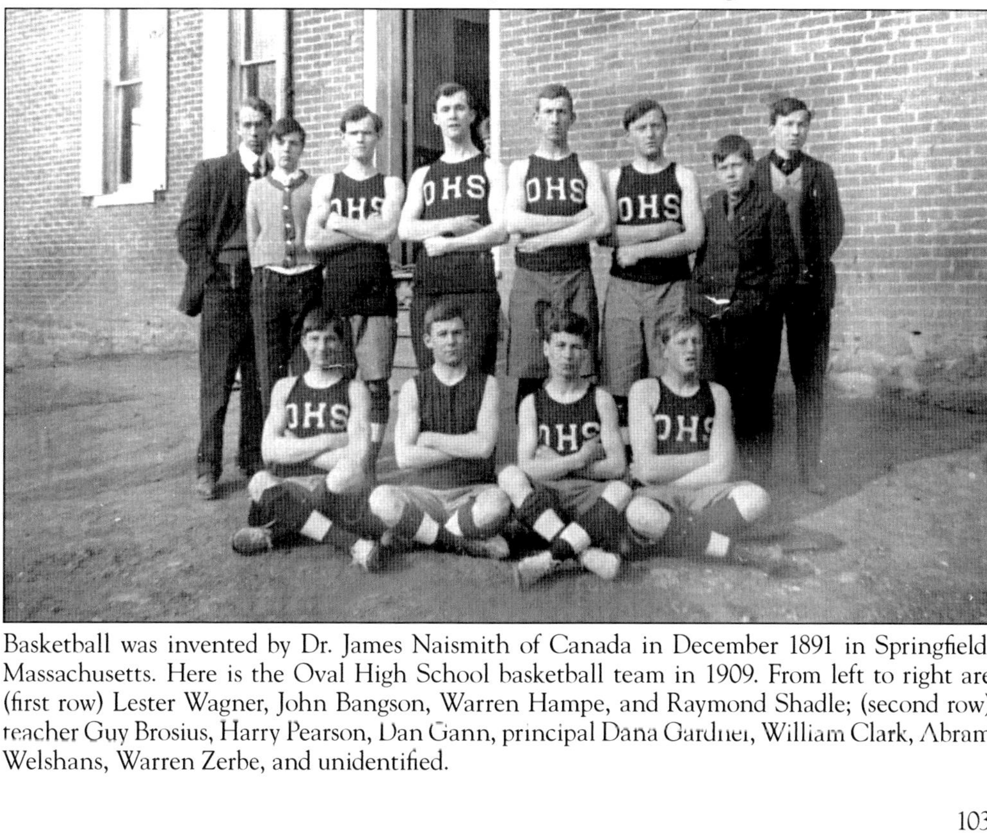

Basketball was invented by Dr. James Naismith of Canada in December 1891 in Springfield, Massachusetts. Here is the Oval High School basketball team in 1909. From left to right are (first row) Lester Wagner, John Bangson, Warren Hampe, and Raymond Shadle; (second row) teacher Guy Brosius, Harry Pearson, Dan Gann, principal Dana Gardner, William Clark, Abram Welshans, Warren Zerbe, and unidentified.

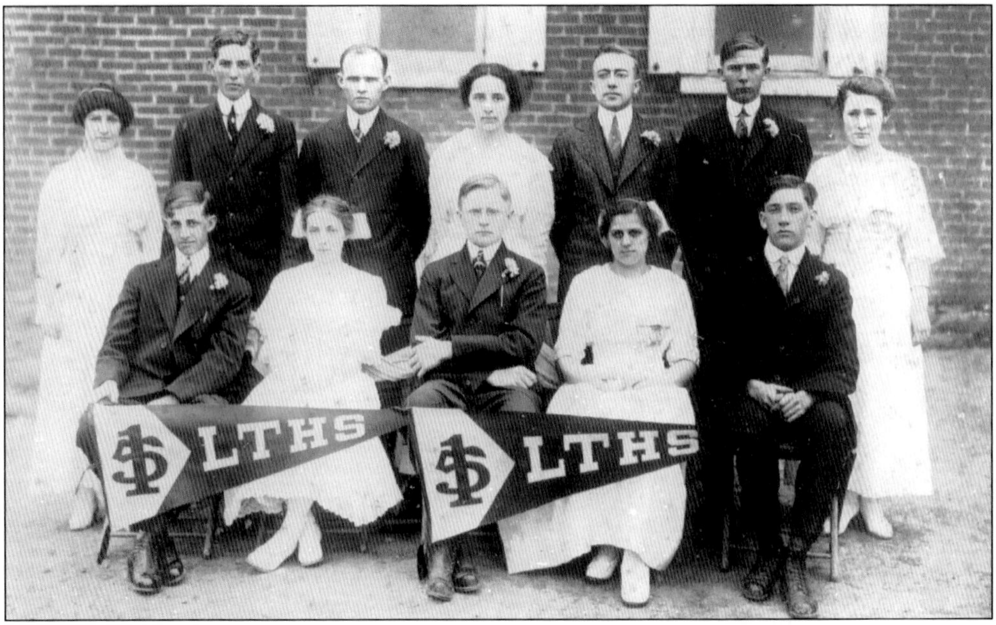

These were the high school graduates of Limestone Township High School in 1915. From left to right are (first row) Robert Pearson, Bertha Pearson, Merrill Sweitzer, Esther Mantle, and Harold von Needa; (second row) Myrtle Curts, Grant Wileman, Dan Gann, Margaret Wells, teacher Glenn Rogers, Giles Yorks, and Hazel Phleger. By December 1918, Gann was killed in France, and notice reached the valley of the deaths of Clarence Eck and Joseph Lorson.

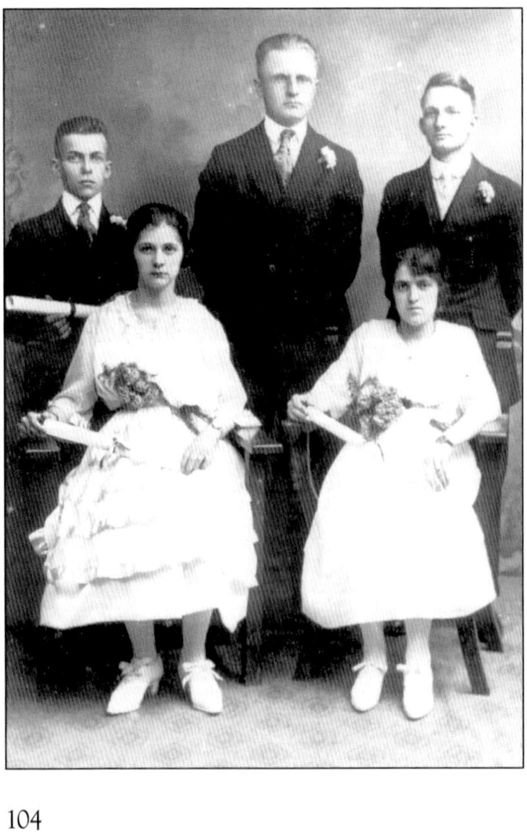

Some graduating classes from the Oval High School were not too big. This class of 1921 had three graduates, including Joe Moore, Evelyn Sweitzer, and Fay Bicksler. Merrill Sweitzer (center) was a 1915 graduate of this school and was its principal teacher by 1921, along with teacher Deloss Ramsey. This 13th graduation was held on April 13; music was provided by the Lutheran Church Orchestra of Jersey Shore.

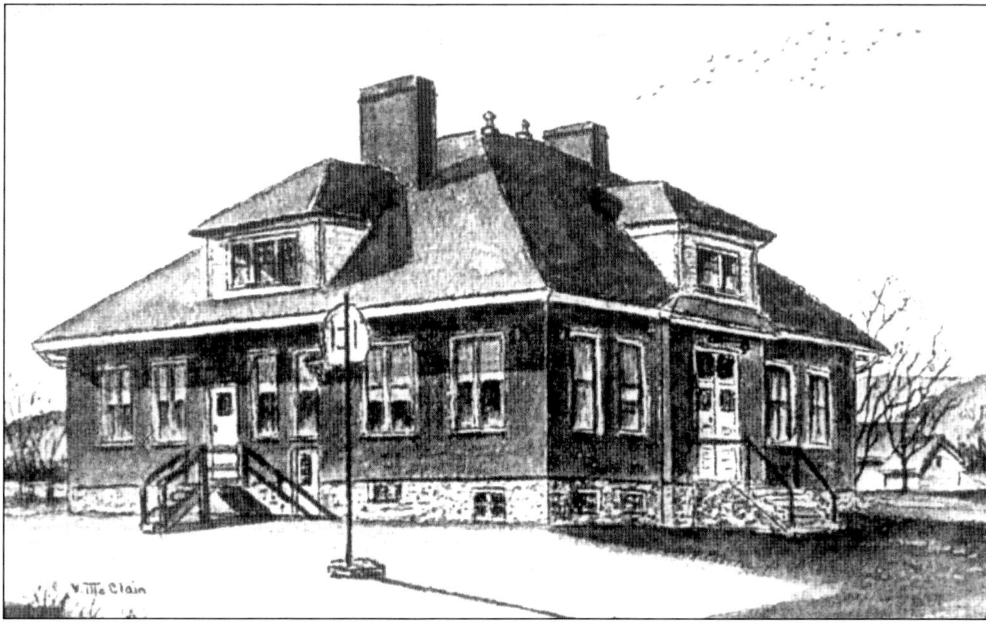

The dedication of this new schoolhouse was held on Saturday evening, September 21, 1918. This structure was built across the street from the 1891 school that had burned the previous year. A special vote held on June 21, 1917, gave the school board the right to borrow $15,000 for the construction. The land was purchased from John D. Barner. This school building was renovated and opened in 2007 as the Nippenose Bible Fellowship Church with Dave McCoy as pastor.

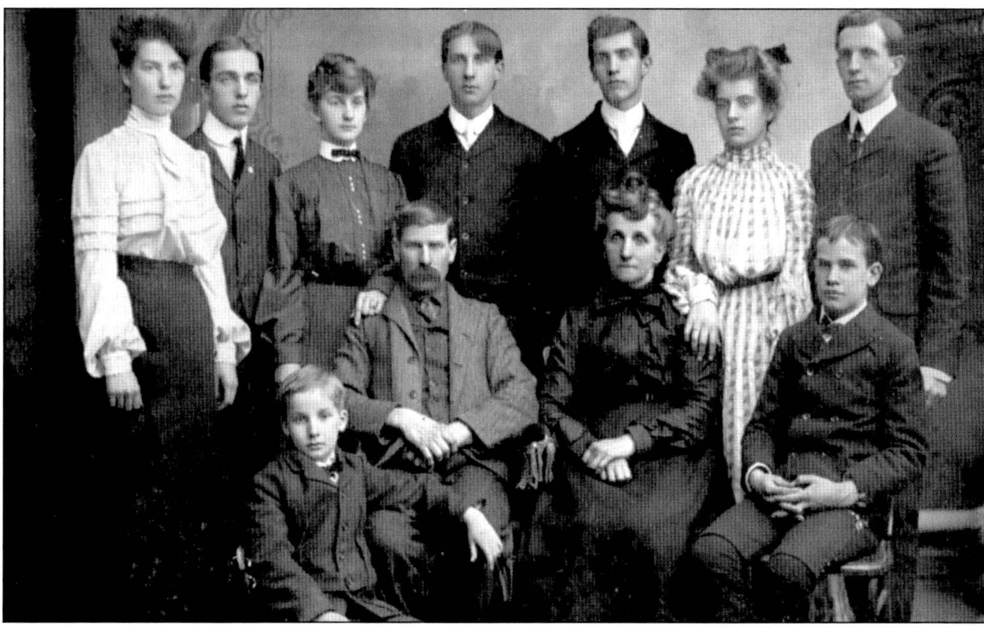

This is the Barner family of Oval. From left to right are (first row) Warren D. Barner (x Margaret Wensel), John D. Barner (1855–1930), Sarah Alice Brownlee (1854–1917), and Charles Barner (x Anna Bergstrom); (second row) Alice Barner (x Harry Miller), J. Merrill Barner (x Violet Hartman), Nellie Barner (x Wesley Barner), Guy Barner (x Myrtle Epler), William Barner (x Bessie Lucas), Emma Barner (x Herbert Young), and George Barner (x Grace Smith).

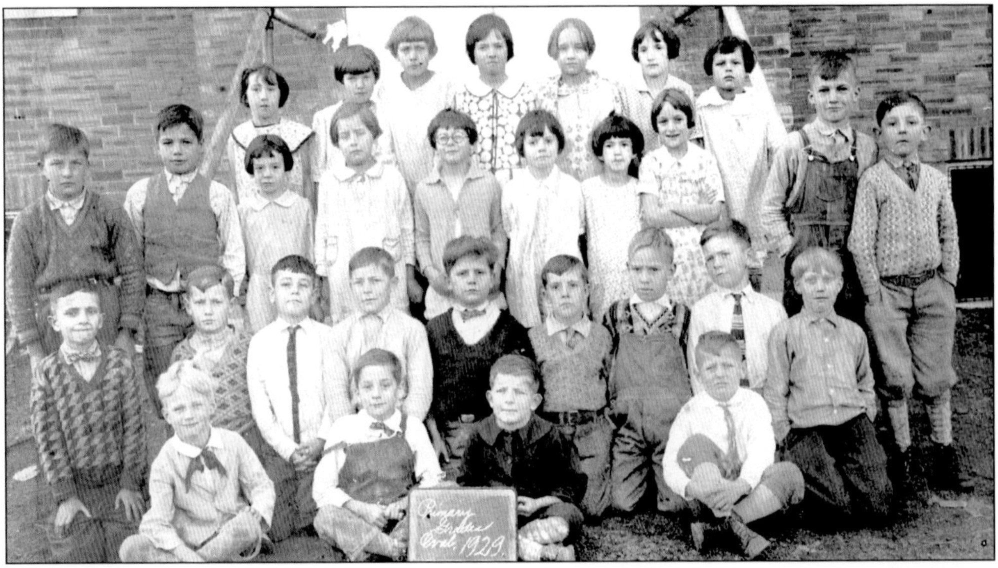

These were Oval primary students in 1929. From left to right are (first row) Nelson Brownlee, Charles Barner, Dale Wagner, and George Hampe; (second row) Malcolm Wagner, John Dougherty, Ted Lehman, Earl Wagner, Bill Garrett, Lee Dougherty, Warren Miller, Bob Krape, and Paul Laubach; (third row) Lynn Wagner, Raymond Eck, Janice Hiney, Gladys Wagner, Doris Kaufman, Betty Kissel, Muriel Snyder, June Barner, John Barner, and Carl Sweitzer; (fourth row) Helen Laubach, June Wynn, Evelyn Wynn, Martha Kissel, Pauline Lehman, Bertha Barner, and Katherine Hampe.

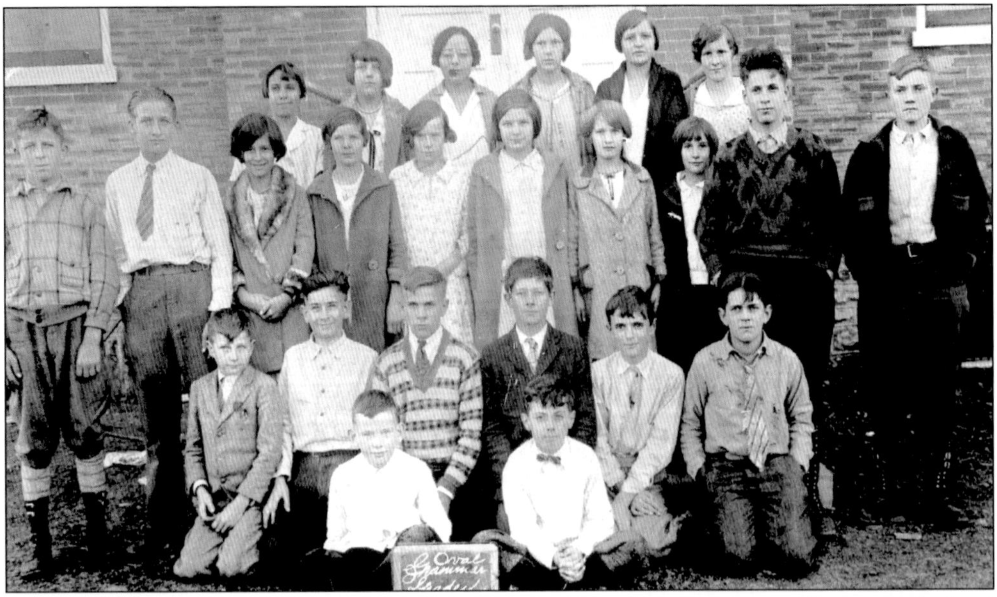

These were Oval Grammar School students in 1929. From left to right are (first row) Richard Aumiller and Bill Kissel; (second row) Larue Sweitzer, Bill Lehman, Earl Snyder, Chester Wynn, Daniel Cohick, and Carl Seifrit; (third row) Kenneth Welshans, Dan Lehman, Gladys Seewald, Gladys Gamble, Marion Aumiller, Carrie Eck, Leona Lehman, Anna Barner, Harry Barner, and Trevanion "Buddy" Clark; (fourth row) Martha Lehman, Madeline Garrett, the teacher, Edith Laubach, Evelyn Brewer, and Florence Laubach.

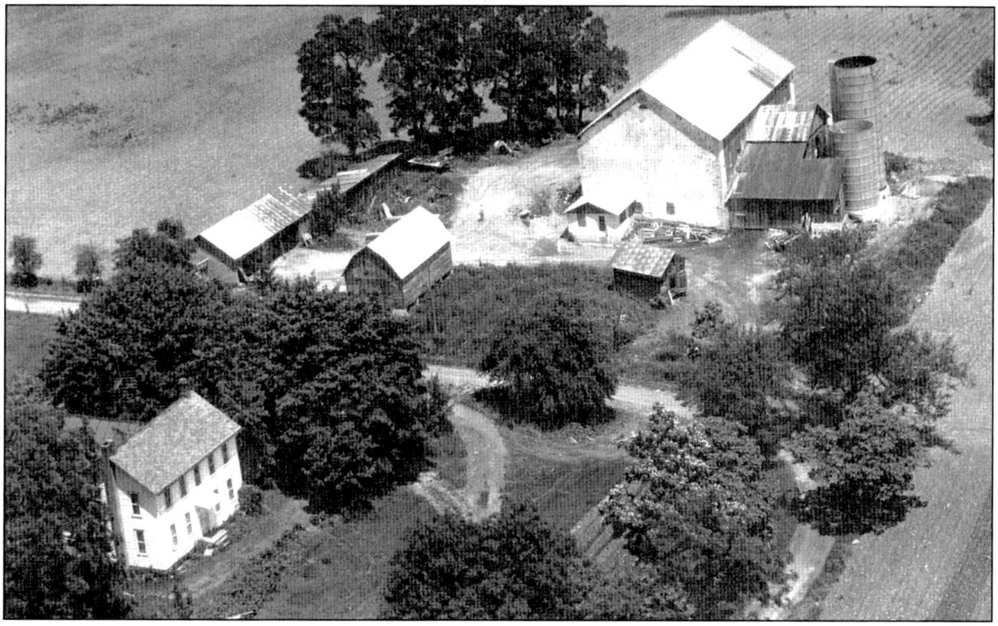

Henry J. Klinger bought this 272-acre farm on October 27, 1827, and it remained in the family until 1861, when it was sold to Fred Knauf. At one time, there was a tannery and the valley jailhouse located here. Jacob Seifrit bought it in 1868 and in 1921 sold it to Alfred W. and Dora Mantle. When Wentworth got it in 1940, it still contained 179 acres. The only barn in the valley with two stone ends is located here.

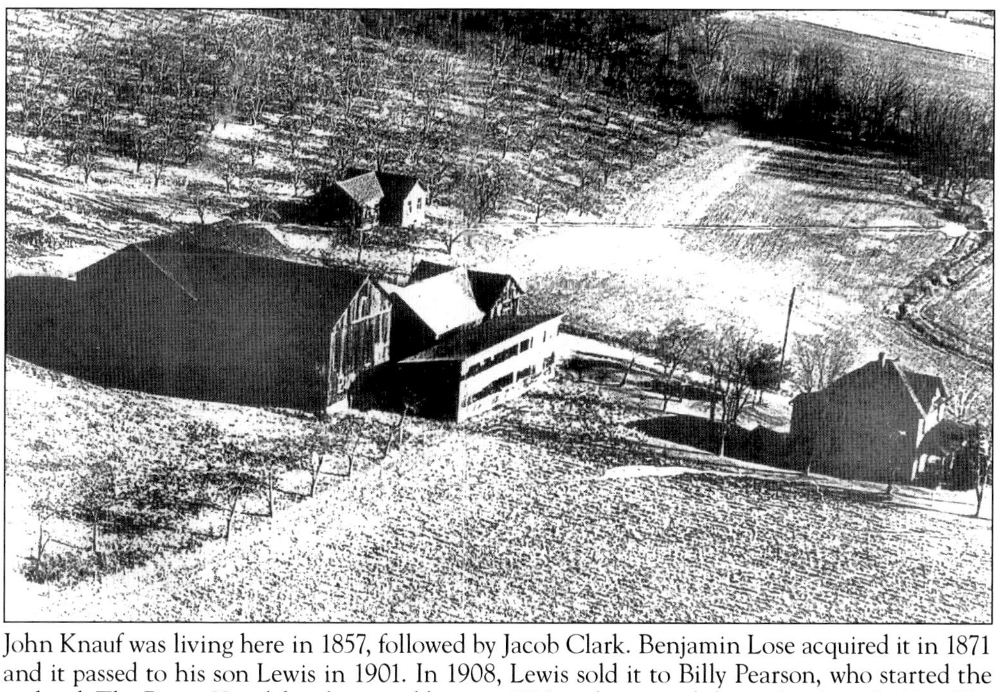

John Knauf was living here in 1857, followed by Jacob Clark. Benjamin Lose acquired it in 1871 and it passed to his son Lewis in 1901. In 1908, Lewis sold it to Billy Pearson, who started the orchard. The Bruce Kissel family moved here in 1923 and operated the orchard until 1984. The house was moved from Mosquito Valley about 1915, and electricity ran to the farm in 1938. Bill Enders was the last man to operate this orchard.

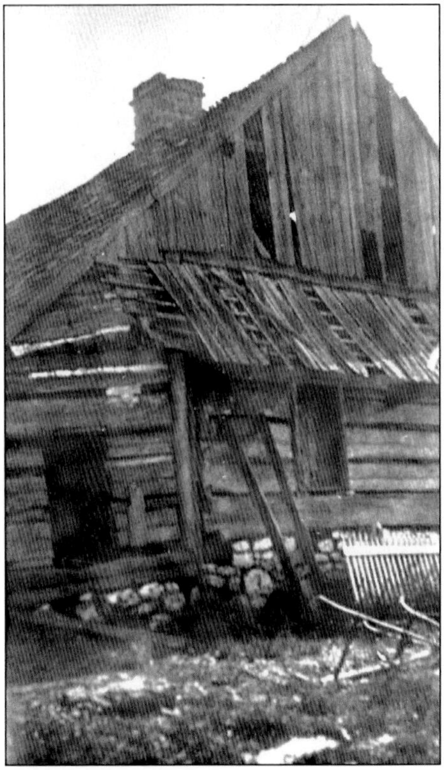

John and Louisa Vandyke were living here in 1857. It was purchased from them in 1884 by Nathan and Catherine Williamson Sweitzer, who moved here from Old Farm at Sweitzer Gap. Water rights were obtained from Andrew Casper's neighboring property in 1899. The farm was sold to Wilson Sweitzer in 1919 and to Nathan Welshans in 1966. The Sweitzer family attended St. Peter Lutheran Church in Collomsville.

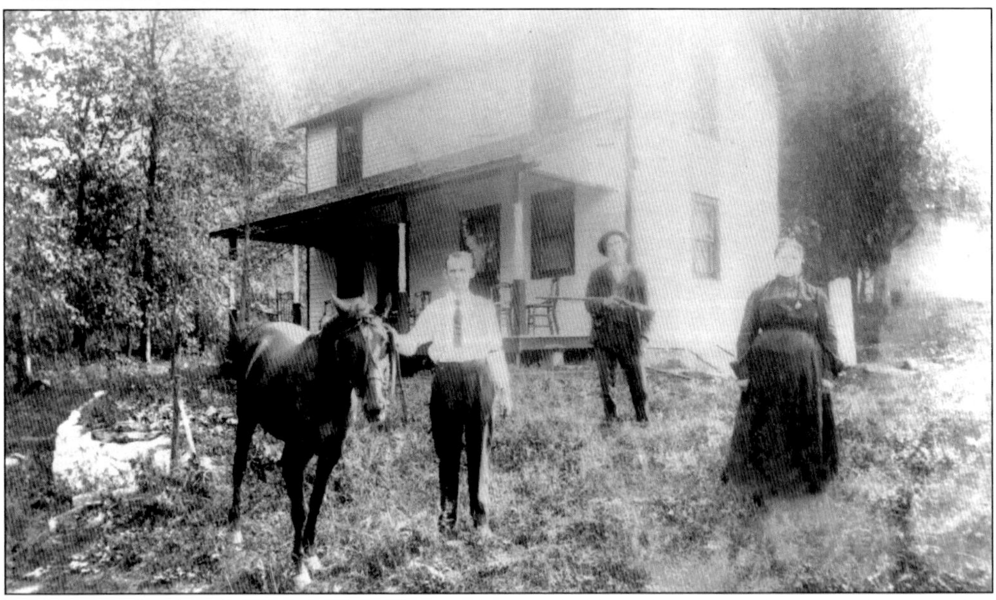

The Casper family was living on this 131-acre farm in 1873. At that time, there were four families living along the farm lane, including the Vandykes, Voneidas, Caspers, and Denworths. The latter three were not yet established in 1861. From left to right, this photograph shows John (Jack) Casper, James Casper, and Amelia Casper. James's parents were Andrew (born in 1813) and Julia Richards Casper (born in 1813). James ran a harness shop here in 1919. There was also a Casper family cemetery located here at one time.

Eight

COLLOMSVILLE

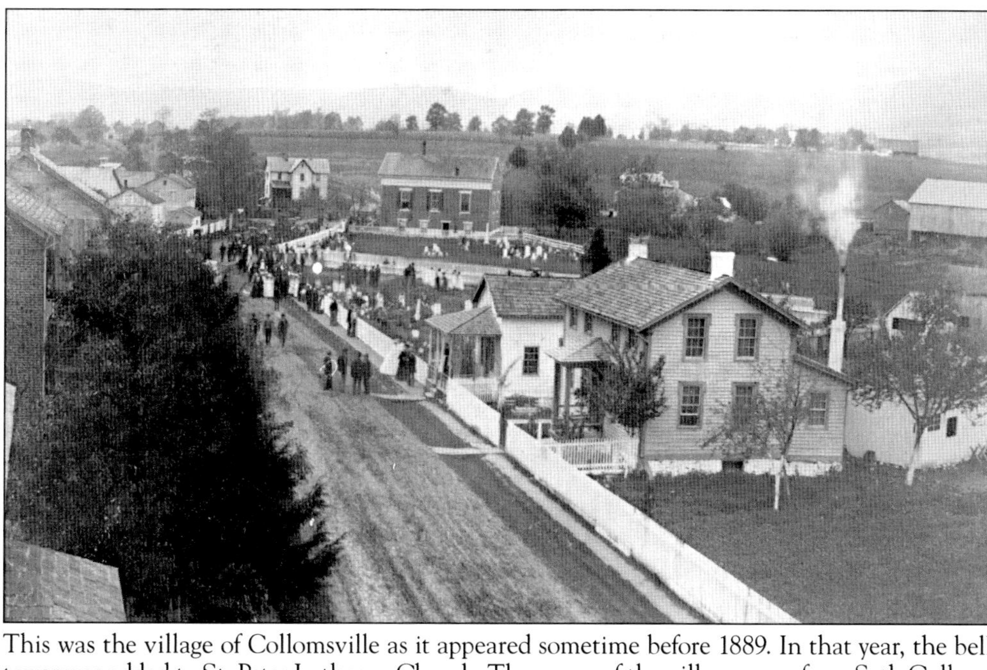

This was the village of Collomsville as it appeared sometime before 1889. In that year, the bell tower was added to St. Peter Lutheran Church. The name of the village came from Seth Collom, a Scotch Presbyterian, who settled here around 1830. By 1840, there were only three houses here, but the 1861 map shows 20, and the 1873 map shows 30. It appears that the western half of the old stone house owned by the Homler, Eck, Hallow, and Croyle families was not yet built.

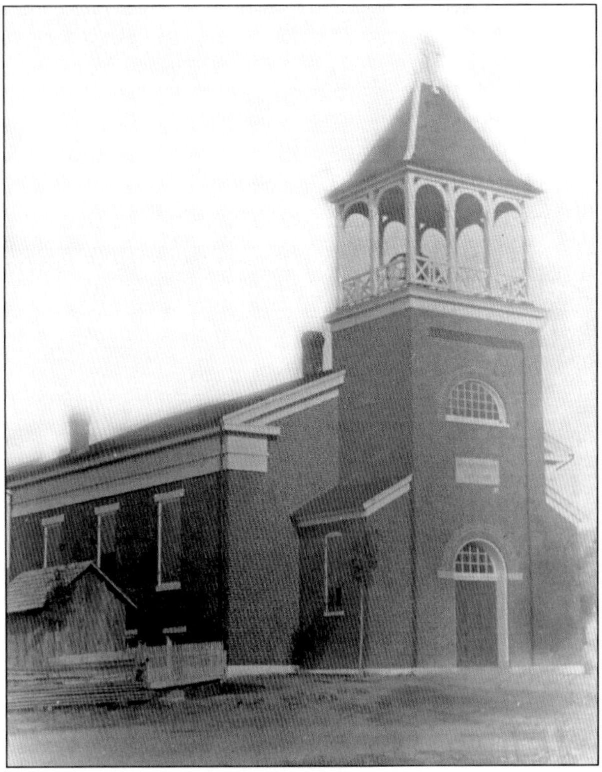

The St. Peter Lutheran congregation organized in 1834 and held services in a log church that stood across the road from this one, which was completed in 1852. The church was both German Reformed and Lutheran at the time. The structure was to be made of brick and be 40 feet by 50 feet with a height of 15 feet. The building contract was given to George Howard of Lock Haven and the brickmaking to David Bowersox of Union County.

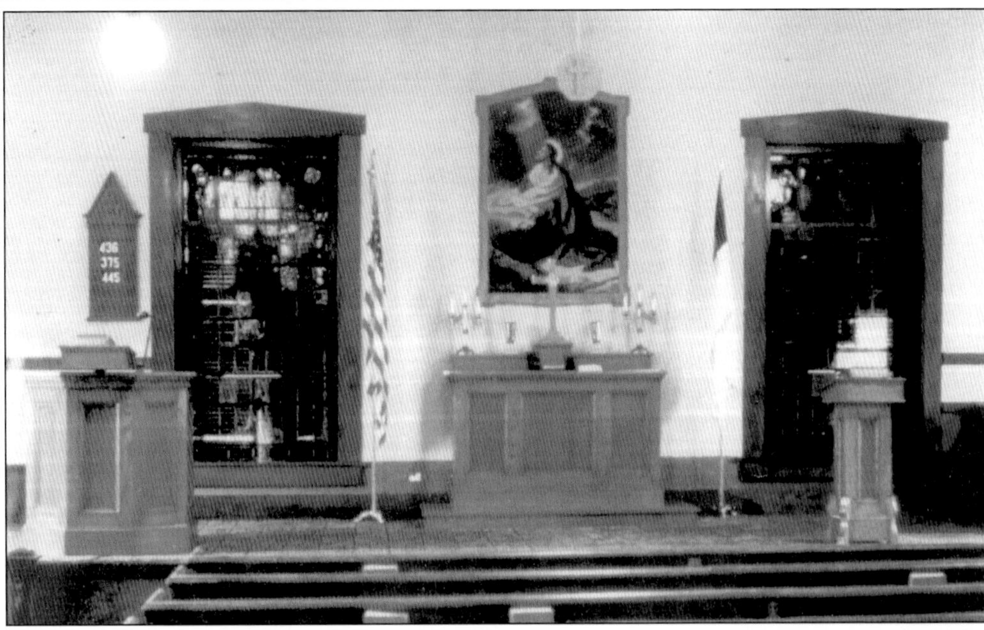

The interior of the church looked like this when it was torn down on November 7, 1987. The original contributing members who paid for this church in 1851 included David Zerbe, Fred Knauf, John Hartz, Jacob Seifrit, Israel Gann, Michael Sypher, Jesse Bower, Jonathan Bixler, John Epler, Hugh Baty Tate, Solomon Bastress, and John Michelly. The stained-glass windows were given to the Holy Cross Orthodox Church in Williamsport, and the bell went to Florida.

Rev. John Hays Grier was the Presbyterian minister who performed the first recorded marriage in the valley in 1815 between John Shaw and Susan Mellon at a place above Collomsville. He also helped establish a Presbyterian church, which was built across from the Clark General Store around 1842. The church began with 13 members. John Gann, James Vandyke, and Solomon Kaufman were mentioned as "Commissioners in Presbytery." The church was closed by 1865.

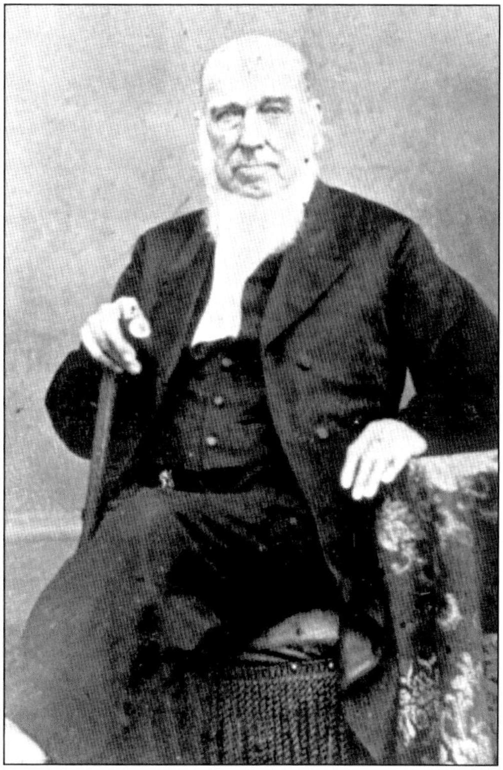

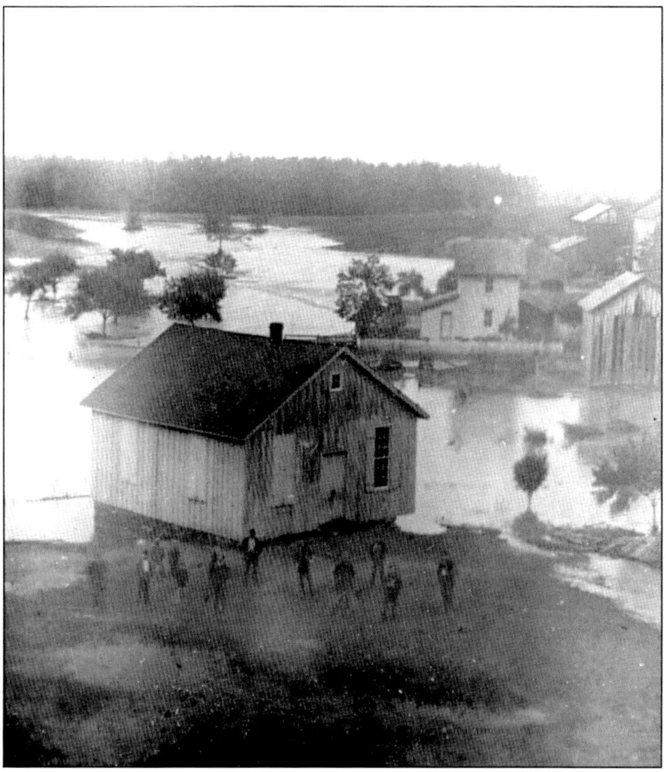

Before 1905, Collomsville had two single-room wooden schools. With the building of a new brick school, one wooden schoolhouse was torn down and the other was used as a voting and gathering place. The old structure was used again as a school when the Oval School burned in 1917. This picture may have been taken during the 1889 flood. Welker's Sink is right behind the building, and once full, it sends water coursing over the valley floor.

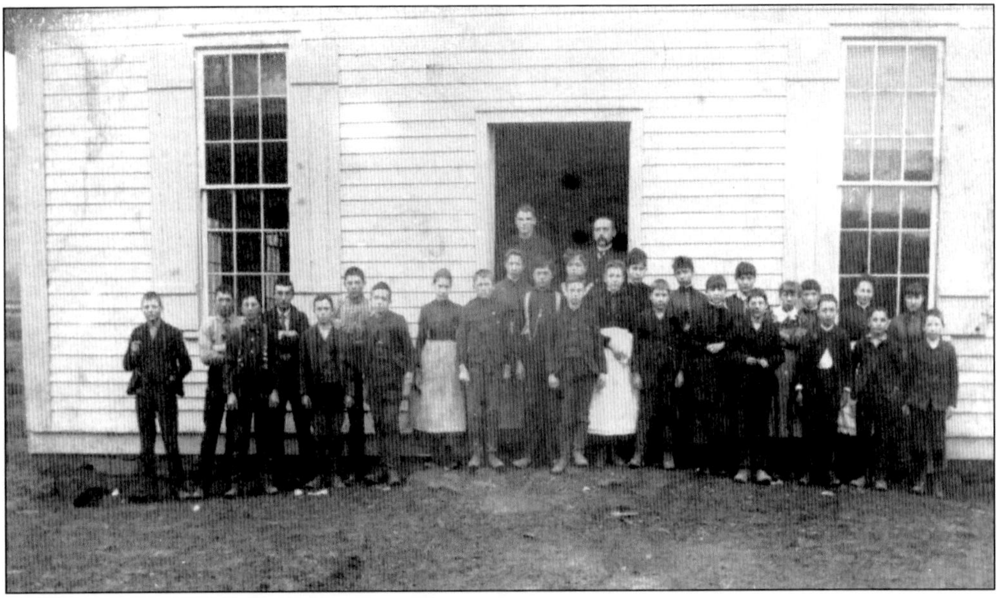

These Collomsville Grammar School students are standing in front of the old wooden school in 1892 with their teacher, James W. Smith. The girls pictured include Clara Grambling, Lizzie Eck, Bertha Axman, Ida Clark, Amanda Sweier, Alice Marks, Ellie Clark, Linnie Zerbe, Zulu DeFrain, Nettie Dougherty, Hattie Clark, and Ella Zerbe. The boys pictured include Elmer Gebhart, Ulysses Grambling, Monroe Wagner, Ernest DeFrain, William Betts, Abe Knauf, Vincent Smith, Ed Gebhart, Robert Moore, Orin Phleegor, James Zerbe, John Bricker, Henry Musheno, George DeFrain, Roy Harrison, and Abram Dougherty.

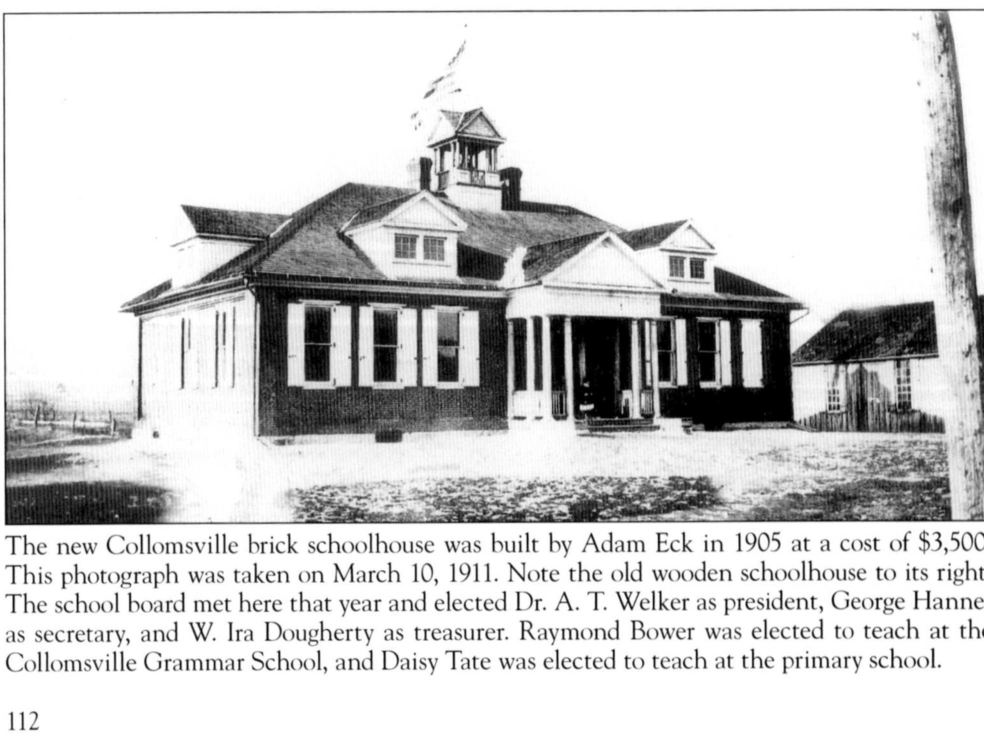

The new Collomsville brick schoolhouse was built by Adam Eck in 1905 at a cost of $3,500. This photograph was taken on March 10, 1911. Note the old wooden schoolhouse to its right. The school board met here that year and elected Dr. A. T. Welker as president, George Hanner as secretary, and W. Ira Dougherty as treasurer. Raymond Bower was elected to teach at the Collomsville Grammar School, and Daisy Tate was elected to teach at the primary school.

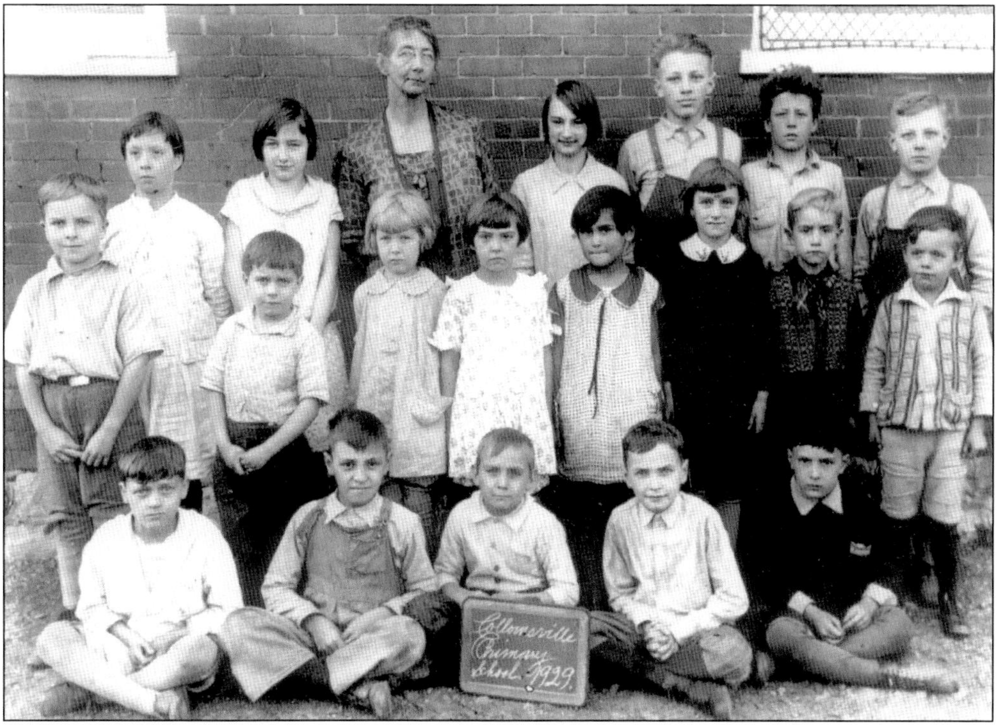

These were primary school students at Collomsville in 1929. From left to right are (first row) Leroy Laubach, James Stephens, Joe Bierly, Harold DeFrain, and Hayes Lose; (second row) Ted Confer, unidentified, Josephine DeFrain, Jeanne Decker, Vivian Knarr, Mildred Young, ? Young, and Bruce Clark; (third row) Marjorie Clark, ? McQuade, teacher Hattie Clark, Geraldine McQuade, Merrill Stephens, Jasper Bower, and Melvin Stephens. Identifications were made by Howard and Vivian Knarr.

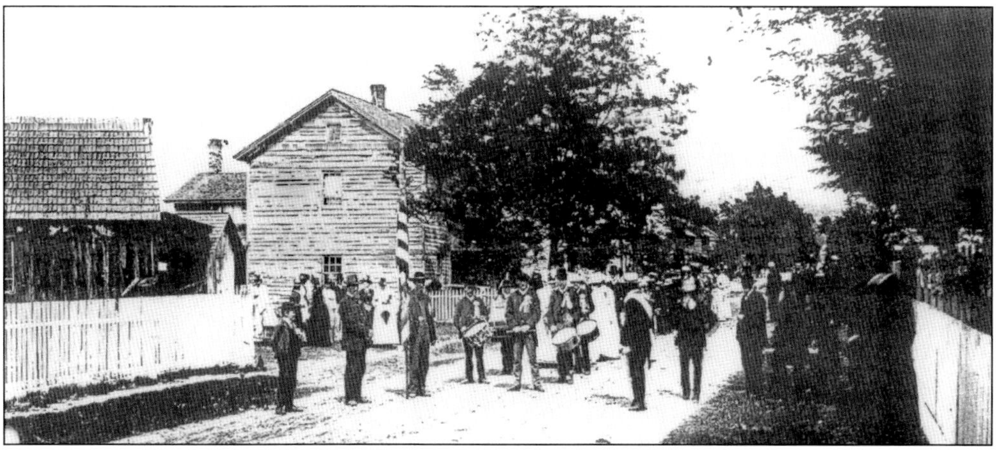

This was the Collomsville Fife and Drum Corps set for the Decoration Day parade in 1876. This little band was organized right after the Civil War and was active for many years. Some members were identified by George DeFrain as John H. Grambling, Ulysses G. Grambling, Clyde Grambling, Edward Gebhart, George Engler, Ebenezer Busler, William Busler, and Leroy Busler. There was also a fife and drum corps in Oval led by Charles Wilson. Such bands were often escorted by a wagon pulled by four horses.

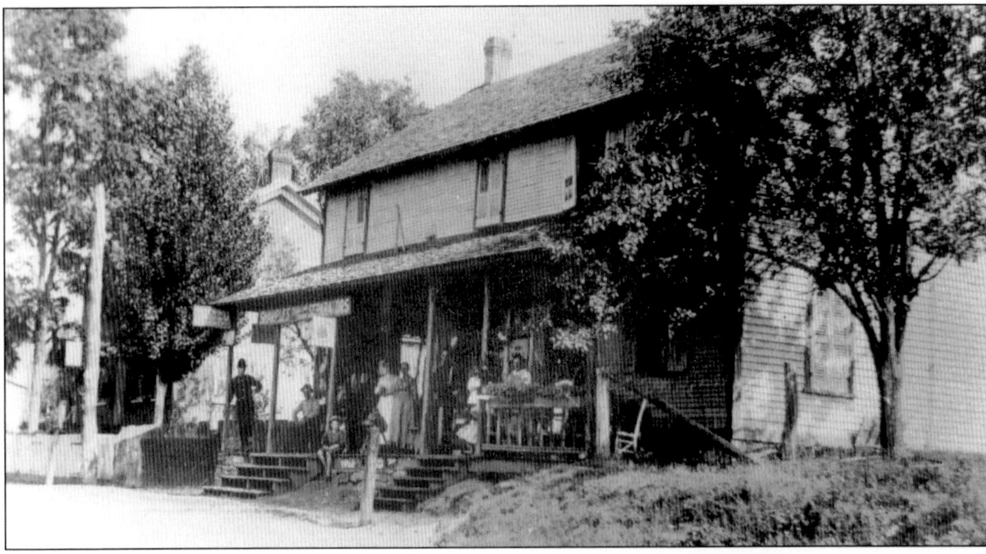

The 1861 map shows a Clark and Smith General Store here, and the 1873 map shows Clark's General Store. George and Clarence DeFrain ran it until 1947 when Clarence became sole owner until he retired in 1969. George was married to Alice Welshans, and Clarence was married to Olive Bixel. Signs on the storefront include Deering Harvesting Machinery, a telephone sign, and a big sign for Sharples Tubular Cream Separators, which were made in Poughkeepsie, New York, in 1890.

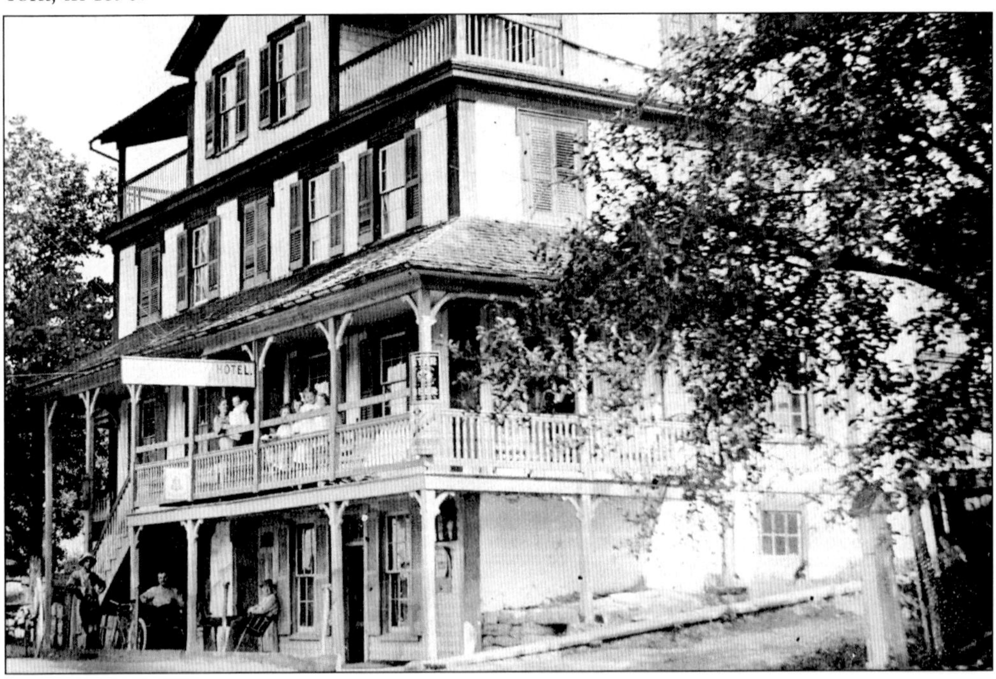

The Collomsville Inn was probably the first hotel in the valley and was a convenient layover between Allenwood and Jersey Shore. In the 1840s, the proprietor was William G. Clark, and by 1861, a general store was added and George Litzelman ran it. Litzelman was followed by Nicolas Young and then George Eoute in 1866. The post office located here that year, and the mail arrived twice a week. Reuben Eck (1877), Joe Frederick (1906), and Hiram Boone (1907) followed.

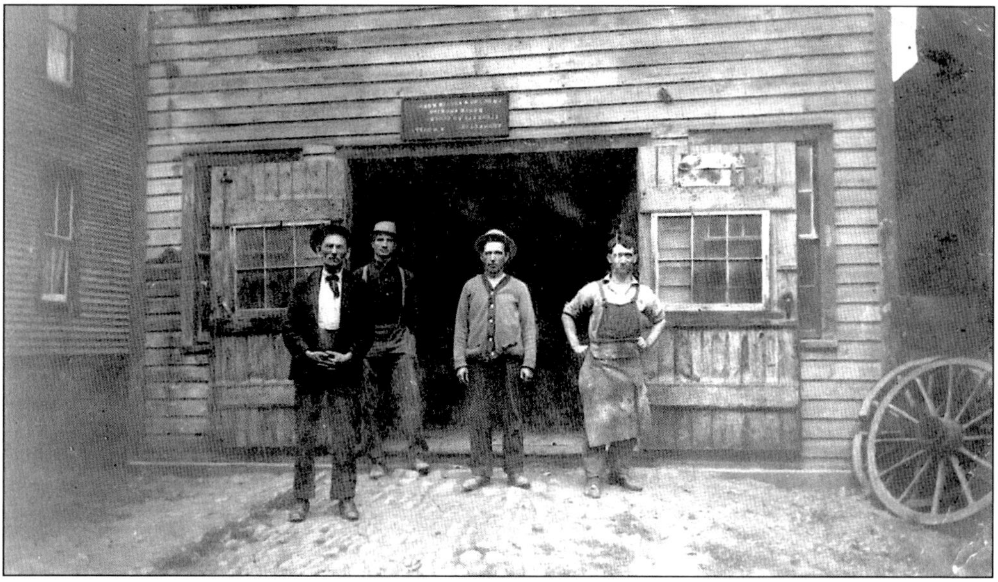

During the early years, blacksmiths, tinsmiths, nailers, and gunsmiths were all vital to their communities. Names of valley blacksmiths include Ambrose Welshans, William Throsell, Jacob Clark, Peter Group, George Wolf, Dougal Grier (tinner), Hepburn Clark, William Moore, Michael Hain, Henry Knauf (gunsmith), David Farley, George Fetterhoof, John Bierly, Matthias Dapp, Traugott Enigk, Christopher Bertin, and Willie Dapp (shown at right in the picture above). Willie was the son of John Dapp, a Civil War veteran, and Juliana Casper. The Dapp family moved into the valley in 1856.

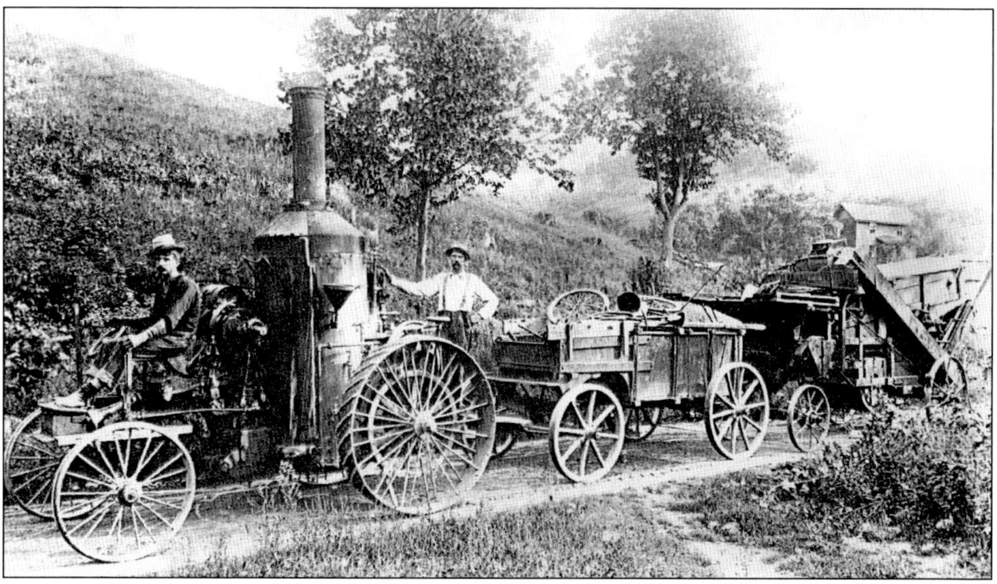

Vincent Smith and his bicycle were riding behind the Westinghouse steam tractor near Collomsville. His father, James W. Smith, began taking pictures in the valley in 1865, and Vincent took thousands of Lycoming County photographs over the years. James was married to Matilda Homan, whose grandfather David Zerbe was an early settler in Nippenose Valley. James taught school in the valley for 43 years and was a justice of the peace for 15 years. The family moved to South Williamsport in 1893.

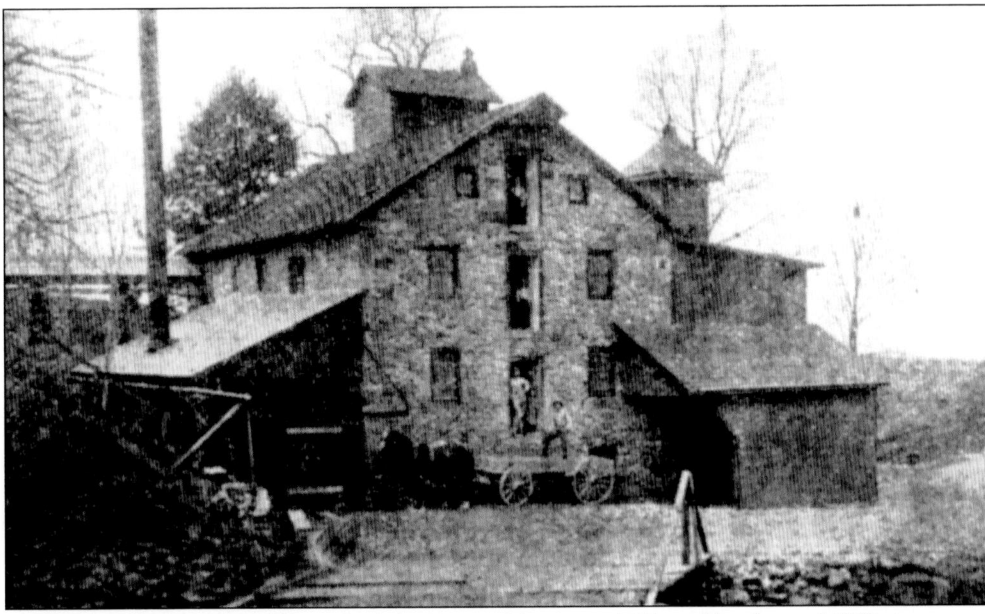

The Collomsville Grist Mill was built by Henry Clinger in 1851, and by the mid-1850s it was run by Elijah Williamson. He died in 1866, and the mill passed to his son Alexander. Around 1885, it passed to Henry Dougherty followed by John Engler (died in 1901), and then it went to his sons George Engler and Joseph Engler in 1905. Peter and Elizabeth Miller bought it in 1925, and then it went to Fred Miller in 1943.

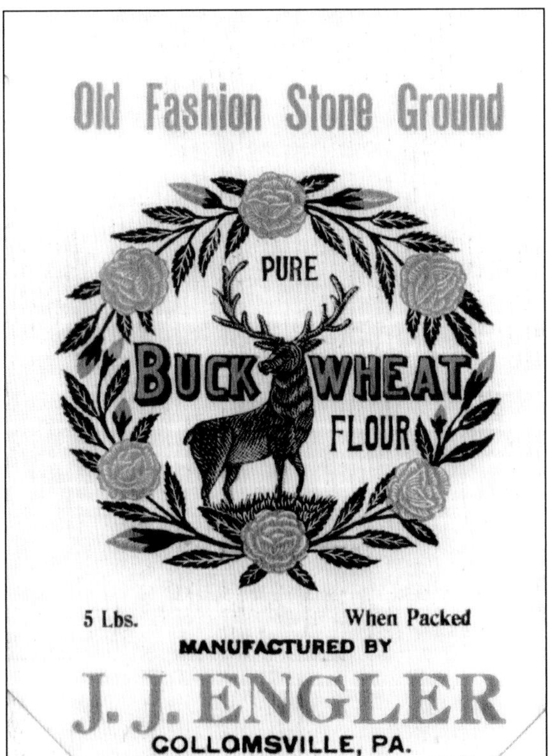

The 40-by-50-foot Collomsville Mill was powered by water from Sweitzer and Nygart streams, and later it was supplemented with a steam engine. Portable hammer mills eventually cut into the profits. Clarence Knarr of Collomsville had the first mill of this type in the area. This mill and power source was carried on a 1932 Chevrolet truck and could go to farms to do custom work. With this mill, he could make chop, shred corn fodder, and make cornmeal and whole and buckwheat flour.

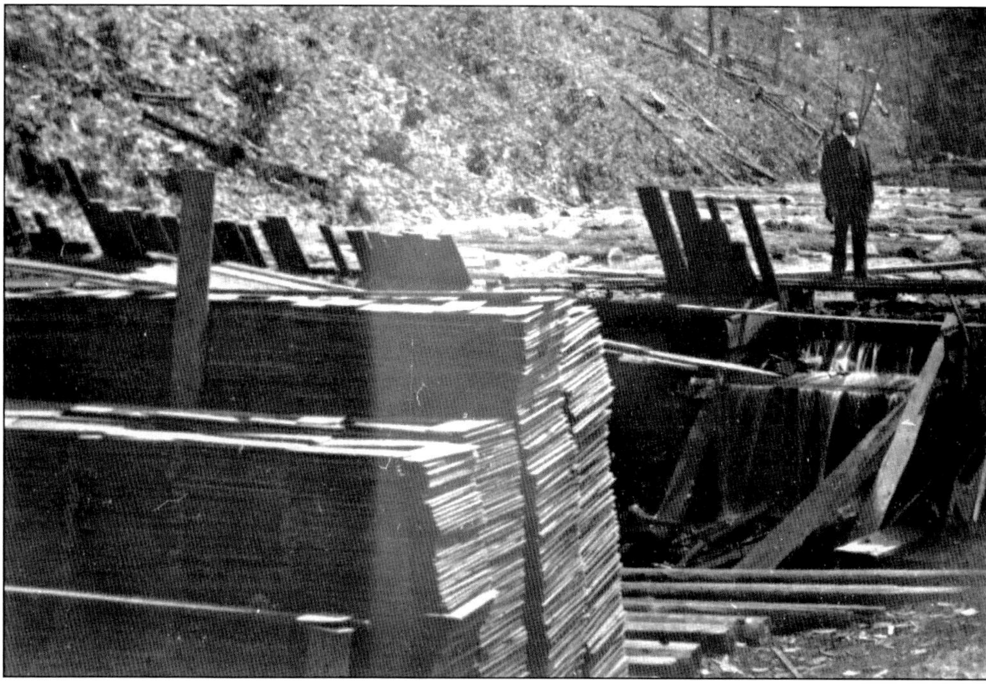

Pictured is John Engler's sawmill, which was located at the lower end of Sweitzer Gap. He was considered "king of the log drivers" on Pine Creek between 1874 and 1894. Besides the gristmill, he owned three farms, ran a general mercantile business, and was postmaster for a time. John came to Nippenose Valley with his parents in 1846. John Sr. was a wagon maker and farmer who moved to Minnesota in 1867.

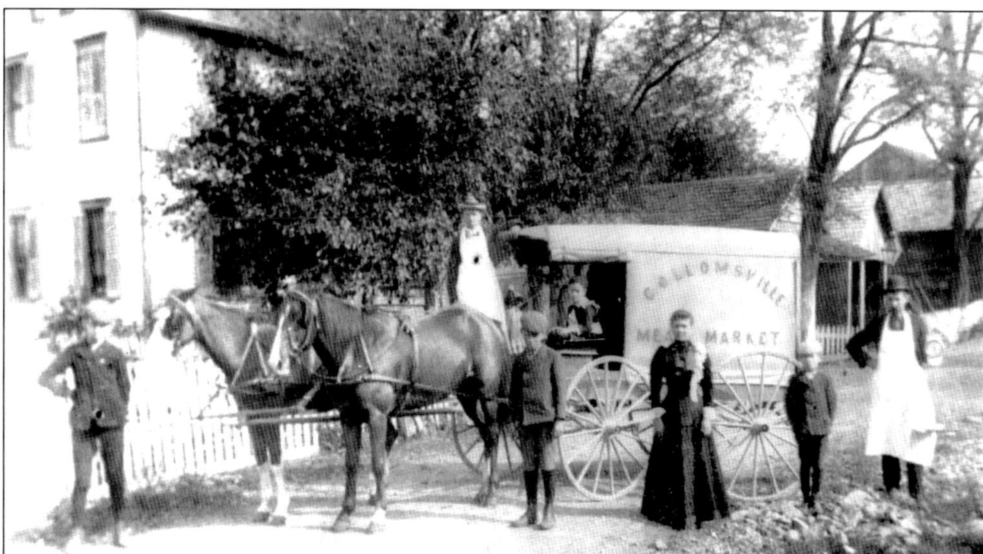

Bill Brownlee (1859–1935) was both a valley constable and butcher for many years. His parents were Bill Brownlee Sr. and Ruth Ann Tate of Oval. He married Elizabeth Esther Voneida in 1882, and together they had five children. By 1906, his business had moved to Oval, and at that time, he completely modernized his shop, making it one of the best in the county. He sold the business in 1914, and his son John carried on the trade.

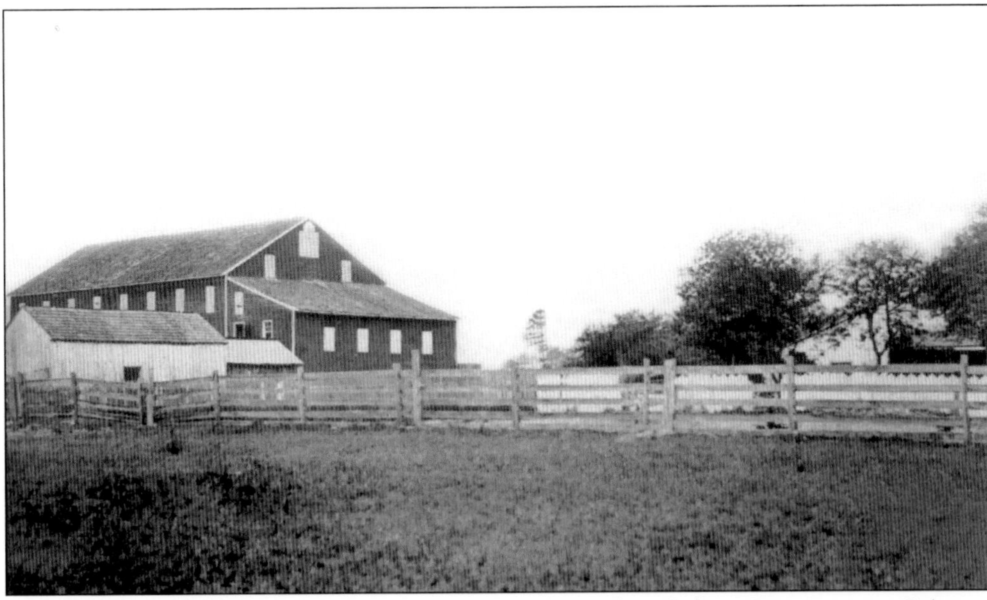

The Kaufman family came to America around 1716 and settled in Germantown. Solomon Kaufman (1804–1886) is listed as owner of this farm on both the 1861 and 1873 landowner maps for Limestone Township. He came to the valley and was first married to Elizabeth Tate, and upon her death in 1840, he got married again to Margaret VanDyke. The farm was also owned by George and Ida Eck Baier and then passed to Richard and Gertrude Schuler Baier, who owned it from 1923 to 1966.

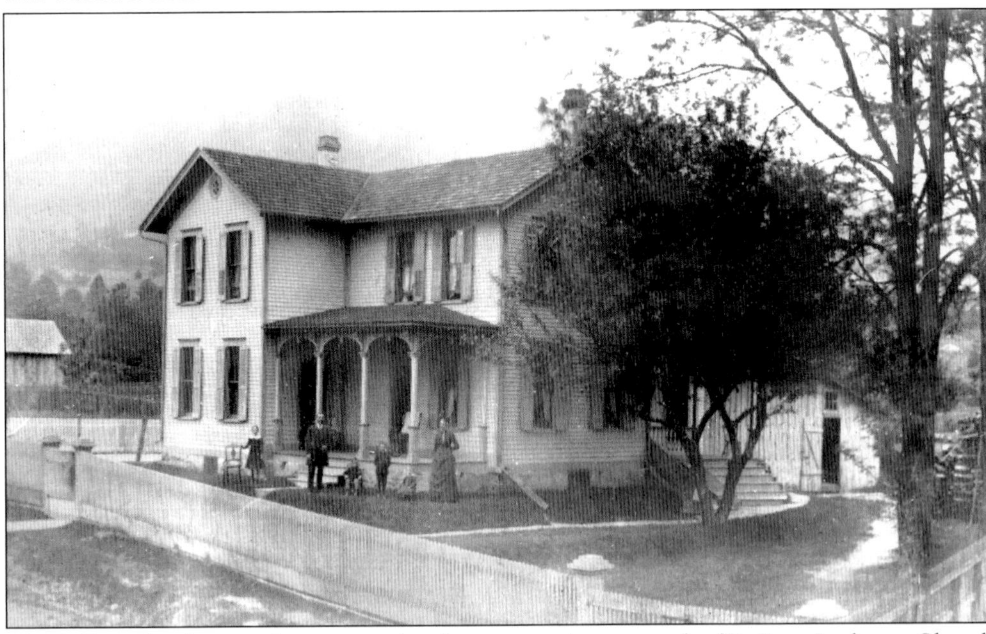

The DeFrain family name first appeared in the communicant records of St. Peter Lutheran Church in 1863. Isaac DeFrain Sr. (1828–1890), a wheelwright, was married to Mary Ann Williamson (1848–1925) and had two children baptized in 1874. DeFrain is listed as a manufacturer of light and heavy wagons in 1873. Isaac Newton (1882–1965) and Mary Koons DeFrain lived here across from the upper blacksmith shop.

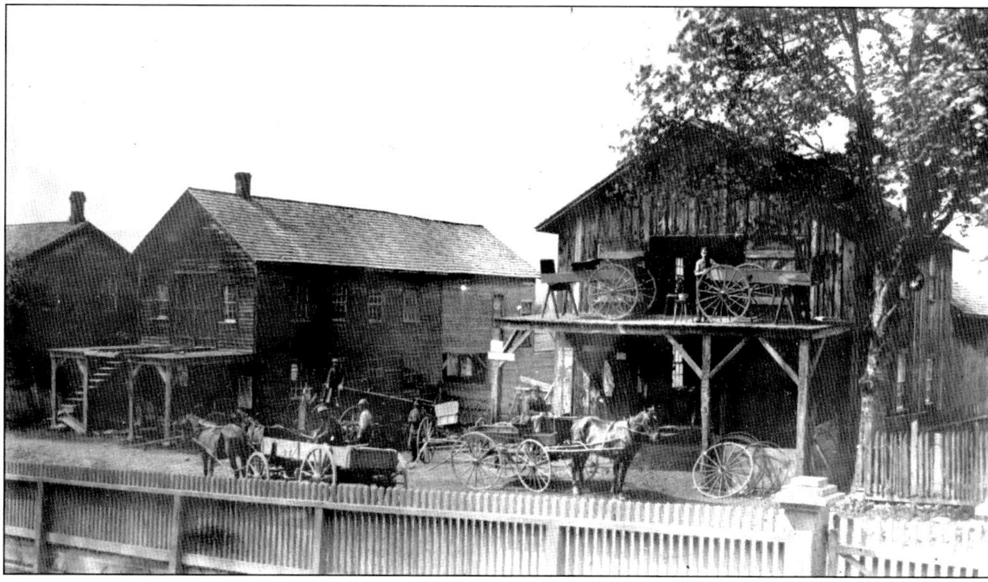

The DeFrain wagon and blacksmith shop was located across the street from their home. Traugott Enigk, George Dapp, and Christopher Bertin (in 1915) were blacksmiths who ran their business here. At the west end of town, Joseph DeFrain (1873–1953) was running the old Clark store until it was bought out by his brother George DeFrain in 1916. George began selling gas that year, and in 1922, he purchased a new International truck with lettering in gold.

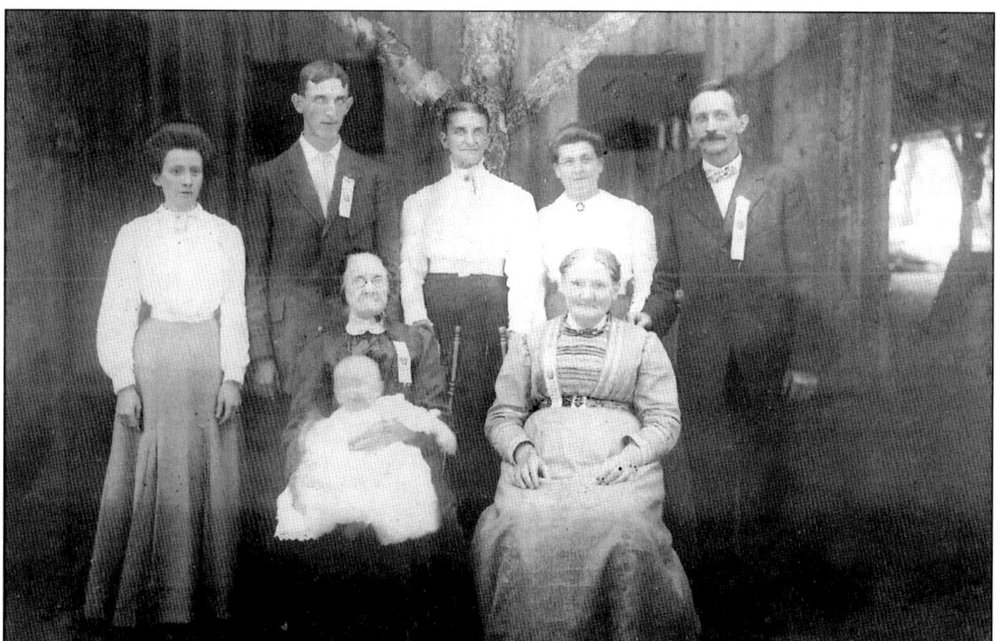

Here are a few members of the DeFrain and Koons families of Nippenose Valley. From left to right are (first row) Ellie ? and Mary Jane Koons (1843–1915); (second row) Anna J. DeFrain (1887–1945), Isaac Newton, Isaac's mother Mary Ann Williamson DeFrain, Clara Koons Ramsey, and Baty Ulysses Koons (1866–1925).

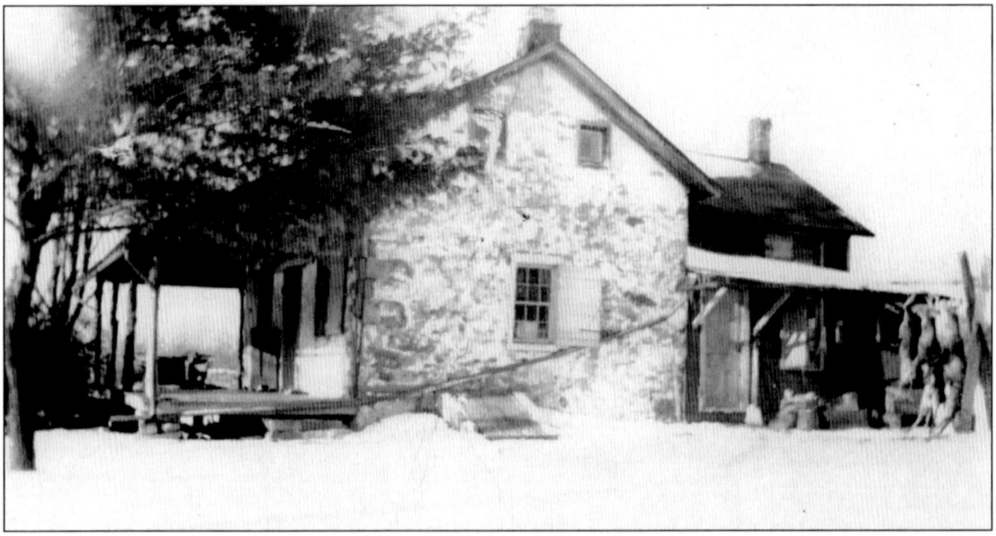

Behind the Seven Sisters lays Little Texas Valley. Prior to 1860, only the Eoute family lived here. By the 1870s, a wagon road developed that connected the western end of Mosquito Valley to Sand Springs and beyond. Families living along it included Zins (Octorora farm), Dapps, Hanleys, and Nygarts. The Joseph Musheno and George Musheno families also lived here along with their wives and 15 children. George was a mason and likely built this home. The Seewalds and the Dapps lived here later.

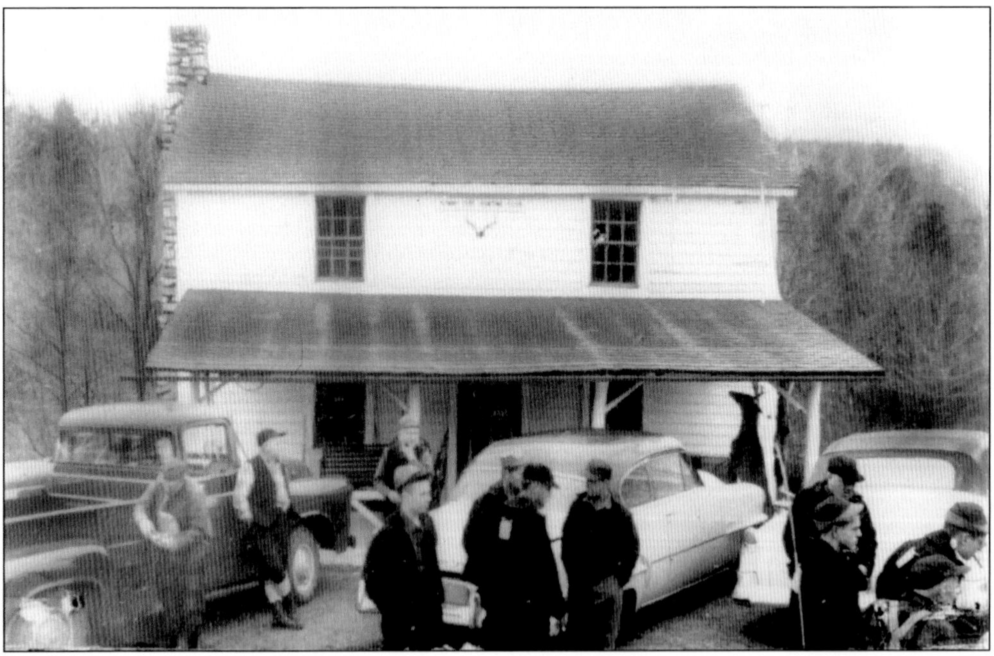

The George Bower home lies along the old Mosquito Valley Road that runs easterly from the Elimsport Mountain Road above Collomsville. This was near the Jake Lambert home and Lone Oak cabin. Today this property belongs to Sunnyside Hunting Camp, which was started with 60 acres by Joe Waldman in 1923 and now contains 364 acres. The Waldman family came from Germany and settled in Nippenose Valley about 1860.

Nine

BASTRESS

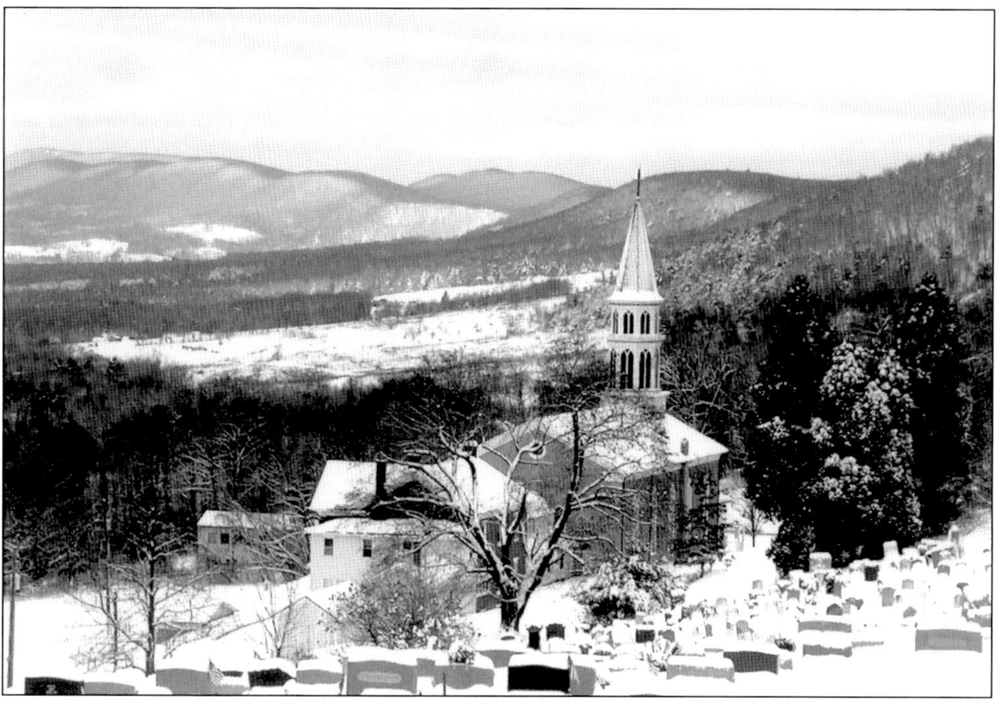

St. Mary's Church of the Immaculate Conception was built of stone in 1860 and was preceded by smaller churches built in 1839 and 1842. This is the oldest Catholic parish in Lycoming County and was started as a German Catholic settlement by Fr. Nicholas Steinbacher about 1838. Steinbacher found three Catholic families living here in 1837. Today the congregation consists of 350 families made up of about 1,000 people.

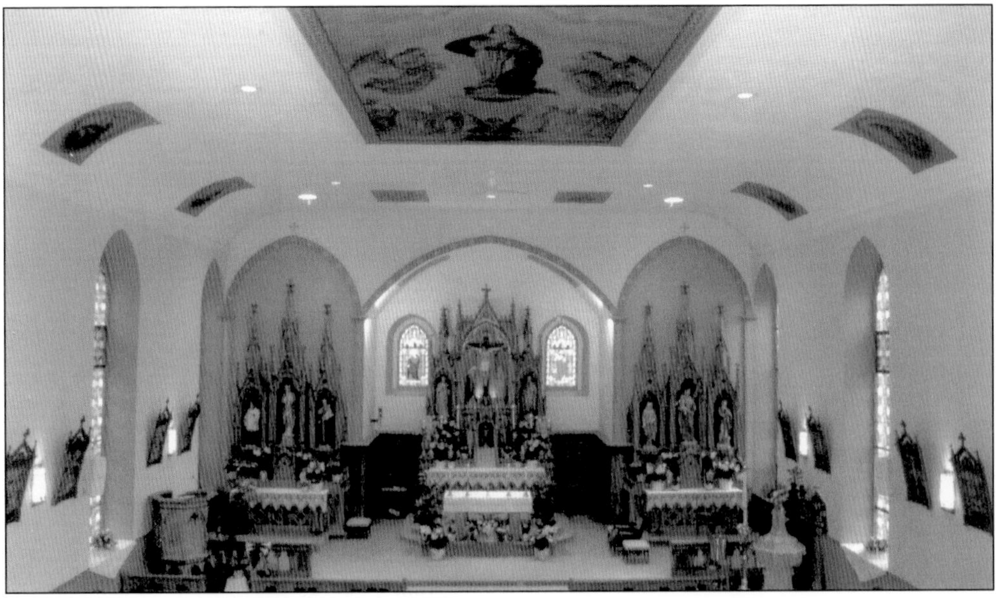

This beautiful church had humble beginnings. The early church members came from the lower counties looking for cheaper land, and already the best in the valley was taken. From this stony and mountainous forestland, they established beautiful farms and this magnificent church. A pipe organ was installed in 1869, the ornate altars were added in 1901, and over the next decade, improvements and repairs, inside and out, were accomplished. The ceiling painting was added in 1910.

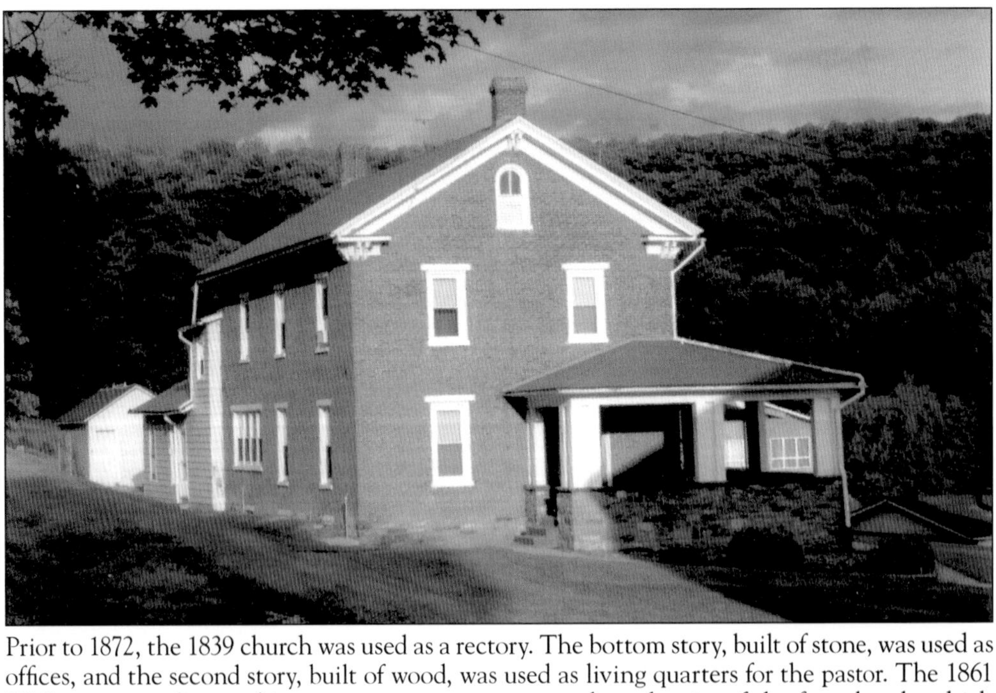

Prior to 1872, the 1839 church was used as a rectory. The bottom story, built of stone, was used as offices, and the second story, built of wood, was used as living quarters for the pastor. The 1861 Walling map indicates this new rectory was constructed on the site of the first church, which was later used as the first rectory. Running water was added about 1905, and a lighting plant was added in 1916.

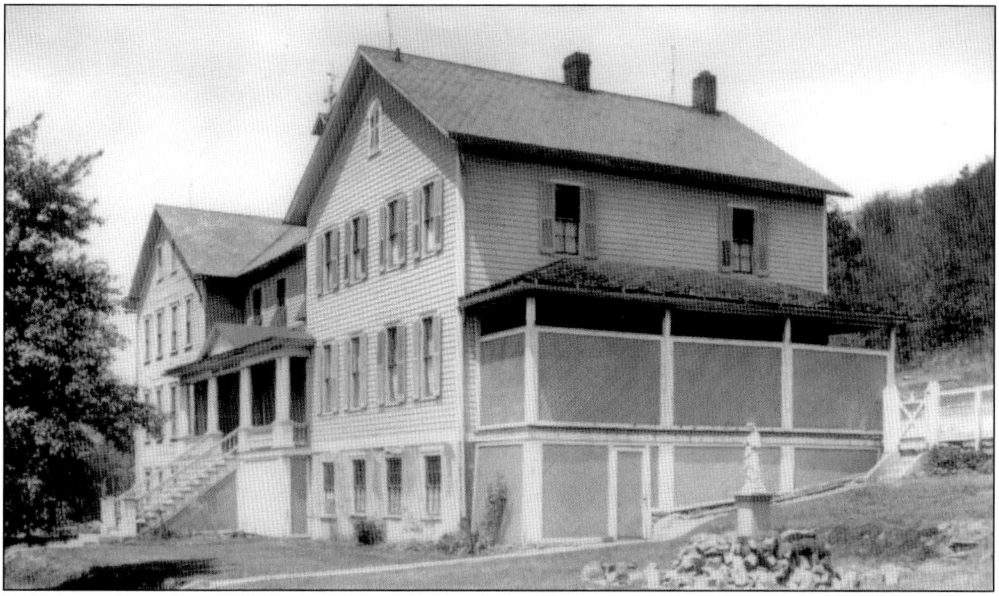

This church complex, including a convent, a chapel, and a school, was built in 1874 and 1875. Up to this time, classes were held in the 1842 church, and John Steinbacher was an early teacher. This was known as the German School since the public school at Bastress was taught in English. An eighth-grade class was added in 1927, and in 1928, the first school bus was purchased. Frank Schuler drove the bus for 13 years and was followed by his wife, Pauline, who drove for 7 more.

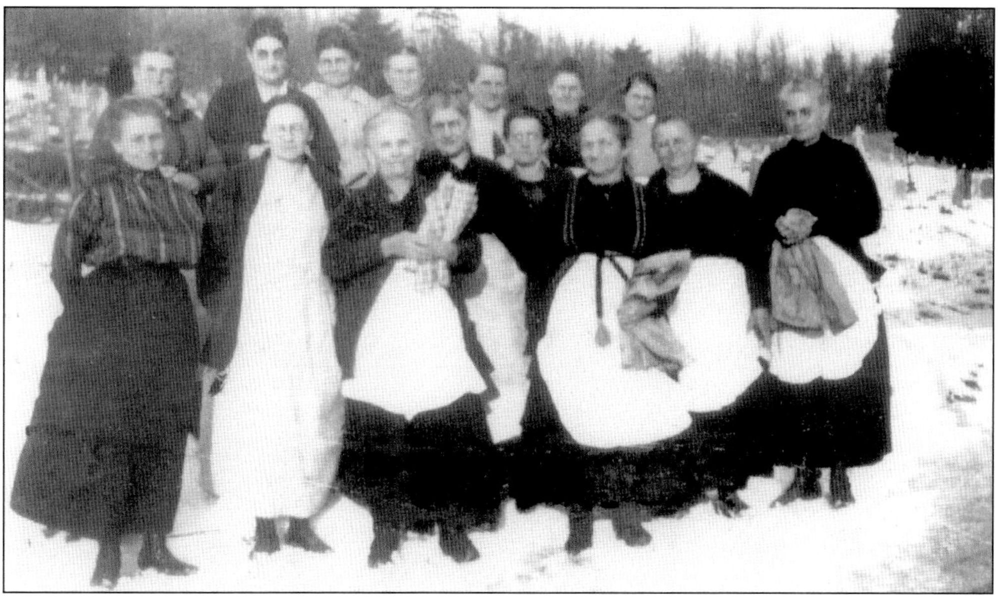

These ladies were members of the Bastress Church sewing group during the 1920s. From left to right are (first row) Alice Eck Moore, Elizabeth Eck Stopper, Susanna Eck Baier, Magdalena Eiswert Eck, Anna von Weldon Wenner, Mary Shurer, Mary Wagenblast Eck, and Elizabeth Lorson Stopper; (second row) Barbara Dincher Ulsamer, Mary Shuhler Hoffman, Clara Sweier Winter, Eva Ulsamer Young, Mary Nittinger, Susanna Bender Dincher, and possibly Ella Hullar Danneker.

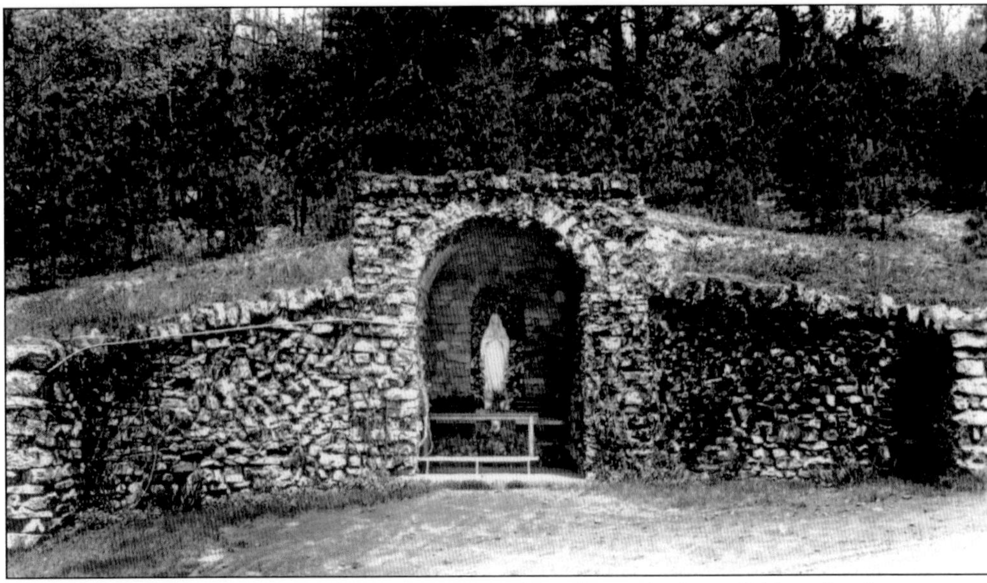

The Lourdes Grotto at Immaculate Conception Church was built in 1915 under the tenure of Rev. George Schmidt. Parishioners did the excavation and hauling of rocks to the site, and Louis Ulsamer did the masonry work. The statue was carved out of a solid block of Carrara marble in Genoa, Italy. May Devotions was started here in the late 1920s by Rev. John Meyer. This is the only such shrine in Pennsylvania built along a public road.

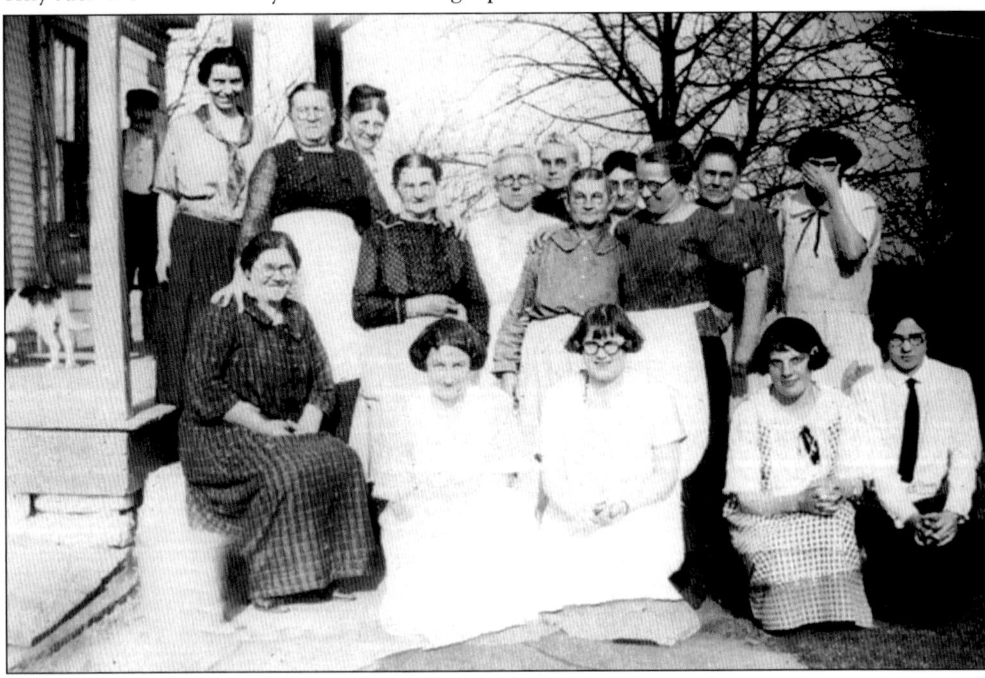

These ladies were gathered for a quilting bee at the Louis Ulsamer farm on Bastress Mountain. From left to right are (first row) Mame Lorson, unidentified, Catherine Lorson, Barbara Miller, and Irene Young; (second row) Louis Ulsamer (on porch), Victoria Miller, Eva Young, Mary Waldman, Tillie Schuler, Lizzie Schuler, Elizabeth Stopper, Barbara Ulsamer, possibly Mary Hoffman, Mary Baier (or Nittinger), Susanna Dincher, and Catherine Miller.

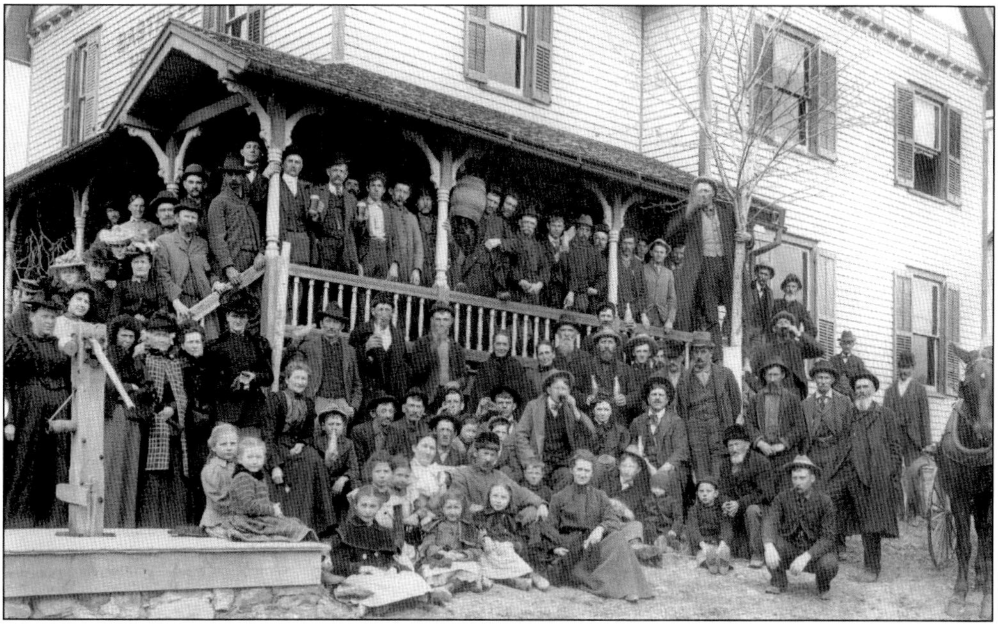

This picture, taken at the Bastress Hotel, shows a group of people either coming from or going to a picnic in the nearby woods. Tony Deitrick is believed to have owned the hotel at this time, followed by Charles Schuler (for one month), John A. Bubb, Mark Keister, Joseph Nittinger (who changed the name to Nippenose Tavern), Whitey "Brooks" Laubach, Pheras "Hus" Eck, Robert Moore, Eugene and Betty Kaboliski, Mike Lupole Sr., Bob Eoute, and Ray Smith in 2008.

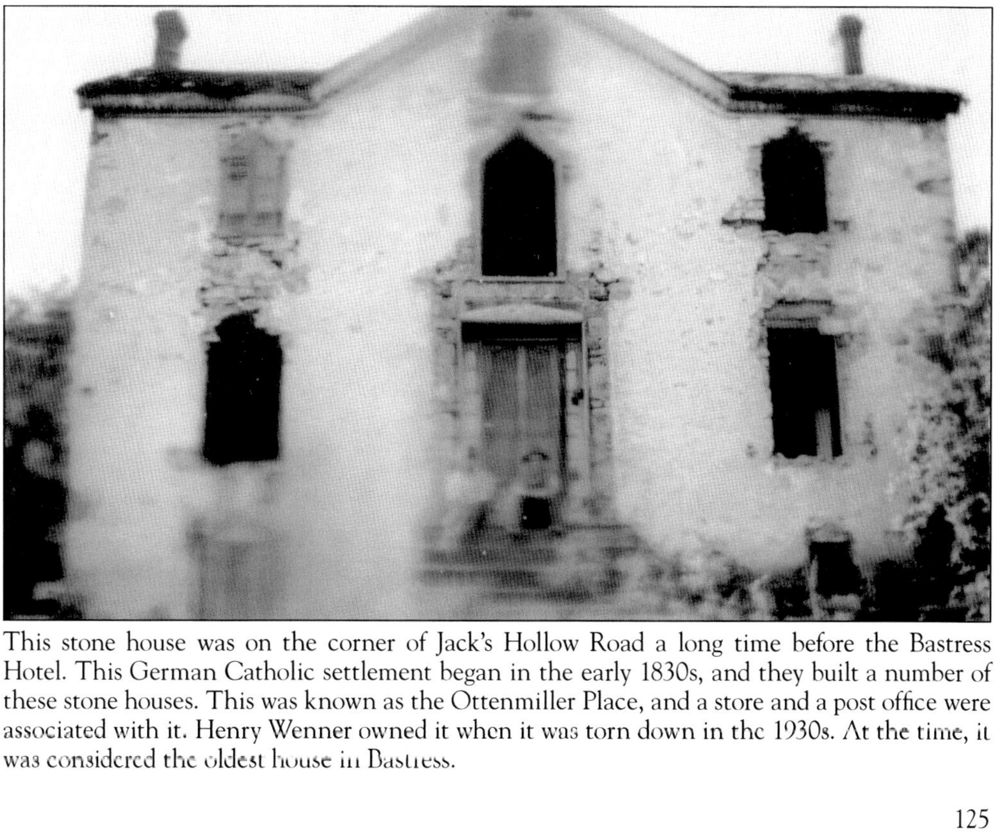

This stone house was on the corner of Jack's Hollow Road a long time before the Bastress Hotel. This German Catholic settlement began in the early 1830s, and they built a number of these stone houses. This was known as the Ottenmiller Place, and a store and a post office were associated with it. Henry Wenner owned it when it was torn down in the 1930s. At the time, it was considered the oldest house in Bastress.

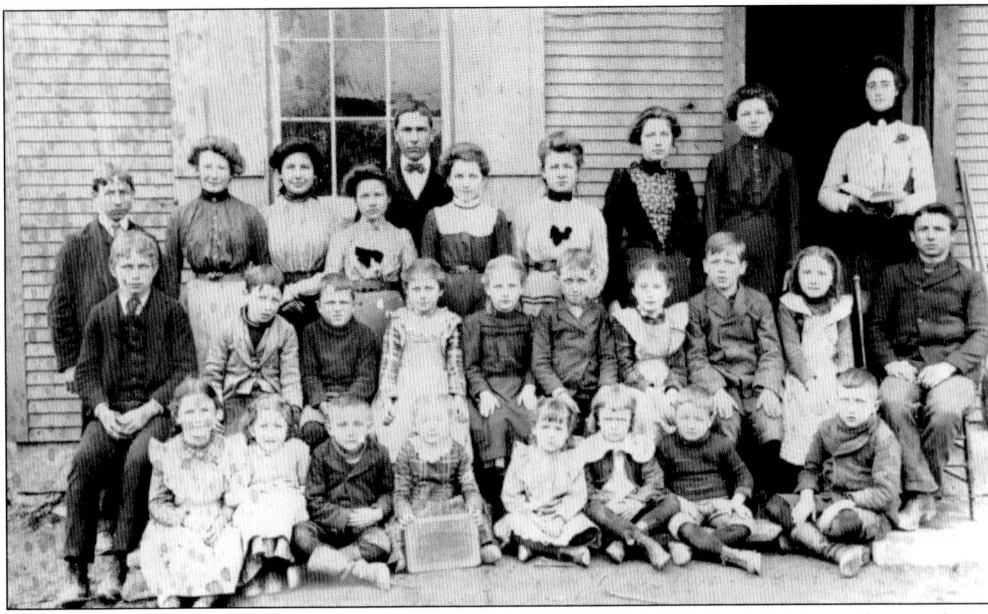

These students attended the Bastress Public School in 1902. From left to right are (first row) Eva Bower, Marian Axman, Andrew Danneker, Emma Axman, Francis Baier, Rudolf Baier, Joseph Baier, and Raymond Danneker; (second row) Edward Eck, Raymond Bower, Ambrose Baier, Theresa Eck, Ellen Bubb, Anthony Steppe, Ruth Axman, Harry Bubb, Margaret Axman, and Robert Baier; (third row) Edward Baier, Margaret Stopper, Helen Bower, Belle Baier, Richard Nau, Amelia Stopper, Martha Baier, Amanda Bubb, Katie Stopper, and teacher Ellen Mansuy. Mansuy was hired to teach for seven months at a salary of $35 a month.

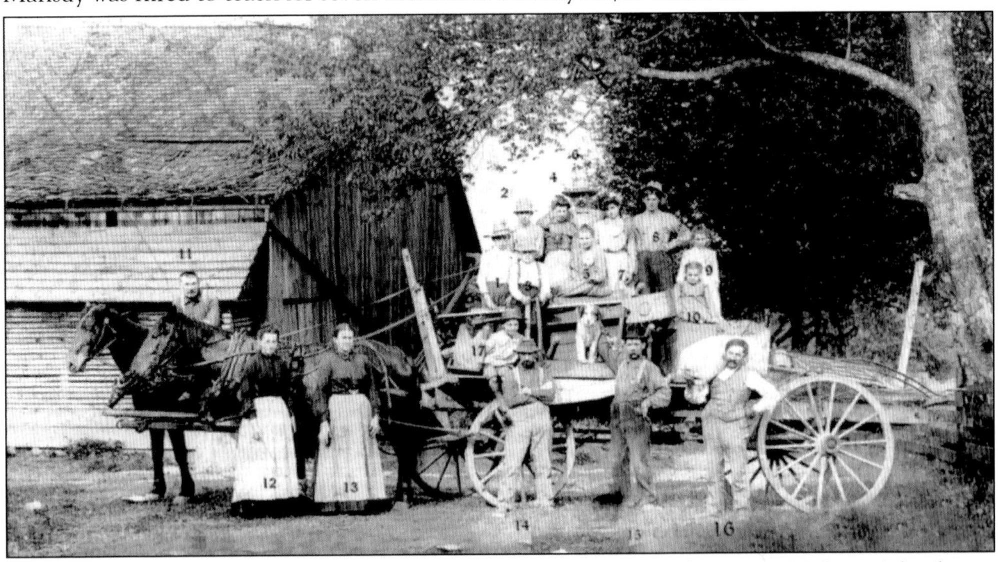

The settlement of neighboring Mosquito Valley began in 1795 with Marcus Huling. After being clear-cut of timber by lumber companies from Williamsport, it was occupied by many farm families. By the early 20th century, the Citizens Water Company of Williamsport forced the sellout of these farms to insure the city's water supply. This photograph shows moving day for the Frank Bower family. Many settled in Nippenose Valley, and some of the homes were dismantled and moved as well.

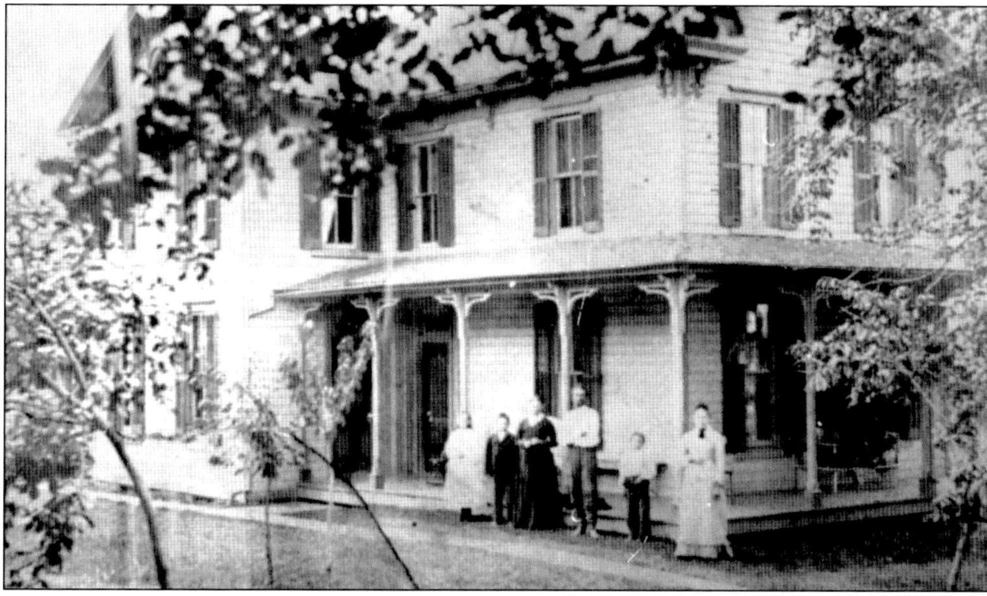

Joseph Riedy (1825–1907) was born in Rathshausen (Black Forest country) and emigrated from Wurttemberg, Germany, in 1849. He bought this farm from Peter DeWald in 1867 and built a two-story springhouse where his family lived until the barn and house were completed. His wife, Christina Higi (1830–1900), was also from Wurttemberg. The original warrant to this farm was for Philip DeWald in 1793. From left to right are Riedy family members Katherine, William, Christine, Joseph, Edwin, and unidentified.

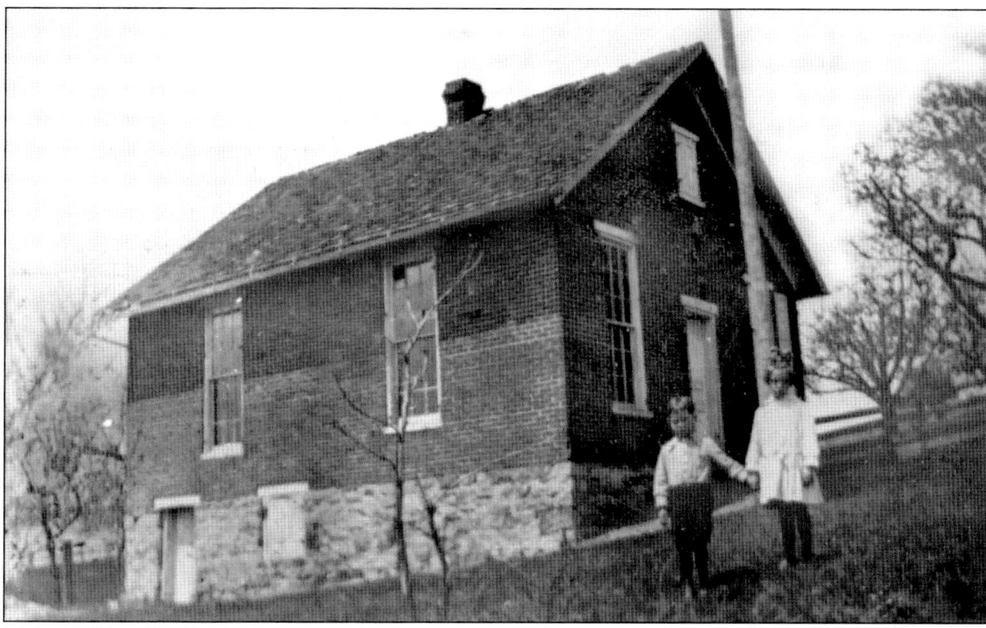

The Riedy School closed in 1920 and is shown here with Francis Edwin Riedy and Verna Frances Riedy. Joseph was a bricklayer and stonemason and may have built this school. Verna (born in 1913), the daughter of Edwin Riedy and Lena Nau, was married to Clarence Stopper in 1935, and the Riedy farm was next owned by Charles and Susan Snyder Stopper. The Ecktown School closed in 1921, and the Moore School was sold at auction that same year.